UNDERSTANDING TH

*By comparing how three major thinkers expl
divine fullness, Dominic Robinson offers us a
issue in Christian theology.*
         Michael Paul Gallagher SJ, Pontifical Gregorian University, Italy

Dominic Robinson has chosen a major Biblical theme – "human beings as the image of God" – and charts its interpretation in the related but contrasting work of three major theologians: Barth and Moltmann from the Reformed tradition and the Catholic Balthasar who engages responsively and critically with the Augustinian Protestant tradition. At stake in the discussion is the question of the human subjective capacity, the role of Jesus Christ in conveying true identity to us and the oscillation within the Western theological imagination about the possibility of a free human response to God. Robinson offers us a well considered, insightful and ecumenically focused contribution to our grasp of these central themes. His work, bringing out the consonance between Balthasar and Pope Benedict, brings out the best of recent Roman Catholic work in this key area of systematic theology.
         John McDade SJ, Principal of Heythrop College and lecturer in Systematic Theology, UK

As theologians across confessional divides try to say something significant about human dignity in our contemporary society, there is fresh interest in the ancient Christian doctrine that the human being is created in the "*imago Dei*". Theology is grounding responsibility for others and for the world around us in this common vision that the human being's infinite horizon lies in a divine calling and destiny. Robinson examines the "*imago Dei*" debate through three giants of twentieth century theology – Karl Barth, Hans Urs von Balthasar, and Jürgen Moltmann. This is placed against a survey of the principle developments and distinctions relating to the doctrine in the history of Christian thought, which in itself will be valuable for all students of theology. A fresh analysis of ecumenical contributions places the development of the doctrine in the context of the ongoing process of ecumenical dialogue on the dignity of the human person, with special reference to this theme in the first encyclical of Pope Benedict XVI, *Deus Caritas Est*.

Whilst "*imago Dei*" is the focus of this book, Robinson invites the reader to see its relevance to theology as a whole on a specifically ecumenical canvas, and relates directly to more general areas of theological anthropology, grace, salvation, and the relationship between God and the world.

Understanding the "*Imago Dei*"
The Thought of Barth, von Balthasar and Moltmann

DOMINIC ROBINSON
Heythrop College, University of London, UK

LONDON AND NEW YORK

First published 2011 by Ashgate Publishing

Published 2016 by Routledge
2 Park Square, Milton Park, Abingdon, Oxfordshire OX14 4RN
711 Third Avenue, New York, NY 10017, USA

First issued in paperback 2016

Routledge is an imprint of the Taylor & Francis Group, an informa business

Copyright © Dominic Robinson 2011

Dominic Robinson has asserted his right under the Copyright, Designs and Patents Act, 1988, to be identified as the author of this work.

All rights reserved. No part of this book may be reprinted or reproduced or utilised in any form or by any electronic, mechanical, or other means, now known or hereafter invented, including photocopying and recording, or in any information storage or retrieval system, without permission in writing from the publishers.

Notice:
Product or corporate names may be trademarks or registered trademarks, and are used only for identification and explanation without intent to infringe.

British Library Cataloguing in Publication Data
Robinson, Dominic.
　Understanding the 'imago Dei' : the thought of Barth, von Balthasar and Moltmann.
　1. Image of God. 2. Barth, Karl, 1886–1968. 3. Balthasar, Hans Urs von, 1905–1988.
　4. Moltmann, Jurgen. 5. Theology, Doctrinal–History–20th century.
　I. Title
　233.5-dc22

Library of Congress Cataloging-in-Publication Data
Robinson, Dominic, 1967–
　Understanding the "imago Dei" : the thought of Barth, von Balthasar and Moltmann / Dominic Robinson.
　　p. cm.
　Includes bibliographical references (p.　) and index.
　ISBN 978-0-7546-6770-4 (hardcover : alk. paper) – ISBN 978-0-7546-9828-9 (ebook)
　1. Image of God. 2. Barth, Karl, 1886–1968. 3. Balthasar, Hans Urs von, 1905–1988. 4. Moltmann, Jurgen. I. Title.
　BT702.R63 2010
　233'.5–dc22

2010047457

ISBN 13: 978-1-138-27916-2 (pbk)
ISBN 13: 978-0-7546-6770-4 (hbk)

Contents

Abbreviations		*vii*
Acknowledgements		*ix*
	Introduction	1
1	"*Imago Dei*": The Historico-Theological Background	5
	The Account in Genesis	5
	Augustine	8
	Irenaeus	12
	Aquinas	14
	Luther	17
	Calvin	20
	The Council of Trent	22
	The Second Vatican Council	24
	Barth, von Balthasar and Moltmann	27
	Karl Barth	29
	Hans Urs von Balthasar	33
	Jürgen Moltmann	38
	Conclusion	41
2	Karl Barth	45
	Understanding of "*Imago Dei*": Objectives and Tensions	45
	The Sources of Barth's Sombre View of Humanity	50
	Critical Analysis: Formulation of Barth's View and Rejection of Roman Catholic Understanding	56
	Critical Analysis: Karl Barth's Model of "*imago Dei*" in Itself	67
	Conclusion	78
3	Hans Urs von Balthasar	83
	Understanding of "*Imago Dei*"	83
	Critical Analysis: Patristic Sources	89
	Critical Analysis: The Barthian Contribution	98
	Hans Urs von Balthasar's Model of "*Imago Dei*" in Itself	120
	Conclusion	126

| 4 | Jürgen Moltmann | 129 |

Understanding of *"Imago Dei"*: Themes and New Directions — 129
The Quest for a Relational Model — 136
Jürgen Moltmann's Model of *"Imago Dei"* in Itself — 144
Conclusion — 156

| 5 | Concluding Reflections: Broader Horizons | 159 |

Deus Caritas Est and the Interface of *Agape* and *Eros* — 162
Closing Recommendations — 166
Closing Summary — 175

Bibliography — *177*
Glossary — *187*
Index — *189*

Abbreviations

CCC	*Catechism of the Catholic Church*
CD	*Church Dogmatics*
GL	*Glory of the Lord*
GS	*Gaudium et Spes*
HK	*Herrlichkeit: Eine Theologische Ästhetik*
KD	*Kirchliche Dogmatik*
LG	*Lumen Gentium*
MP	*Mysterium Paschale*
ST	*Summa Theologiae*
TD	*Theo-Drama: Theological Dramatic Theory*
TDK	*Theodramatik*

Acknowledgements

At the completion of this project I am very conscious of the many people to whom I owe a debt of gratitude. As this book is based on the doctoral thesis I submitted to the Pontifical Gregorian University in Rome as recently as 2007 I must first and foremost express my thanks to those who guided me in my research. I must express my particular gratitude to the three individual professors at the Pontifical Gregorian University who have played such a major part in this. I would like to thank Fr. Philip Rosato, S.J., who, as my first professorial contact before his illness sadly took him back to the United States, encouraged me to pursue my area of research. I owe a great debt of gratitude to Fr. John O'Donnell, S.J., who as my original Director, guided me through the research and the initial stages of the writing. His untimely death was a great loss for so many. Finally, I owe a great debt of gratitude to my Director of two years, Fr. Michael Paul Gallagher, S.J., who, despite his other considerable responsibilities, directed me so conscientiously, with an eye for detail matched with perspective and insight.

In addition, I would also like to thank Professor Richard Bauckham, of St Mary's College in the University of St Andrews, for his expert guidance in my research on Jürgen Moltmann, a kindness for which I was most grateful.

A number of individuals helped in the final stages of preparing the text. I thank Fr. Michael Rosinski, S.J., for his help with some word processing matters. I am very grateful to Sarah Pawlett for her invaluable assistance in house style editing and managing liaison with publishers of quoted works.

I am grateful to the publishers who gave their permission to quote extensively from their material: for *Church Dogmatics* Volumes I/1, II/1, II/2, III/1, III/2, III/3, IV/1 and IV/2: by kind permission of Continuum International Publishing Group; for *Theo-Drama: Theological Dramatic Theory* Volumes II, III and IV: by kind permission of Ignatius Press.

Finally, I add my sincere thanks to my Jesuit brothers at the Collegio di San Roberto Bellarmino in Rome and at the Mount St Jesuit Community in London for their personal and spiritual support.

Dominic Robinson, S.J.

Introduction

The doctrine which states that the human being is created in the "*imago Dei*" has been the subject of much theological debate throughout the history of Christianity. This study brings an ecumenical angle to this debate through an examination of the understanding of the doctrine in three twentieth-century theologians, Karl Barth, Hans Urs von Balthasar and Jürgen Moltmann. Through a historical, analytical and critical research into the work of these three writers, it attempts to show an appropriate way forward for the contemporary presentation of the doctrine, which will propose above all a renewed ecumenically-inspired Christocentric understanding of the human person as the "*imago Dei*".

Why is this important? Above all the recent resurgence of interest in the doctrine among Christian authors of different traditions suggests how theology is trying to say something significant about human dignity in our contemporary society. There is a new recognition of the power here to show how it is in Christ that the human being finds his sense of true value and his infinite horizon in a divine calling and destiny. The doctrine underlines Christ's presence in the world shining through humanity. This affects how theology speaks of contemporary concerns as it underscores our understanding of our responsibility for others graced with the same dignity, our care for the world around us, and so of the ethical values which form a Christian conscience.

At this time in the history of theology this message is being proclaimed more powerfully through a doctrine of human identity which is rooted all the more firmly in Christ and his new creation, humanity made in *his* image and given new life through *his* infinite redeeming love. This was one of the foremost concerns of Pope John Paul II, and is echoed by Pope Benedict XVI in his programme of magisterial teaching.

John Paul II introduced this theme in his first Encyclical *Redemptor Hominis*,[1] when he declared that:

> The Church's fundamental function in every age and particularly in ours is to direct man's gaze, to point the awareness and experience of the whole of humanity toward the mystery of Christ, to help all men to be familiar with the profundity of the Redemption taking place in Christ Jesus. At the same time man's deepest sphere is involved – we mean the sphere of human hearts, consciences and events.[2]

---

[1] Pope John Paul II, *Redemptor Hominis* (Vatican City: Libreria Editrice Vaticana, 1979).

[2] Ibid., no. 10.

This theme was highlighted throughout the pontificate of John Paul II, as the Pope called on Christians to examine their collective consciences as to how they uphold and respect the dignity of the human person, in particular in the face of new threats to its fundamental place in morality, law and political ideology. This call was rooted in the belief in the human being's new creation in Christ as his image on earth and in a vision of his supernatural calling. "Man is called to a fullness of life which far exceeds the dimensions of his earthly existence", teaches Pope John Paul in his Encyclical *Evangelium Vitae*,[3] "because it consists in sharing the very life of God". "Every individual, precisely by reason of the mystery of the Word of God who was made flesh (cf. Jn 1:14), is entrusted to the maternal care of the Church. Therefore every threat to human dignity and life must necessarily be felt in the Church's very heart."[4] It is from this perspective of the firm belief in humanity's dignity made possible through the incarnation that he makes his important call to humanity to reawaken its moral conscience, as he declares:

> Through sin, man rebels against his Creator and ends up by worshipping creatures: "They exchanged the truth about God for a lie and worshipped and served the creature rather than the Creator" (Rom 1:25). As a result man not only deforms the image of God in his own person, but is tempted to offences against it in others as well, replacing relationships of communion by attitudes of distrust, indifference, hostility and even murderous hatred. When God is not acknowledged as God, the profound meaning of man is betrayed and communion between people is compromised.
>
> In the life of man, God's image shines forth anew and is again revealed in all its fullness at the coming of the Son of God in human flesh
>
> [...]
>
> God's plan for human beings is this, that they should "be conformed to the image of his Son" (Rom 8:29). Only thus, in the splendour of this image, can man be freed from the slavery of idolatry, rebuild lost fellowship and rediscover his true identity.[5]

Pope Benedict has been setting out a similar message. In his first Encyclical, *Deus Caritas Est*,[6] the Pope states that he is going to the very heart of the Christian message in turning to the theme of Christian love. This is in no way a vague theological concept. It is clearly based on a strong reaffirmation of the doctrine that the human person is made in God's image. Pope Benedict's first words are

---

[3] Pope John Paul II, *Evangelium Vitae* (Vatican City: Libreria Editrice Vaticana, 1995).

[4] Ibid., Introduction.

[5] Ibid., no. 36.

[6] Pope Benedict XVI, *Deus Caritas Est* (Vatican City: Libreria Editrice Vaticana, 2006).

the quotation from John's Gospel which gives the Encyclical its title, but then he makes clear the work's doctrinal foundations:

> "God is love, and he who abides in love abides in God, and abides in him" (1 Jn 4:16). These words from the First Letter of John express with remarkable clarity the heart of the Christian faith: the Christian image of God and the resulting image of mankind and its destiny.[7]

For the Pope, however, this is not an idea based first and foremost on an ethical choice or on any ideology. Rather, building on the teaching of his predecessor, Pope Benedict wishes to takes us to the heart of the Christian faith in humanity's dignity by drawing us to *Christ*, in whose image the human being is made:

> Being Christian is not the result of an ethical choice or a lofty idea, but the encounter with an event, a person, which gives life a new horizon and a new decisive direction.[8]

This particular work on the "*imago Dei*", however, will also address questions which are of considerable importance on a related level. This is in the field of ecumenical dialogue. Given the contemporary need to reaffirm a Christocentric understanding of the human person, theology must engage itself in discussion on this theme across Christian Churches and traditions. Through this we can appreciate the insights behind doctrines, and so be better disposed to proclaim in a more unified manner this key teaching about humanity at the root of Christian belief and witness in the world.

This study will address the specifically ecumenical challenge through focussing on three twentieth-century writers from different theological traditions, each of whom advocate a reaffirmation of the doctrine of the "*imago Dei*". In these three writers we can detect an ecumenical movement which deserves closer attention. Protestant theologians are now considering the value in a doctrine which has been largely disregarded in their tradition up to now. The work of Balthasar represents a Catholic perspective which has tried to understand theologians of the Reformation and to dialogue with them. Notwithstanding their different approaches and conclusions, each of these three writers has returned to similar sources in the Patristic, medieval and Reformation traditions. Thus we will consider closely their interpretation of the tradition to uncover the reasons for divisions and so suggest possibilities for closer understanding and united witness in the future.

From this emerges a proposal for the contemporary reception of the doctrine which has particular emphases. It tries to recapture the drama of the descent of God to earth in the person of Christ. It aims in particular to hold together the two dimensions, which I will be arguing in the history of theology have formed

---

[7] Ibid., Introduction.
[8] Ibid., Introduction.

a doctrinal, and also specifically ecumenical, divide. These two aspects I have termed the "descendant", that which stresses God's descending to earth in Christ, and the "ascendant", that which focuses on the human person's orientation towards God. Through my research into the roots of the contemporary debate I focus on how the work of Hans Urs von Balthasar in particular points us towards a doctrinal and ecumenical rapprochement as he is able to place the "descendant" and the "ascendant" in one integrated dynamic. In such a way I will argue that this gives us a fuller understanding of the doctrine which enables the Christian community in the twenty-first century to speak more powerfully of human dignity and vocation.

Chapter 1
"Imago Dei":
The Historico-Theological Background

The Account in Genesis

> God created man in the image of himself,
> in the image of God he created him,
> male and female he created them.
> (Genesis 1:27)[1]

This single verse of scripture presents the basic teaching that the human person is made in the image of God, in the *imago Dei*. For the theological community who seek to understand this teaching it is the fundamental scriptural reference. Thus, if we are to understand the history of the theological debate we must first place this verse of scripture in its own context.

The verse in question comes towards the end of the first chapter of the book of Genesis, the narrative account of the origins of creation in the Old Testament. This chapter tells us how God created heaven and earth, day and night, water and dry land, plant life, fish and birds, animals, and then, after this God created humans in the image of himself. Then we are told that this final element of God's work, humanity, represents the pinnacle of the created order. The world which God has created is in fact created for humanity. The environment in which man and woman will live is his and her dominion. "God blessed them, saying to them, 'Be fruitful, multiply, fill the earth and conquer it. Be masters of the fish of the sea, the birds of heaven and all living animals on the earth'" (Genesis 1:28). Then we are told at the beginning of Chapter 2 that after God had finished this creative work, and having pronounced that all that had been created was very good, God rested.

The following two chapters focus on this pinnacle of God's excellent created order, humanity, made in God's own image. In Chapter 2 we read how God fashions man from the earth and breathes life into him. Thus he becomes a living being. God plants a beautiful garden, a "paradise" as it is translated in the Septuagint, and places man there. God gives an admonition: "You may eat indeed of all the trees in the garden. Nevertheless of the tree of knowledge of good and evil you are not to eat, for on the day you eat of it you shall most surely die" (Genesis 2:16–17). Then God creates woman as a companion for man.

---

[1] All scripture quotations, unless otherwise stated, are from *The Jerusalem Bible* (London: Darton, Longman and Todd, 1966).

It is then, in Chapter 3, in this paradise called Eden, that we are given the narrative of what will later be known as the Fall. Tempted by a serpent, for the Judaeo-Christian tradition that is to say the power of evil or the Devil, the woman eats of the fruit of the tree of good and evil, and gives some to the man who also eats of it. Both realise that they are naked and hide. God appears and because they have done what was forbidden expels them from Eden to live in the ordinary world. Because of what human beings had done there would be pain and hard labour for them and their descendants. "For dust you are and to dust you shall return", God says to the man. God also condemns the serpent to crawl on its belly, eat dirt and to be forever the enemy of the woman and her offspring.

This basic narrative has given rise to volumes of interpretation over the centuries. However, if we are to first of all place it in its own context, it seems worthwhile asking ourselves who actually wrote it. For Biblical scholars this can be a complex question. What we can affirm is that the authorship of Genesis is unknown. Furthermore there is a basic disagreement as to whether the text we see today is more the work of an editor or that of a single writer. Clifford and Murphy, writing in *The New Jerome Biblical Commentary*,[2] favour the widely accepted view that the Genesis narrative was originally an oral epic. This was recorded by editors in written form and then edited several times more down to as late as the sixth century BC. This view has been widely credited by many Old Testament scholars who have traced the sources of the narrative.

Biblical criticism since the eighteenth century has generally regarded there to be four main editorial traditions at work on these ancient accounts of the origins of the world in Genesis and the ancient accounts which formed the other four books of the Pentateuch. Murphy, in his introduction to the Pentateuch in *The New Jerome Biblical Commentary*,[3] introduces these briefly, stating clearly that these generalisations he makes are not absolute. The tradition Old Testament scholars have called "J" is marked by vivid storytelling and promise of fulfilment. "E" emphasises morality and the call to faith and fear of the Lord expected by Israel. "D" stresses adherence to divine commands under threat of punishment. "P" is concerned with cult, ritual and genealogies. This editing process was surely complex and so, if we are to accept this view of how the text was formed, we are to conclude that the text of Genesis we read today is a complex mixture of different teachings on the divine origins of the world and of the place of human beings within it. It is good to be aware of that as a mark of caution at the outset of our study.

Nevertheless, today not all scripture scholars agree that the creation of the text of Genesis is so complex. Wenham, in the recently compiled *Eerdmans Commentary*

---

[2] Richard J. Clifford and Roland E. Murphy, "Genesis", in *The New Jerome Biblical Commentary*, Raymond E. Brown, Joseph Fitzmyer and Roland E. Murphy, eds (London: Geoffrey Chapman, 1989), 9.

[3] Roland E. Murphy, "Introduction to the Pentateuch", in *The New Jerome Biblical Commentary*, 4–7.

on the Bible,⁴ entertains the real possibility that the work of one single creative author is an important factor in the compilation of the book. Wenham, while leaving the question of authorship open, returns to the ancient tradition that Moses was the author. "The brilliantly told narratives and tight structure of the book of Genesis make it difficult to believe that it simply evolved out of oral tradition or was the compilation of a mere editor. It bears the stamp of a powerful creative author, but who that was we cannot know. If Moses was as significant as biblical tradition paints him, we may credit him with the first draft of the book."

However, let us step back from the question of authorship and turn to the narrative itself which the Judaeo-Christian has inherited. For regardless of exactly who wrote or edited this narrative, it is generally agreed that this seminal narrative was for centuries embedded in the tradition of the people of Israel and the ancient near East before theologians began to interpret it. Clifford's introduction to Genesis in *The New Jerome Biblical Commentary*⁵ highlights how in Mesopotamian culture scribes explored the origin of things through narrative. There were many creation epics in circulation. In particular the Atrahasis story contains themes similar to those in the narrative of the creation and Fall of humanity. Human beings are created by the gods to maintain creation. They offend the gods because they spread and make noise. The gods punish the humans. Then a fresh beginning is made through one surviving man. So the Genesis account is not alone in exploring major questions about the relationship between God or the gods and humanity through a narrative of creation. What is true is that, however it was compiled and against whatever cultural background, this account has formed a significant basis of the Christian understanding of the relationship between God and humanity. At the very centre of this understanding is the assertion that humanity is made in God's image. So let us state in straightforward terms what this seems to mean.

God made humanity in his own image. Thus God placed humanity in a unique position vis-à-vis himself. Humanity is, as is all creation, very good, but human beings are created with a special dignity. Human beings are given such a special dignity as creatures made in God's image that they are placed in a paradise, the Garden of Eden. So the *Catechism of the Catholic Church* teaches: "the first man was not only created good, but was also established in friendship with his Creator and in harmony with himself and with the creation around him".⁶ Then came the Fall. In the Christian tradition what humanity did to be expelled from Paradise has generally been understood through what we term original sin. Because humanity, although very good and made in God's image, was expelled from paradise, so humanity inherits the tendency to sin. Thus our being created in God's image,

---

⁴ Gordon J. Wenham, "Genesis", in *Eerdmans Commentary on the Bible*, James D.G. Dunn and William Rogerson, eds (Grand Rapids and Cambridge, UK: William B. Eerdmans Publishing Company, 2003), 35–6.

⁵ Ibid., 8–9.

⁶ *Catechism of the Catholic Church*, revised edn (London: Geoffrey Chapman, 1999), no. 374. [This will now subsequently be referred to as *CCC*].

because of that first sin, entails our tendency to sin. As the *Catechism* explains the teaching:

> God created man in his image and established him in his friendship ... A spiritual creature, man can live this friendship only in free submission to God. The prohibition against eating "of the tree of the knowledge of good and evil" spells this out: "for in the day that you eat of it, you shall die".[7] The "tree of the knowledge of good and evil"[8] symbolically evokes the insurmountable limits that man, being a creature, must freely recognize and respect with trust. Man is dependent on his Creator, and subject to the laws of creation and to the moral norms that govern the use of freedom. Man, tempted by the devil, let his trust in his Creator die in his heart and, abusing his freedom, *disobeyed* God's command. This is what man's first sin consisted of.[9] All subsequent sin would be disobedience toward God and lack of trust in his goodness.[10]

Such is the basic teaching we inherit. It is now time to turn to the interpretation of Christian theologians down the centuries.

Augustine

By far the most influential of the Fathers on the developing understanding of *imago Dei* was Augustine. Early in his career, in his work *De Diversis Quaestionibus*[11] he stated:

> Because man is able to participate in Wisdom through the inward man, it is according to the latter that he is said to be created *ad Imaginem*, in order that he might be fully formed by this Image with nothing intervening and in such a fashion that nothing could be closer to God. Thus he would truly know, and live, and be. No created thing could be greater.[12]

It is important to be clear about what Augustine seems to mean. This requires us to make some distinctions. Firstly, Augustine identifies humanity's being created "*ad Imaginem*" with the interior ability of human beings to participate in Wisdom, that is to participate in the life of the true image of God. For Augustine the image

---

[7] Genesis 2:17.
[8] Genesis 2:17.
[9] Cf. Genesis 3:1–11; Romans 5:19.
[10] *CCC*, no. 396–7. Italics in the text of the Catechism.
[11] St Augustine, *De Diversis Quaestionibus*, Latin text in *Patres Latini Tomus 40* (Paris: Garnier Fratres et J.-P. Migne Successores, 1887).
[12] I am citing St Augustine in the English translation given in Eugene TeSelle, *Augustine the Theologian* (New York: Herder and Herder, 1970) of *De Diversis Quaestionibus LI.2*.

of God himself is the second person of the Trinity, the Word. It is according to this relationship to the true image of God himself that humanity is said to be "*ad Imaginem*". Humanity itself is not in fact *the* "*imago*", the image of God as though we reflect God in a mirror. Rather humanity is placed in a special *relationship* with God. This basic relationship marks off humanity from all other creatures.

This basic truth, however, allows us to say that each individual human being has a "likeness" ("*similitudo*") to God. Each individual human person has a special dignity proper to himself which constitutes his own particular relationship with God and his fellows. It presents to each and everyone the possibility of living, knowing and being in a way which begins to find beyond himself the God according to whose image one has been created. Thus, at the very heart of Augustine's thought, we have the basic notion that humanity is made with a special dignity which is generic yet also deeply personal to each individual. Thus we may draw close to God or distance ourselves from him. As Farrugia puts it, quoting Augustine in *De Trinitate*:

> [I]t is *likeness* that constitutes and accounts for either closeness or distance between God and the human person: "For one does not approach God across intervals of time and space but by likeness, and by unlikeness he draws away from him".[13]

So how does Augustine explain the next stage of the narrative of this special personal relationship? In other words, how does he understand human beings' response to grace as actually an incorporation into the life of Christ who has claimed him? This narrative will be crucial for trying to understand the theological traditions which flow from it. First of all we must be clear that Augustine affirmed the fundamental Judaeo-Christian faith in a Creator God who makes all things, including humanity, good. This straightforward interpretation of the Genesis account is a fundamental starting point. "All of nature, therefore, is good, since the Creator of all nature is supremely good."[14] So, in making humanity "*ad Imaginem Dei*", God made humanity good.

Now, however, there is an important distinction to make which will underscore an aspect of Augustine's thought which would serve to play down the emphasis on human dignity but highlight the negative tendency in humanity to turn away from God. The basic intrinsic difference between God and humans made "*ad Imaginem Dei*" is in fact a characteristic distinguishing us from God which we share with angels. God is immutable but human beings and angels are mutable. On this distinction he forms the basis of his teaching on the Fall in Chapters VIII–XIII

---

[13] Mario Farrugia, "Gn1: 26–27 in Augustine and Luther: 'Before you are my strength and my weakness'" (*Gregorianum* 87, 3, 2006), 501, quoting St Augustine, *The Trinity*, VII, 6, 12. Emphasis Farrugia's.

[14] St Augustine, *Enchiridion on Faith, Hope and Love* (Philadelphia: Westminster Press, 1955), IV.12.

of his work *Enchiridion on Faith, Hope and Love*. Augustine declared that "the cause of the evil is the defection of the will of a being who is mutably good from the Good which is immutable".[15]

It is through this mutability that the Fall occurs. Through it humanity can be both ignorant of the good and desire that which is not good. "This was the primal lapse of the rational creature, that is, his first privation of the good. In train of this there crept in, even without his willing it, ignorance of the right things to do and also an appetite for noxious things."[16] When the first human chose to turn away from the good this had a catastrophic consequence for the whole human race:

> From this state, after he had sinned, man was banished, and through his sin he subjected his descendants to the punishment of sin and damnation, for he had radically corrupted them, in himself, by his sinning. As a consequence of this, all those descended from him and his wife (who had prompted him to sin and who was condemned along with him at the same time) – all those born through carnal lust, on whom the penalty is visited as for disobedience – all those entered into the inheritance of original sin … This, then, was the situation: the whole mass of the human race stood condemned, lying ruined and wallowing in evil.[17]

For the sin of the first human in Eden humanity was banished. This entails the punishment of sin and damnation. Because of the effects of sin human beings were at one point all damned. We all inherited what is termed "original sin". Thus Augustine has laid the foundations of a theology of humanity which, while created good and in a special relationship with the God according to whose image he is made, at the same time has inherited the tendency to turn away from God, to sin and thus to be damned.

From this position Augustine develops the framework of his theological anthropology. From the perspective of the "*massa damnata*" Augustine develops a theology of humanity's salvation through grace. Not all humans will be condemned. Just as with the angels, who in his scheme had fallen before humans, so "those who had remained loyal through the revolt should go on rejoicing in the certain knowledge of the bliss forever theirs", the life of the "heavenly Jerusalem",[18] that is oneness with God according to whose image they were made. In fact our human nature, despite the Fall, still yearns for this state of "*beatitudo*", "blessedness", "happiness". "Yet such a nature, even in its evil state, could not lose its appetite for blessedness".[19] A portion of humanity will be saved. Others will be damned. We are mutable and inherit a tendency to sin. Yet we all have an "appetite" for "blessedness", made as we are according to the image of God. So how can we

---

[15] Ibid., VIII.23.
[16] Ibid., VIII.24.
[17] Ibid., VIII.26–7.
[18] Ibid., VIII.29.
[19] Ibid., VIII.25.

be saved? The basic answer for Augustine was to follow St Paul's teaching in Romans. Our salvation came through Jesus Christ. God incarnate in Jesus Christ gave His life as a ransom for the human race. Salvation comes through the sacrifice of Christ.

> Since men are in this state of wrath through original sin – a condition made still graver and more pernicious as they compounded more and worse sins with it – a Mediator was required, that is to say, a Reconciler who by offering a unique sacrifice, of which all the sacrifices of the Law and the Prophets were shadows, should allay that wrath. Thus the apostle says, "For if, when we were enemies, we were reconciled to God by the death of his Son, even more now being reconciled by his blood we shall be saved from wrath through him".[20]

That portion of humanity which *can* be saved, that is the portion which is not damned, can do nothing on its own. Human beings cannot attempt to be saved themselves. They can only be saved by Christ who has paid the ransom for us. "But now, can that part of the human race to whom God hath promised deliverance and a place in the eternal Kingdom be restored through the merits of their own works? Of course not! For what good works could a lost soul do...?"[21] Augustine then goes on to say that we find no "freedom" in attempting our own salvation. Rather we discover our true freedom in the divine Son, the incarnate Word, Wisdom, the one to whom we are oriented as creatures made according to God's image. Our own human nature, despite our being made "*ad imaginem Dei*", cannot save us. We need a saviour and all salvation is a free gift, that is what we call grace.

Thus Augustine gave the Church a framework for understanding how human beings were constituted in this special relationship with God. After the Fall there would be no relationship without the grace of Christ. This is the faith we inherit and it is through our faith in Jesus Christ that we have the possibility of being saved. How this faith relationship will be depicted will be significant for the centuries of theological discussion which follow. Human beings after the Fall can do nothing except through the grace of Christ but to what extent are we merely passive spectators in the special relationship with God according to whose image we are made? Yet does not Augustine also open up a picture of the special relationship as in many ways reciprocal, reflecting the "*via*", a life of pilgrimage towards "*beatitudo*" in the "heavenly Jerusalem", and so prepare the ground for a theology of the moral life which make us in a sense active participants in that relationship as we grow towards his likeness? These will be important themes to which we will return later in Augustine.

---

[20] Ibid., VIII.33.
[21] Ibid., VIII.30.

Irenaeus

It is generally agreed that Irenaeus, writing 200 years and more before Augustine, has had less significance on the development of the understanding of "*imago Dei*". Although tradition had taught that he provided a direct link with the teaching of the apostles, the less voluminous writings of this Greek Father did not take root to the same extent as the prolific Augustine. However, he is an important link for us. The twentieth-century theologians we will study later returned to the teaching of Irenaeus. Furthermore it may be argued that, whilst it is not always clear through the scant original material we have, exactly what Irenaeus believed, he presents an alternative vision to what was to become a rich Augustinian tradition in the Church.

It has been argued that Irenaeus made a sharper distinction between the Greek terms "εικών", translated into Latin as "*imago*" and English as "image", and "ομοίωσις", translated into Latin as "*similitudo*" and English as "likeness". What did this distinction mean? J.N.D. Kelly,[22] who has traced Irenaeus' use of the distinction, explains it as follows. Inasmuch as Irenaeus taught that human beings were created in God's "image" he meant that the first human enjoyed the power of reason and of freedom of will. Inasmuch as he taught that human beings were created in God's "likeness" they enjoyed a supernatural endowment through the action of the Spirit.

Adam was created in God's "image" and "likeness". However, just because he was made in the "likeness" of God, supernaturally endowed by the Spirit, this did not prevent him from exercising the reason and freedom which constituted his humanity made in God's "image". As for Augustine it is Adam's exercise of these human faculties in the paradise of Eden which leads to the Fall. But for Irenaeus it is at this point, as a consequence of the wrongful exercise of these faculties, that humanity loses its "likeness" to God. However, this Fall and loss of God's "likeness", while having consequences for the human race which involve sin, suffering and damnation, is by no means a catastrophe. In fact Irenaeus seems to paint what some may argue is a more optimistic picture of the Fall than that we have inherited from Augustine.

For Irenaeus our being made in God's "image" was of great significance to understanding why Adam fell and so humanity's retention of this "image" after the Fall becomes the key to his view of our relationship with God now. It would seem that for him this faculty of free will and reason is of crucial importance to humanity's growth through life on the earth as we move back towards the perfection of God's "likeness". For Irenaeus Adam's being created with the ability to choose freely and to reason meant that he was not created perfect as God is perfect. Thus he was in fact divided from God at the very outset in a different and far greater

---

[22] J.N.D. Kelly, *Early Christian Doctrines*, 4th edn (London: Adam & Charles Black, 1958, 1968), 171. I am indebted here to Kelly's paraphrasing and translation of the Greek text in Migne, *Patrologiae Graecae, Tomus VII* (Paris: Garnier Fratres et J.-P. Migne Successores, 1882).

way to that taught by Augustine. He was not just mutable so distanced from the God who is immutable, as Augustine had taught. In fact he was also, from the very outset, created in a child-like state of imperfection which necessarily tended towards acting in a way which distanced him from God. Through this experience the child would grow towards the perfection the sovereign God intended for him. As Kelly puts it, explaining the section in *Adversus Haereses*, "Adam was necessarily far removed from the divine perfection and incorruptibility; an infinite distance divided him from God".[23]

The exegetical keys to Irenaeus' view seem to be his interpretation of Genesis 2:7 and of St Paul's letter to the Ephesians. When God infused into the first human being "the breath of life" this did not constitute him at this stage as an adopted son of God. Rather "[I]t was by a long process of response to grace and submission to God's will that Adam, equipped as he was with free choice, was intended to advance towards ever closer resemblance to His maker".[24] The opportunity of this fresh start, this life's pilgrimage back towards God, is offered to us, through and only through the grace of Christ. As with Augustine we cannot work our way back to God on our own. However some would note that, whereas Augustine has focussed more on the retention of our original sin and the possibility, or in the case of some inevitability, of our damnation, Irenaeus has focussed more on how the grace of Christ offers humanity in general a fresh start.

Irenaeus develops the teaching of St Paul to present a very particular understanding of our redemption. "Because of His measureless love He became what we are in order to enable us to become what He is."[25] In other words the point of the incarnation was to draw us human beings into Christ, the one who is fully God and fully human. What we lost in Adam we are now enabled to regain in Christ as God's purpose is, as Paul had written, "to sum up all things in Christ".[26] Christ is the "second Adam", heralding a fresh start, as he has "recapitualated in Himself all the dispersed peoples dating back to Adam, all tongues and the whole race of mankind, along with Adam himself".[27] Thus in Irenaeus later theology inherited a different perspective on the doctrine of "*imago Dei*" to the more widely accepted model of Augustine. Later on, when we turn to our twentieth-century theologians, we will consider the influence on them of these two early Church Fathers and in so doing address some of the nuances in their writings. For now we are able to summarise the key difference between the two models of "*imago Dei*" Augustine and Irenaeus present. For Augustine being made in God's "image" stresses how the human being is made perfect and falls from this state of perfection before God. For Irenaeus being made in God's "image" represents an original state

---

[23] Ibid., 171, referring to *Adversus Haereses* 4, 38, 1–3.
[24] Ibid., 171, referring to *Adversus Haereses* 4, 37, 1; 4, 38, 3.
[25] Ibid., 172, referring to *Adversus Haereses* 5, Preface.
[26] Ephesians 1:10.
[27] Ibid., 173, translating *Adversus Haereses* 3, 22, 3.

of immaturity which is part of God's plan for us as we grow towards perfection in being restored to the divine "likeness".

What are the implications of these divergent models? We might say that whereas Augustine emphasises how the Fall led to God's punishment and damnation of the human race, for Irenaeus the Fall leads to negative consequences as we lose our "likeness" to God but this is all part of the necessary environment for human growth. For both it is Christ who offers us the possibility of being restored in his mystical body. However, for Augustine there remains the possibility of laying greater emphasis on how our being made in "*imago Dei*" involves a belief in the inevitable damnation for some and salvation for others. This is not one of Irenaeus' emphases. Rather for him the human being's creation in the "*imago*" places him on life's pilgrimage as responding to God's grace, a theme more reminiscent of the more teleological aspect of Augustine's thought.

Such are the different emphases in these two Fathers of the Church. This is certainly not to say that we may highlight flaws in both these Father's writings nor to say that one ought to be endorsed in favour of the other. The wisdom of the Church accepts them both as complementary to each other.

Aquinas

Aquinas had a vast influence on the debate which was to take place at the time of the Reformation. It was the thought of this writer which was to become the benchmark of orthodox teaching and which the reformers were to object to so strongly. Indeed some would argue that the direction in which Aquinas took theological reflection was a major factor in the Reformation divide. For Aquinas moved away from exposition of the narrative of creation by God, the first sin, and our redemption in Christ, to probe much more deeply the more scientific and philosophical question of what that narrative then says about our identity, about God's, and the relationship between the two. If we take the narrative as written these questions, which rely on a more philosophical and scientific way of writing theology, are valid ones to ask. However, this moved theology into a new area which would raise contentious questions. To these questions Aquinas provided some clear answers.

First of all we need to affirm that in basic general respects Aquinas accepted the narrative the medievals inherited from Augustine.[28] We can trace this through

---

[28] This general statement requires clarification. I must point out that of course it is true that Aquinas' version of the narrative also differs in certain respects from Augustine's. Aquinas, it is true, developed a greater distinction between man and woman than had Augustine. Also Aquinas' view of how man is created in a specifically Trinitarian image of God is different in respects. These differences indeed are due to particular interpretations of both the Greek and Latin Fathers and to the influence of Aristotelian philosophy on his thought. However these divergences in emphasis, while they would be of significance to a

the pages of the *Summa Theologiae*.²⁹ Humanity is created in the divine image and so at the outset is placed in a special relationship with God.³⁰ Then comes the Fall. The first human sinned and thus sin and death entered the world.³¹ Jesus Christ, through his death and resurrection, restored us to himself thus giving us the possibility of salvation.³²

When considering what the narrative teaches us about our identity vis-à-vis God Aquinas focussed, as had Irenaeus, not solely on the motif of "image" of God but also on that of "likeness" to God. But the method and perspective of his enquiry differed from that of Irenaeus. For Aquinas was chiefly interested in the more scientific and philosophical question of how we can know God. In *De Veritate* he states:

> We cannot say ... that whatever is predicated of God and creature is predicated purely equivocally, since if no real likeness of creature to God existed, his essence would not be the likeness of creatures and then he would not know creatures through knowing his essence. So we must state that the name "knowledge" is predicated of God's Knowledge and of ours neither wholly univocally nor purely equivocally, but by analogy, which merely means according to proportion.³³

Thus Aquinas concludes that humanity is like God in terms of "analogy". We can indeed say that humanity is like God but the analogical distinction between creator and creature is important. Because of Adam's sin humanity's likeness to God is coloured by our sin. Nevertheless likeness to God is still our true identity and so fuller participation in this reality is our true calling. These two motifs, namely identity and participation, are important.

Aquinas had set the stage for the theological community to debate the consequences of an accepted narrative involving belief in a sovereign Creator God whose creatures then fell from some elevated state yet could still, through Christ, attain salvation. If we accept this, who exactly are we and how do we attain full participation in that for which we were made? As one influenced by the Platonic school of philosophy this way of approaching the subject was also

---

longer study of Aquinas, are not of significance to a general introduction to the theological debate.

²⁹ Throughout I am using the New Blackfriars edition: St Thomas Aquinas, *Summa Theologiae*, New Blackfriars edn (London and New York: McGraw-Hill Book Company, 1960–1981), subsequently referred to as *ST*, and cited according to section of the text and volume of the New Blackfriars edition.

³⁰ *ST* Ia.93, Volume 13: *Man Made to God's Image*.

³¹ *ST* IaIIae.81–85, Volume 26: *Original Sin*.

³² *ST* IaIIae.106–114, Volume 30: *The Gospel of Grace*.

³³ St Thomas Aquinas, *De Veritate*, consulted in *Opera Omnia Tomus IX* (New York: Musurgia Publishers, 1949), II.1. Here I am following the translation in *An Aquinas Reader*, Mary T. Clark, ed. (London: Hodder & Stoughton, 1974), 99.

present in Augustine. This is an important strand in his multi-faceted theological picture which we will naturally return to later in depth. However it was Aquinas, recovering Aristotle, who made this line of enquiry his theological starting point.

As creatures the first question we must ask is regarding our very existence.[34] Aquinas had started his enquiry with the question of God's existence. God, as uncaused cause of all things, is the being from whom all created things receive their existence and so to whom they tend. The very essence of God is to exist. Humanity exists but in a limited way. We discover our existence through our participation in the life of God in whom we find the perfection of existence. We are not just encouraged to participate in the life of God on earth but to set it as our goal. Union to God is the final end of our lives on earth because then we will be one with he in whose image and likeness we were made, the God who is our true identity.

So how do we participate in the life of God?[35] For Aquinas this is only possible through the grace of Christ. Thus the grace of Christ is necessary. However, as limited creatures who nonetheless are oriented towards final union to the infinite God, God infuses his creatures with virtues, especially of faith, hope and charity, which help us on our journey back to him. Sin hampers us on our journey but through God working in us, that is through what Aquinas calls "grace", we are given the opportunity to attain at the end of our lives the goal which was our origin, namely "*beatitudo*", the "blessedness" of union to God.

Thus as in Irenaeus, and in the Platonic strand in Augustine, we have a teleological picture of our salvation after the Fall. God through the merits of his incarnate Son on the cross has made possible the way back for sinful humanity. The necessity of grace is absolutely central to the picture. Yet we in our limited sinful "nature" are granted the possibility and indeed are oriented towards the final end of our existence, a reunion with God. We are indeed participators in the work of our restoration after the Fall, not merely passive spectators as some are saved and others damned, as might be argued to be a central strand in the classical Augustinian position. Rather our being made in God's image and likeness involves us in a personal pilgrimage and quest in which, through grace, we can discover our true identity and home in God. Thus in Aquinas and the teaching of other scholastics who followed him our special human dignity as creatures made in God's image and likeness plays a more and more active part in the special relationship we have with God. The "grace" of Christ builds on our human "nature". It is this development which would lead to great debate as the Reformation dawned.

---

[34] I refer here to the following sections in the *Summa Theologiae*: Ia.2–11, in Volume 2 of the New Blackfriars edn: *Existence and Nature of God*, and Ia.75–83, in Volume 11, *Man*.

[35] I refer here to the following sections in the *Summa Theologiae*: IaIIae.106–114, in Volume 30 of the New Blackfriars edition, *The Gospel of Grace*, and IaIIae.1–5, in Volume 16, *Purpose and Happiness*.

Luther

The question of what caused the Reformation is very complex, involving political and cultural considerations as well as theological. However in theological terms differing perspectives on the relationship between God and human beings were at the heart of the dispute. Reformation theology still accepted in general terms the account of the narrative inherited from the Fathers and medieval scholastics. Human beings have a special dignity and special relationship with God as they are made in his image. They fall from the state of goodness in which they were created, and through this fall the relationship between God and human beings is distorted. Jesus Christ, through his death and resurrection, however, heralds salvation. So much is agreed and thus is common ground. But it is in the particular understanding of the special relationship between God and human beings after the Fall that we find crucial points of departure for a whole tradition of theology loosely termed Lutheranism.

Luther believed that medieval theology's concentration on the role of human nature in the God–human relationship after the Fall implied our ability to work our way back to God to the extent that an affirmation of belief in the total gratuity of salvation in Christ was jeopardised. His intention was to correct this error and reclaim the true teaching of scripture and rightful account of what it means to say that we are creatures made in God's image. His view seems, at first sight, to be close to Augustine's, emphasising our human depravity as sinners and our need of and utter dependence on God's saving work in Christ. For Luther humanity's creation in God's image does not entail the natural ability to prepare for God's justice which had characterised some medieval theology. We are able to make moral choices but this ability is totally unconnected with God's justice which is totally gratuitous. Human beings are called simply to accept that as creatures made in his image we have been put right with God through the sacrifice of his Son Jesus Christ.

It is important to note that Luther's position does not translate today into a homogeneous theology in the Lutheran churches or what is loosely termed Lutheranism. A note of caution must be entertained before moving to such a simplistic presentation of this particular strand in the Reformation as Luther, like Augustine and Aquinas indeed, has been interpreted in different ways in different traditions. Lutheranism today is not at one on every aspect of Luther's teaching. However this belief in humanity's utter dependence on God's justice in the person and work of Christ is fundamental to classical Lutheran thought. Indeed the Lutheran Formula of Concord attributes this clear statement of belief to Luther himself:

> Our free will has no power whatsoever in virtue of which man could prepare himself for justice or even seek it out. On the contrary, blind and captive man gives exclusive obedience to Satan's will and perpetuates thereby things offensive to God ... Fallen man does not cease to be a rational creature ...

> furthermore, in civil and external matters he is able somewhat to discern the good from the bad and even freely to do some things and desist from others ... Before conversion man is, indeed, a rational creature, having intellect and will (though no understanding of divine realities nor will to do what is good and salvific). He is, nonetheless, able to contribute nothing to his conversion.[36]

Luther's role in the development of theological thinking on humanity's creation in God's image is important. He aims to steer the doctrine away from the scientific and philosophical enquiry of the medieval period. He rejects the up to this point accepted notion of the earthly pilgrimage culminating in the beatific vision such as we found in Aquinas and in the more Platonic strand of Augustine. Instead he introduces a different emphasis, stressing how humanity's identity can only be defined in terms of Christ's justification. In so doing Luther was not merely returning to the strand of Augustine's thought which stressed the human being's need of grace. He is not merely saying that in the Fall God's image in humanity has been distorted and we rely on God's grace to restore us. When we examine Luther more carefully we find a very radical account of human identity before God, which claims to represent faithfully the teaching not of any early Church Father or medieval writer but of St Paul, especially in his letter to the Romans.

The result of Luther's exegesis is an altogether more dynamic view of what happens when we are reconstituted in a special relationship with God after the Fall. For Luther we are reconstituted in Christ even though God's image in us will always be distorted. This teaching is generally known as "justification by faith alone". For Luther we are called to an assurance that we are here and now as sinners made right with God in Christ. It is by our "faith" in this fact of our salvation in Christ that we are "justified" while at one and the same time we are still, and always will be, sinners. We are "*simul*" and "*semper*" "*iustus et peccator*". Our "faith" is not the kind which is moved, whether by God's grace or anything else, to fulfil our destiny in being reunited with Christ through the exercise of faith, hope and charity. This is not necessary. Our faith is for Luther "*fiducia*", simply a "trust" in the fact that we are right with God in Christ. The true radicality of Luther is clearly present in his own testimony of this incredibly personal and dynamic realisation of what is at the heart of the Gospel:

> Although I lived an irreproachable life as a monk, I felt that I was a sinner with an uneasy conscience before God; nor was I able to believe that I had pleased him with my satisfaction ... At last, God being merciful, as I meditated day and night on the connection of the words "the righteousness of God is revealed in it, as it is written: the righteous shall live by faith", I began to understand ... this sentence,

---

[36] Formula of Concord, *Solida Declaratio*, 879–96 *passim*, quoted in translation in M.B. Schepers, "Lutheranism", in *New Catholic Encyclopedia*, Editorial Staff of the Catholic University of America, Washington, District of Columbia (New York: McGraw-Hill Book Company, 1967), 1095–6.

"the righteousness of God is revealed," to refer to a passive righteousness, by which the merciful God justifies us by faith ... This immediately made me feel as though I had been born again, and as though I had entered through open gates into paradise itself.[37]

To accept this teaching in "justification by faith alone" in fact answers all questions about our human identity as creatures made in God's image and entails the freedom of the Christian. Not to accept God's justification of us in Christ is for Luther a rejection of our true identity, that is identity in Christ, and represents the true meaning of sin. We are either free in our acceptance of our righteousness or we are slaves to the sin of rejecting this. We might question whether in Luther's system we are in fact free not to accept. Luther believes that we are and must be but also seems to regard true freedom as impossible if we reject our justification. We will return to this later when we examine how Luther's picture has influenced all three twentieth-century theologians we are studying and how they inherit this problematic.

However, if our true identity as creatures made in God's image lies in simply accepting that we are here and now right with God there is another question we must address. Is our role in the God–human dynamic purely passive as in fact all human beings are saved? In a complex and multi-faceted theological picture the Church Father Origen had taught universal salvation in Christ after the Fall and this had been condemned as heresy. As we shall clarify shortly, in turning to the Council of Trent and to Vatican II, Luther has of course departed from Catholic teaching and been condemned but not necessarily on the grounds that he teaches universal salvation. It is unclear from Luther's writings how he saw this issue. Some scholars believe that his call to be assured of salvation amounted to a belief that we can hope that we are all saved. However others note his emphasis on the elect and see in his picture the teaching that, while we can all hope, some are saved and others condemned.

Nevertheless, regardless of this uncertainty over universal salvation, Luther leaves theology with a model of "*imago Dei*" which, while claiming that humanity is free in accepting the righteousness of God, at the same time portrays the believer's relationship with God as necessarily passive. There appears to be no reciprocity in the special relationship between God and humans. On the one hand Luther's new model, in placing renewed emphasis on Christ, may be said to cut through the medieval preoccupation with our ability with God's grace to become once again like God. However, in doing this and giving the glory back to God in Christ, the human person's creation in God's image ceases to involve a reciprocal relationship with God played out actively on our earthly pilgrimage. This shift in perspective was to be highlighted even further in the thought of another reformer, John Calvin.

---

[37] Martin Luther, *Preface to the Latin Works*, in *D. Martin Luthers Werke: Kritische Gesamtausgabe*, Volume 54 (Weimar: Böhlau, 1938), 185.12–186.21, quoted in translation in *The Christian Theology Reader*, Alistair McGrath, ed. (Oxford: Blackwell, 1995), 228.

Calvin

The work of John Calvin provided early Protestantism with a clear theological synthesis which expressed starkly the shift in perspective we noted in Luther. For Calvin we are made in "*imago Dei*" but at the Fall the image was distorted to the extent that we are rendered incapable of participating in a reciprocal relationship with God. The relational distance between God and the creatures made in his image becomes most clear. God now becomes totally other as human beings passively accept their righteousness.

Calvin's theology is laid out in the pages of the *Institutes of the Christian Religion*.[38] Here Calvin accepted, defended and taught Luther's doctrine of justification by faith alone and in doing so emphasised through it God's sovereignty and humanity's depravity. For him we must not ask the medieval question "*quis est Deus?*" because God's "essence is incomprehensible; hence his divineness far escapes all human perception".[39] We cannot attain any knowledge of God except through the teaching of scripture.[40] When we look to scripture what we find is a picture of the utter sovereignty and otherness of God vis-à-vis humanity whose being made in God's image, while not totally destroyed, "was so corrupted that whatever remains is frightful deformity".[41] After the Fall human beings are totally incapable of maintaining right relation with God because we are bound by the slavery of sin.

Our salvation comes through faith in Christ, the sole mediator, who takes away our sins and places us at one and the same time in right relation with God. This faith of the Christian, Calvin is intent on making clear, involves no ability on the part of the human to draw close to God. Instead it comes from outside of us. The faith through which fallen humanity is made righteous comes from the sovereign God himself. Faith is "the principal work of the Holy Spirit".[42] Saving faith is "a firm and certain knowledge of God's benevolence towards us, founded upon the truth of the freely given promise in Christ, both revealed to our minds and sealed upon our hearts through the Holy Spirit".[43] Faith itself has no power in itself. It "merits righteousness for us ... because it is an instrument whereby we obtain free the righteousness of Christ".[44]

The otherness of the sovereign God and humanity's depravity is brought into such close relief in the Calvinist system that a clearly stated doctrine of double predestination naturally follows. As such for him it becomes a necessary foundation.

---

[38] I am using the following English translation: John Calvin, *Institutes of the Christian Religion* (Philadelphia: Westminster Press, 1960).
[39] Ibid., 1.5.1.
[40] Ibid., 1.8.13.
[41] Ibid., 1.15.4.
[42] Ibid., 3.1.4.
[43] Ibid., 3.2.7.
[44] Ibid., 3.13.8.

The work of salvation has absolutely nothing to do with fallen humanity and so is totally in the hands of God. For Calvin, if we truly accept this, then we must believe that God wills salvation and condemnation. Nothing can get in the way of this plan. The elect conform to God's desires but others will in a manifestation of God's glory be justly condemned. God is absolute and we are powerless. "We call predestination God's eternal decree, by which he determined with himself what he willed to become of each man. For all are not created in equal condition; rather, eternal life is foreordained for some, eternal damnation for others."[45] Thus, on this point, he accepts Augustine's doctrine of double predestination.

To conclude, in the theologies of Luther and Calvin the Reformation represented a clear shift in thinking on how humanity is made in the "*imago Dei*". They moved the doctrine's point of reference from asking the medieval philosophical and scientific questions about the nature of the human being per se and focussed instead first and foremost on the sovereignty of God in whose image humanity is made and, in particular, on Christ, who has restored us to this image. The emphasis shifts towards Christ's action in the life of the believer and away from the believer's growth and fulfilment as he finds his way back to God.

It is important to note, on the one hand, how this may be seen to be a positive shift in the development of the doctrine yet, on the other, how it represents a weakness. On a positive note we find a fresh emphasis on the person of Christ, the power of grace and the inability of the human person to fulfil himself without God. Yet the human being's creation in the "*imago Dei*" does not seem to involve a reciprocal relationship with the God who in Christ has redeemed him. The Reformation thus represents an impoverishment of the theme of relationship between God and the human being. Inasmuch as humanity is unable to actively participate in fulfilling his own destiny as a creature made for God he loses a sense of his dignity. If Christ's action in human lives is not merely the reference point, but this Christ is benevolent, merciful, loving, even though his special creation is sinful, is there not room for a picture of humanity's personal quest for relationship with such a God founded on a belief in the prior grace of Christ?

This question will be an important one. Later theology, and especially the three theologians of different traditions we will be considering, will shed light on this question. Barth, Balthasar and Moltmann are at the forefront of addressing this key ecumenical issue. All three theologians were strongly influenced by this shift in emphasis that took place at the Reformation. Each will incorporate this renewed emphasis on Christ's action in human lives. Yet each will also try to develop in a different way a picture of the human being's creation in the "*imago Dei*" as necessarily involving a personal relationship with Christ. Shortly we will introduce these three twentieth-century theologians. Firstly, however, we must turn to the response of the Roman Catholic Church in the sixteenth century, to the declaration of the Council of Trent which was to condemn the teaching of the

---

[45] Ibid., 3.21.5.

reformers and after much debate state more clearly the teaching of scripture, the Fathers and, especially, Aquinas.

The Council of Trent

The Fathers of the Council of Trent reacted strongly to the Reformation position. First of all the Council restated a clear belief in the necessity of God's action in Christ in restoring humanity's original holiness and justice which was lost through the sin of Adam. For the Fathers at Trent this distortion of our creation in the "*imago Dei*" placed us all in a state of original sin. Clearly it is not our own human nature but only Jesus Christ who can make us right with our Creator.

> If anyone asserts that this sin of Adam which, one by origin and passed on to all by propagation and not by imitation, inheres in everyone as something proper to each, is removed by human and natural powers, or by any remedy other than the one mediator, our lord Jesus Christ … let him be anathema.[46]

However it was necessary to clarify how God's grace was mediated and so how original sin was taken away and we were thus restored to an ongoing relationship with God. For Trent this was done through the infusion of grace in the sacrament of baptism. This applies to both adults and infants. Righteousness is not simply the justification which we accept in our sinful state as we turn towards God in fiducial trust that original justice has been restored in Christ. It is in fact mediated through the sacraments of the Church which set us on a pilgrimage back towards union with the God in whose image we are made.

> If anyone says that recently born babies should not be baptised even if they have been born to baptised parents; or says that they are indeed baptised for the remission of sins, but incur no trace of the original sin of Adam needing to be cleansed by the water of rebirth for them to obtain eternal life, with the necessary consequence that in their case there is being understood a form of baptism for the remission of sins which is not true, but false: let him be anathema.[47]

Baptism thus sets the Christian made in "*imago Dei*" on a path which is directed to oneness with God. The baptised Christian is now said to be "justified" but this is merely the start of a life's journey, not a final reality. The relationship between God and the new Christian, between grace and human nature, is an active dynamic through life. The Christian must dispose himself to receive sanctifying grace. This

---

[46] Council of Trent, *Decree on Original Sin*, no. 3. I am using the translation of this Decree and of the *Decree on Justification* given in Tanner, whose edited footnotes I also include.

[47] Ibid., no. 4.

is infused in the form of virtues which enables us to become more and more like God for whom we were made through the exercise of good works. We are not simply made right with God through faith alone as Luther and Calvin maintained. We can actually progress in holiness and so towards the beatific vision, that is the restoration of our likeness to God.

> So those justified in this way and made friends and members of the household of God,[48] going from strength to strength,[49] are (as the Apostle says)[50] renewed from day to day by putting to death what is earthly in themselves[51] and yielding themselves as instruments of righteousness for sanctification[52] by observance of the commandments of God and the church. They grow and increase in the very justness they have received through the grace of Christ, by faith united to good works, as it is written: *Let him who is holy become more holy*;[53] and again, *Do not wait until death to be justified*;[54] again, *you see that a person is justified by works and not by faith alone.*[55] Indeed, holy church asks for this increase of justice when it prays, *Lord, give us an increase in faith, hope and charity.*[56] [57]

Thus, through grace working in us, we are granted a restored dignity as God's special creation which nevertheless we must actively work on throughout life as we work towards our goal of becoming more like God. We must avoid sin and live out our baptism if we are to be granted the vision of God in the next life. For Luther we were already "*coram Deo*" but Trent needs to place us on a relational path of gradual restoration to oneness with our Creator. New Christians, once baptised, have a duty to preserve this dignity and relationship with God:

> Thus, receiving true and Christian justness in exchange for that which Adam, by his disobedience, lost for himself and for us, the reborn are immediately ordered to preserve the justice freely granted to them through Jesus Christ in a pure and spotless state ... so that they may carry it before the tribunal of our Lord Jesus Christ and possess eternal life.[58] [59]

---

[48] See Ephesians 2:19.
[49] Psalm 83:8.
[50] See 2 Corinthians 4:16.
[51] See Colossians 3:5.
[52] See Romans 6:13, 19.
[53] Apocalypse 22:11.
[54] Ecclesiasticus 18:22.
[55] James 2:24.
[56] In the prayers of 13th Sunday after Pentecost.
[57] Council of Trent, *Decree on Justification*, no. 10. Italics Tanner's.
[58] See *Rituale Romanum (Roman Ritual)*, administration of baptism.
[59] *Decree on Justification*, no. 7.

In responding clearly to the challenge of the Reformation the Council aimed to correct the emphases of Luther and Calvin. The human being's creation in the "*imago Dei*" involves a belief in the God-given ability of the human being to actively become holy, to become more like God. Being created in God's image entails an ongoing relationship with God before whom, through our baptism and fortification in the other sacraments of the Church, we are graced with a special dignity. Trent thus restores to the doctrine this important aspect of the personal human quest for meaning, fulfilment and dignity.

Some might argue that Trent missed the point of the Reformation's shift of emphasis away from the human being per se and towards God's action in human lives. For followers of Luther and Calvin, and for some within the Roman Catholic Church, the emphasis on the ongoing relationship with God leads to undue emphasis on working out our salvation, on sin and guilt, and above all trying to get to heaven. They would argue that in the Catholic response to the Reformation we do not find a perspective on the human being's creation in "*imago Dei*" which reflects the human being's special dignity in actively seeking to fulfil his vocation through an ongoing relationship with God yet also integrates an emphasis the Reformation puts on how our dignity is already assured on the earth through Christ. In response to this accusation it is interesting to turn to the teaching of the Second Vatican Council. The teaching of Vatican II is totally in line with that of the Council of Trent as it recognises the deficiencies in the Reformation doctrines. Yet here we do find an explanation of how this emphasis on the assurance of Christian dignity is contained within the Catholic doctrine of grace. Let us now turn to this.

The Second Vatican Council

Here we see how in the doctrine of "*imago Dei*" humanity finds its meaning and destiny in the gift of Christ. The Council was to ground its theological anthropology in a renewed understanding of the ancient doctrine centred in Christ. It was to teach that, through common baptism, Christ has joined himself to fallen humanity and restored it to a special dignity as we are called into his company here on earth. It is in the documents *Lumen Gentium* and *Gaudium et Spes*[60] *that we are to find this emphasis. Lumen Gentium* was to set forth a vision of the vocation of each human being as, through baptism, called to participate here on the earth in the life and mission of Christ in which they have already been constituted as a pilgrim people.

This does not amount to a break with the teaching and tradition of the Council of Trent. Trent had stated this teaching implicitly but expressed it in a different way for a different time. Rather it represents a continuity and development of Trent's teaching. For Trent, needing to correct Reformation theology's stress on the passivity of the God–human relationship, our call to a life of holiness

---

[60] Second Vatican Council, *Lumen Gentium* [hereafter referred to as *LG*], and *Gaudium et Spes* [hereafter referred to as *GS*].

emphasised the struggle of the individual's ascent back to God as fallen creatures. So it laid great emphasis on our ultimate sanctification, on our becoming less earthly and more like God, that is, through what became known as "mortification". "Mortification" for the Tridentine Decree on Justification is the "*mortificando membra carnis suae*", translated by Tanner as "putting to death what is earthly in themselves".[61] It is important to be clear that this is still a very important and necessary part of our understanding of the Christian life for the post-Vatican II Church. An ongoing relationship with God does involve putting to death our earthly desires. This now was to be expressed in a renewed focus on our common baptismal dignity expressing a common identity in Christ.

For *Lumen Gentium* the baptised are called into a relationship with Christ the new Adam in whom they have been reborn. So in our baptism we are already marked as holy in Christ. All are called "by God not in virtue of their works but by his design and grace, and justified in the Lord Jesus" (*LG* 40). Those "justified in the Lord Jesus" "have been made sons of God in the baptism of faith and partakers of the divine nature, and so are truly sanctified" (*LG* 40). The Council was to develop this renewed emphasis on our relationship with Christ in a way which spoke very specifically of the dignity of the human person made in God's image. Whilst some may argue that, in rooting the doctrine firmly in Christ, the Council was on a basic level heeding the insights of the Reformation, the shift in emphasis is a more subtle and dynamic vision of the insights of Catholic doctrine. It takes us further into discussion of the mystery of the human person and his role in the world. It is above all *Gaudium et Spes* which develops these themes.

Christ, states no. 22, is the "'image of the invisible God' (Col. 1:15),[62] is himself the perfect man who has restored in the children of Adam that likeness to God which had been disfigured ever since the first sin. Human nature, by the very fact that it was assumed, not absorbed, in him, has been raised in us also to a dignity beyond compare" (*GS* 22). Christ not only puts us right with God but explains our vocation and special dignity as creatures made in God's image. For Christ is construed here not as counter to fallen human nature. On the contrary it is Christ's own humanity, assumed not absorbed, which joins himself to our humanity and represents to us the perfect image of God. Our humanity is not lost. Rather our human nature is, through him, as Ladaria puts it, "exalted to its supreme dignity".[63]

Thus each human being made in God's image and reborn in Christ is above all worthy of great respect and his or her vocation is not simply to return to the Creator but to make Christ present here on the earth. Our ongoing relationship with Christ involves a communal and social dimension. So *Gaudium et Spes* was

---

[61] Council of Trent, *Decree on Justification*, no. 10.
[62] Cf. 2 Cor. 4:4.
[63] Luis Ladaria, "Humanity in the Light of Christ in the Second Vatican Council", in *Vatican II: Assessment and Perspectives*, R. Latourelle, ed. (New York and Mahwah: Paulist Press, 1989), 391.

able to outline a belief in the essential dignity of the human being who, while made for God, we must affirm "by his innermost nature [man is] a social being" (*GS* 12). Our vocation is to grow in our likeness to Christ but this cannot be construed in any way as purely individualistic or divorced from the reality of life here on earth. Rather, because in baptism we are conformed to Christ, image of the invisible God on earth, we are called to active participation in his mission in the life of the Church in the world. So *Lumen Gentium* can proclaim:

> It is therefore quite clear that all Christians in any state or walk of life are called to the fullness of the Christian life and to the perfection of love, and by this holiness a more human manner of life is fostered also in earthly society. In order to reach this perfection the faithful should use the strength dealt out to them by Christ's gift, so that, following in his footsteps and conformed to his image, doing the will of God in everything, they may wholeheartedly devote themselves to the glory of God and to the service of their neighbour.[64]

The document goes on to develop a communitarian view of the God–human relationship. Our conformity to God's image directs us outwards to our fellow humans. This communal dimension flows into the Second Vatican Council's renewed emphasis on the Christian disciple's active role in society. *Gaudium et Spes* goes on to proclaim the need to transcend an individualistic morality. From this teaching flow sections on marriage and the family, economics, culture and the political realities of today. The keynote is the fundamental respect for each human person as a child of God in Christ and the heightened role of the Christian in building up a society which promotes this. This has become more and more the orientation of the postconciliar Church in its social and ethical teaching. Pope John Paul II's call, throughout his pontificate, to proclaim a culture of life enshrining the respect for human dignity, has as its theological background the firm belief that the human being is made for God. Schindler explains the connection well in his recent article in *Communio*: "To be a creature is, *eo ipso*, to bear a relation to God that 'demands' and presupposes a 'space' inside what is deepest and most original in the creature, that reaches from within the roots of the creature outward."[65] It is the fundamental teaching about the human being, that his very existence places him in special relationship to God, which gives meaning to his life on earth in relationship with his fellow humans.

In short Vatican II has brought two motifs to the fore which will also be important to the study of the three twentieth-century theologians to whom we now turn. On the one hand the Council wished to emphasise how Christ is the answer to all questions about our human identity. However, it also wanted to reassert that we

---

[64] *LG*, no. 40.

[65] David L. Schindler, "The Dramatic Nature of Life: Liberal Societies and the Foundations of Human Dignity" (*Communio: International Catholic Review* 33, Summer 2006), 183–202, 184–5. Emphasis his.

cannot simply passively accept our justification. Christ calls us into a relationship with him which at one and the same time affirms our special dignity as creatures made in God's image and draws us into his company. This directs us outwards towards others as partners on his mission. Our ongoing relationship with him is not just about our future destiny but represents a communal call to build up the Kingdom here on the earth.

Barth, von Balthasar and Moltmann

This first exploration of the writings of Karl Barth, Hans Urs von Balthasar and Jürgen Moltmann intends to do the following. For each in turn I will introduce their life and times and their theological system in general. I will then briefly outline their perspective on the doctrine of *"imago Dei"*. My aim is to show how they fit into the history of the doctrine I have been outlining and discussing up to this point. In particular I hope to show how they interpret the major themes and tensions in the history of the doctrine and point a way forward for its development now.

What are these major themes and tensions? We have seen how Vatican II interpreted the doctrine in terms of God's action in our lives in Christ and aimed to avoid turning to the question of human fulfilment in itself. Heavily influenced by Reformation thinking and the culture of his time the Protestant theologian Karl Barth insists on this emphasis too within his own integrated theological system. Balthasar and Moltmann, both influenced by Barth, by the Reformation, and by the culture, will do the same. It will be my conclusion that all three thus represent a clear thread in the twentieth-century history of the doctrine. They all represent the importance of grounding the doctrine in Christ and his action in our lives. They all, we might say, start their doctrine from above, not from below. The human being's creation in God's image is a theological topic which must be firmly rooted in the light of the truth about God, and in particular his descent to us in Christ. Only then can we explore the human condition from the perspective of its own ascent, desire and quest for God.

Yet, this agreed, there is another challenge with which all three of these theologians will engage with varying degrees of success. For a full picture of human dignity theology cannot avoid entirely looking at the human condition in itself. It also needs to continue to talk directly of the human response to God's creating us in his image. It requires us to speak of our ongoing relationship with Christ which propels us outwards towards others. So it must find ways to speak of the human search for meaning, fulfilment and destiny. It must also address how we live out our calling to be God's image on earth in our relationship with others with whom we share a like dignity. We have seen how, always against a clear Christocentric background, *Lumen Gentium*, *Gaudium et Spes* and postconciliar Catholic teaching has intended to explore this. It has been sure to focus the doctrine on Christ's descent to us as had the Reformation. Yet Vatican II and postconciliar Catholic teaching also recognise the importance of an account of our ascent, of our call to transcendence, above all of our ongoing friendship with God, and of the relationship with our fellow human beings which ensues.

This relational dimension has been a keynote of the development of the doctrine throughout the twentieth century in both the Catholic and the Reformation traditions. Through our examination of the three theologians which now follows I hope to show how, across the ecumenical divide, this fuller picture of human dignity, always rooted and centred in Christ's descent to us, has emerged as a vital part of contemporary theological narrative. Through attention to this dimension theologians across the ecumenical divides of the past may now begin to speak a common language which gives new meaning to the human situation. Both traditions, I will show, have learned to integrate aspects of the other. Taking this as a starting point for my study, however, we must be positively critical of the three theologians. Their contrasting attempts to restate the doctrine for contemporary theology shows us potential pitfalls. These will show us what to avoid in a contemporary doctrine of "*imago Dei*" if we are to do justice to a theological account of human dignity for the twenty-first century which learns from the whole tradition across the Reformation divide. Before I start this study of Barth I will be clear from the outset that my own general view will be two-fold. Firstly, the one theologian among the three who has done this most clearly is Balthasar. Secondly, we can only see his real strengths in this regard against the background in particular of Barth.

Barth aims to develop a more relational model of "*imago Dei*" but we shall see how his theological system restricts him from developing this aspect in a way which concedes a more substantive picture of human dignity as participation in Christ's life and mission. Balthasar, however, would learn from Barth's seminal work. His will be a more vocational model, expressing ongoing relationship with Christ who calls us as disciples in the world. His proposal will clearly be rooted in Christ's action in human lives, but will express a more integrated, substantive and overall optimistic picture of human dignity. The key will be his use of aesthetics and a dramatic narrative of Christ's immersion in the world.

Finally, we will be turning to Moltmann. Writing at the end of the twentieth century, he represents a theologian still living and working who is attempting to interpret the tradition as a whole. He will present a model which tries to hold together the centrality of Christ and our response in engagement with God, our fellow humans, and the whole created world with which we share a common dignity. Here, however, it will be my view that the balance has moved back to constructing a view of humanity which is insufficiently rooted in Christ as the perfect image of God. Moltmann will in fact show us some of the challenges of a more ecumenical and holistic doctrine, but above all some of the dangers to be aware of if we fail to learn from the groundwork done by Barth and Balthasar to develop it.

Karl Barth

The first twentieth-century theologian we will be considering is Karl Barth. It is generally recognised that the work of this Swiss Protestant thinker has had an enormous influence on twentieth-century theology in different traditions. Barth was born in 1886 into an intellectual and deeply religious Swiss Reformed Church family. He was to follow his father into the Swiss Reformed ministry. Through his university education in Germany he was nourished in the ascendant Liberal Protestant tradition, attending Harnack's Church History lectures in Berlin. In his early years indeed it would seem that he accepted this prevailing tradition of the time in Protestant theology.

In general terms this tradition of the earlier twentieth century laid greater and greater emphasis on the importance of human experience and consciousness of religion and of God in individuals, in traditions, and in whole cultures. Disciples of the German Romantic period theologian Friedrich Schleiermacher were beginning to construe the God–human relationship more and more from the perspective of our individual and collective "God-consciousness" rather than from the perspective of the revelation of God in himself. Scholars would agree that in Barth's early formative years he tended to be accepting of this way of approaching theology.

It was, however, at some point in his early life that Barth would break with this tradition. Scholars are still divided and new studies continue to be pursued on the extent and nature of the break. In contrast to his early leanings he would develop an entirely different perspective on the theological task. This perspective would be rooted in a return to the Fathers of the Reformation tradition, Luther and Calvin, and in his view, to the Fathers of the Early Church. More importantly it would return to the Word of God in scripture. Above all it would restore a fundamental belief in God's revelation in Christ over any creeping tendency to define God and the God–human relationship in terms of our own experience. In short, to begin to understand what Barth was trying to do, we might say that his aim throughout life was to return to the priority of the revelation of God in Jesus Christ and how this has made humanity new.

To preach and to preserve this revealed truth he was to develop a coherent theological system. This system, supporting and regulating the absolute priority of God in Jesus Christ in his dealings with human beings, has been attractive to twentieth-century theologians in different traditions, including the Catholic. Moreover such is the coherence of this system that, in order to understand Barth and his followers' particular contribution to the understanding of how God's new creation is constituted in Christ, it is important to take a brief look at his theology as a whole presented in his monumental work the *Church Dogmatics*.[66]

---

[66] Karl Barth, *Church Dogmatics*. Throughout I am using the translation of the *Church Dogmatics* given in the following series: Karl Barth, *Church Dogmatics*, G.W. Bromiley and Thomas Torrance, eds (Edinburgh: T&T Clark, 1957–1975). Hereafter the series will be referred to as *CD*, and this will be followed by the number and title of the

For Barth the most fundamental doctrine of our faith is that of "election". First and foremost God chooses to reveal himself in Jesus Christ. This foundational theological truth means that God chose to manifest himself to the world in human form, namely in his Son Jesus Christ, with whom he is one in the Trinity. This means that God determined himself to be *pro nobis*. Not to accept this as the foundation of theology is to treat God abstractly. It is to conceive of God in general rather than in the concrete fact of his self-revelation *pro nobis*. Furthermore this truth, as it is within the very inner self of God in the eternal Trinity, is eternally true. The very inner being of God is as "*logos ensarkos*", *pro nobis*. Humanity's free response to God's self-disclosure is secondary. God's self-revelation is primary.

> In virtue of this self-determination of His, God is from the very first the gracious God. For this self-determination is identical with the decree of His movement towards man. The reality and revelation of this movement is Jesus Christ Himself. This movement is an eternal movement, and therefore one which encloses man in his finitude and temporality. It is free, and therefore it is entirely grounded in the good-pleasure and the will of God. It is constant, and therefore it cannot deceive, nor can it be withdrawn or rejected.[67]

So what does this say about the state of humanity in virtue of Christ? In point of fact for Barth the salvation of humanity cannot be divorced from God's election of Jesus Christ. Christ is not just oriented towards the salvation of humanity but in fact Barth wants to say that God's revelation in Christ necessarily entails and incorporates our election. Christ, in virtue of his full humanity and full divinity, bears the burdens of the sins of the world as substitute for us. In *CD II/2* he goes on to affirm this truth about Jesus bearing the sins of humanity on himself:

> from all eternity God sees us in His Son as sinners to whom He is gracious ... For all those, then, whom God elects in His Son, the essence of the free grace of God consists in the fact that in this same Jesus God who is the Judge takes the place of the judged, and they are fully acquitted, therefore, from sin and its guilt and penalty.[68]

So for Barth the redemption of fallen humanity is already entailed in the election of Christ. This is a pledge for us. Rather than hold a traditionally Calvinist doctrine of double predestination Barth wants to preach the acquittal of sinful humanity

---

volume as it appears in the English translation, with, where applicable, the edition of this work. In addition, where appropriate in my detailed study of Barth's theology in Chapter 2, I will be quoting from and commenting on the original German, in: Karl Barth, *Die Kirchkliche Dogmatik* (Zurich: Evangelischer Verlag A.G. Zollikon, 1932–1969), which will be referred to hereafter as *KD*.

[67] Barth, *CD II/2: The Doctrine of God*, 91–2.
[68] Ibid., 123–5.

wholesale as part of God's self-determination from all eternity. It is not simply that there is nothing we can do to merit salvation. Rather we must not entertain any thoughts that maybe this God who carried out an eternal plan to substitute himself for us would will the salvation of some and not others. "The concept" of double predestination "which hampered the traditional doctrine was that of an equilibrium or balance in which blessedness was ordained and declared on the right hand and perdition on the left. This concept we must oppose with all the emphasis of which we are capable". It is an idea which portrays God's dealings with humanity in terms of a "rather sinister type of love".[69]

So are we all saved, according to Barth? It would seem that this doctrine of Christ's vicarious substitution would come close to saying this. Barth has without doubt returned Reformation theology to an emphasis on what God *has* done for us, all of us it might seem, in Christ. We are, perhaps all of us, in this graced position before God here on the earth and later in heaven. All the glory clearly rests with and within God. God's action in the world is clear and this re-orientation towards God's redemptive love in Christ has been developed in his own tradition and in others, including the Catholic.

However this does not mean that we have to accept the whole Barthian system. We should legitimately ask if the Barthian system, although giving a sense of finality, can be the last word on God's dealings with humanity. We are drawn to ask ourselves how Barth preserves the freedom and dignity of the human being in such a system which, we might argue, leaves humanity so passive. Whilst Barth can help us to affirm how humanity is made new in Christ, it is also true that for him the human being, whilst saved, is still, fundamentally, fallen, apart from God and unable to do anything to alter that.

Our unalterably sinful state comes across powerfully when we turn to Barth's specific understanding of "*imago Dei*". He affirms belief in the traditional chronology of the narrative. Humanity was once in a satisfactory position concerning God. Then, in virtue of the Fall, we came to be in a defective position. This position entailed a certain distance from God. Our fallen human state represents an independence, a sense of being apart from the Creator. Because of Christ's life, death and resurrection, humanity is now in a more favourable position regarding God. Christ has made that situation different. We are a new creation in Christ.

Barth, however, seems to find himself torn over fitting the doctrine of "*imago Dei*" into this cohesive theological system in which Christ appears to have completed the will of the Father in restoring us to himself. We might wonder what place there is left for a concept of ongoing relationship with God and so a fuller picture of human dignity. In fact Barth is drawn to restating the doctrine in terms of the relationship between the persons in the Trinity as the basis for our relationships with our fellow human beings. In *Church Dogmatics III/2* he states how the doctrine is vital to endorse an appropriate picture of our human dignity and vocation as relationship with others. In particular as God gives himself to us

---

[69] *CD II/2*, 171–2.

in Christ so we relate to other human beings. The meaning of human existence is therefore encapsulated in the way all human beings made in God's image have a special relationship with him as "covenant partners". However, the relationship does not involve infinite possibility through communion with God in Christ.

In fact in *I/1* he says that he is still suspicious of the doctrine of "*imago Dei*" as it implies this infinite, the possibility of fallen humanity accessing God. For Barth the relationship we have with God still holds him at a clear distance. It is not possible for us to know God. We either accept the situation we are in, saved yet still fallen, through faith in Christ, or we do not. The relationship we have with Christ is more one of assent, not of ongoing incorporation into his life and mission. Despite Barth's recognition of the need to develop a relational model of "*imago Dei*", for him the relationship is more passive as it was for Luther and Calvin. Acceptance or not of our salvation marks the distinction between serious Christians and others. Through looking to faith in Christ we open ourselves to the reality of what God in Christ has done for us. Others are deceived by looking to fulfil their divine destiny, falsely believing that they can find God. They cannot and will not find fulfilment in their quest as what they are attempting is, in the very way of defective humanity apart from God, fundamentally sinful. It is God in Christ who has come to us and is for us. We now share that with others. To want anything for ourselves in addition to this is proud, disobedient and sinful.

A Note on Analogy

Before we end this general introduction to Barth it is vital to note at this stage how it is limited. Barth's thought is more nuanced and has been interpreted in different ways. This is exactly why, in order to understand the enormous influence he has had on twentieth-century theology, we must look at his work in depth. This is exactly what we will set out to do in the next chapter.

In particular we will turn to Barth's treatment of the father of so many traditions, Augustine. Barth discusses Augustine in depth in *Church Dogmatics I/1*. Here he would seem to interpret Augustine in a way which rules out the possibility of human access to God after the Fall. It is on this interpretation of Augustine that so much of Barth's belief system concerning humanity's creation in "*imago Dei*" rests. From this Barth will then reject the Catholic notion of analogy, the doctrine of "*analogia entis*" proposed in the medieval period by Aquinas. It is this doctrine which he believes is close to a more integrated model of "*imago Dei*" expressing humanity's likeness to God and participation in the divine life. Thus it is rejection of this notion of analogy which leads him to what is in the final analysis a less relational model of "*imago Dei*" that he at times seems to favour. The only analogy between God and humans will be an analogy of faith. In taking the Lutheran interpretation of Augustine that we are justified by faith alone Barth will not be able to give to his doctrine of "*imago Dei*" the relational dimension which represents a more integrated picture of human dignity.

In Chapter 2 I will have important questions to raise on this key aspect of Barth's thought. Is Barth's a fair interpretation of Augustine or does it concentrate on one important but not solitary aspect of his theological anthropology? Did Augustine rule out the possibility of our participation in the divine after the Fall? Catholic theology would want to portray the more Platonic Augustine. It would want to reject Barth's view of him and leave an important place in his thought for our search for the transcendent and infinite as finite creatures made in his image, for the human quest for God, for human participation in divine reality, our "*deification*" as well as our "*justification*".

In Barth's work as a whole, however, we do have an important foundation for a new way of looking at the teaching that human beings are made in the "*imago Dei*" which will serve Christian theology as a whole. The distinct advantage of his model of "*imago Dei*" is that it is fundamentally rooted in Christ's action in human lives. Yet he also attempts to give this new meaning by developing the relational dimension. It will be my contention that within the structures of his own thought he fails to develop this second dimension. However, we shall also see how it was the Catholic theologian Hans Urs von Balthasar, who was to integrate much of Barth's model into his own vision, and was thus able to develop it more productively. This theologian, working in the post-Vatican II Catholic tradition, rather than reject Barth, saw in his thought a new movement in the Reformed tradition from which Catholic theology could learn much. Balthasar will be the second twentieth-century theologian we examine. So we must now introduce him and place him in the context of the history of theology and the understanding of "*imago Dei*".

Hans Urs von Balthasar

Hans Urs von Balthasar's background was in respects similar to Karl Barth's yet in others very different. Balthasar was also Swiss, born in Lucerne, in 1905. From an early age, through family and schooling, he was steeped in religious culture but for him this was distinctively Catholic. As a young man he was attracted to both the arts and to the academic life. His original research interest was German literature. Thus it was that by the time of his entry into the Society of Jesus at the age of 24 he was already formed and fashioned in the culture of the German-speaking Catholic world. In fact we might say that the young Balthasar was to an extent shielded from any other cultures, religious traditions and peoples. In one sense his formation as a Jesuit would continue to be very sheltered. His philosophy studies were in the fiercely traditional city of Munich, a city alive with art and music, steeped in cultural history, and very Catholic. He was to continue with his theology studies in the Jesuit centre Lyon-Fourvière.

As for Barth the period of Balthasar's formation as a theologian was one of great cultural change in the world and in theology. In the middle of all the beauty and cultural tradition the seeds of German devastation and European disintegration were being sown. The city where Balthasar spent a number of years as a Jesuit scholastic and young priest, Munich, had become one of the principal foci for Nazi rallies and propaganda. In the midst of beauty was ugliness. In the midst of worship of God was worship of human perfection and desire for supremacy. Whilst this new secular gospel of human supremacy was being proclaimed across the German-speaking world of the 1930s the young Balthasar was embarking on what would be an important course in his theological journey. This was, in a similar vein to Barth, lived out as a call to preach the true Gospel of God's glory in Christ as the only truth which gave humanity its special dignity.

At Lyon-Fourvière Balthasar was thrust into a stimulating world of theological enquiry. Here he found that two of his French Jesuit teachers, Jean Daniélou and Henri de Lubac, were also searching for new ways to recover a sense of the absolute primacy of God's power in human lives. With them he returned to a study of the Fathers of the Early Church, especially Augustine and Irenaeus.

Balthasar moved to Basel as university chaplain and lecturer in the 1940s. It was here that he began to appreciate the theology of Karl Barth. Barth's objection to any theological system which gave glory to human beings rather than gave the glory to God interested him. We might say, in general terms, that he was imbued with a common theological desire. The relationship between Barth's and Balthasar's theological vision is complex but I believe it is worth pursuing if it helps us to understand this common desire and paradigm shift in the history of twentieth-century theology. In this study we shall see how much of Barth's vision Balthasar has taken to himself, refined and moulded into his own theological anthropology.

In Balthasar's formation of a theological vision, however, he has drawn on many other sources. Thus his vision of the human being vis-à-vis God is also very different to that of Barth. The next period of his life, from 1950 onwards, shows how other influences in this complex theologian are brought to bear. Barth's early mission had been to preach the Word of God in Reformed Church pulpits in Berlin. Balthasar was more immersed in the arts and especially the German liberal arts tradition. This was to impact on Balthasar's way of preaching the Word of God. The glory of the Lord was to be communicated through media.

For him one chief medium was what we might call aesthetics. The truth about God in Christ is portrayed in terms of beauty. Christ is the "*Gestalt*", the "*form*" of God, which attracts us, beckons us and draws us into relationship with him. Thus in his theological anthropology there is room still for a theological vision which speaks of a more integrated human quest for God as the beautiful and sets us on a path to the beatific vision.

However for Balthasar human identity is also clearly rooted in the person of Christ and his involvement in human lives. Balthasar's theological anthropology is not working in the traditional Catholic framework of Trent, Aquinas and a more teleological interpretation of Augustine, all of which place great emphasis on our human striving for the beatific vision. Rather he is placing his emphasis on how our lives are transformed through the appearance of Christ on the human horizon as the revelation of God. So our Christian response to God is not first and foremost about a quest for God in the next life. Rather the "*Gestalt*" is a human person Jesus, with real flesh and blood, who in the world here and now is immersed in our human condition, and through this meets us. The emphasis is not so much that we sinners need to turn to God. God comes to us in Christ as the beautiful immersed in the ugliness of our world. Precisely in this appearance of Christ on the horizon of our lives is our personal loving call to participate with him on his mission here and now. To this we cannot but respond as actors in this drama of the beautiful amidst the ugly.

Balthasar expresses the truth through another significant medium which Barth had not used. This is dramatic narrative. This drama is also based on another important influence, namely the visions of the Catholic lay doctor whom Balthasar was to befriend, Adrienne von Speyr. Balthasar turns one of von Speyr's most vivid visions into a dramatic narrative. This is the drama of Christ's descent into the underworld.[70] In doing so he places the drama of our redemption in the action of Holy Saturday. This is the day when humanity sees Christ with eyes of faith. Jesus had descended into the underworld in obedience to the Father's will and in solidarity with sinful humanity. Christ is at one with humanity in humanity's ugliness. "By it [the descent into the underworld]", says Balthasar, "Christ takes the existential measure of everything that is sheerly contrary to God".[71]

This dramatic divine immersion into the earthly realm transforms ugliness into beauty and thus transforms humanity's position vis-à-vis God. In fact Balthasar's emphasis is such that this final act of Christ's obedient engagement in the plight of humanity, disfigured through disobedience, may be construed as necessary in an account of redemption. "The Son", he states, "must 'take in with his own eyes what in the realm of creation is imperfect, informed, chaotic', so as to make it pass over into his own domain as the Redeemer".[72] It is this action of Christ on Holy Saturday, when he is at one with the fallen, which then draws us back to him on our pilgrimage through life. This pilgrimage now ties us to Christ as we follow him as disciples on mission here on earth and it culminates in our oneness with him in heaven. Thus a more teleological vision of human pilgrimage and deification comes into play as Balthasar now returns to the Early Church Fathers to develop a fundamentally Christocentric but also dramatic and aesthetic theological anthropology which emphasises our earthly encounter with and participation in Christ's mission. Irenaeus' perspective, as well as Augustine's, will be significant for him. "The vision of chaos by the God-man has become for us the condition of our vision of the Divinity."[73]

---

[70] Hans Urs von Balthasar, *Mysterium Paschale* (Edinburgh: T&T Clark, 1990), 164–81 [hereafter referred to as *MP*].

[71] *MP*, 174.

[72] Ibid., 175. Balthasar states that he is quoting from the Gospel of St John.

[73] Ibid., 175, quoting St Irenaeus, *Summa Alexandri* 3.7.1.1. Quaracchi 4, 205 (Balthasar's own notes).

So how would Balthasar approach the doctrine of "*imago Dei*"? At the outset of our study it is very important to affirm one certain fact which follows from a consideration of the influences which were forming him throughout his life. His understanding of how the human being is made in "*imago Dei*" is multi-faceted. Indeed we might venture that, whereas for some in both the Reformed and the Catholic tradition, there is a clearly defined dogmatic system, in Balthasar, with his myriad influences impinging on his portrayal of post-Vatican II Catholic dogma, we see more of a tapestry of ideas and pictures. Furthermore, we ought to be circumspect, in this general introduction, in defining exactly what Balthasar believed. He himself was extremely cautious about giving any early definitions. After his long excursus on aesthetics, *The Glory of the Lord*, the opening volume of "*prolegomena*" to his volumes laying out his "theo-dramatic" vision, that is *Theo-Drama: Theological Dramatic Theory*, he considers the understanding of humanity made in "*imago Dei*", but still declares that the topic is "a little premature here".[74]

However, Balthasar's tapestry is not simply patchwork. Rather there is a colour scheme and to have understood something of this general scheme is important. For then we see how any definition of "*imago Dei*" at this stage would be indeed premature. Absolutely central to his scheme is the fact that human beings are fundamentally indefinable except through reference to Jesus Christ. So Balthasar cannot appropriately define how we are created "*imago Dei*" except through proclaiming how it is Christ who has restored us to our divinely-willed dignity:

> In a Christian theodramatic theory we have the right to assert that no other, mythical or religio-philosophical anthropology can attain a satisfactory idea of man, an idea that integrates all the elements, but the Christian one. It alone can release man from the impossible task of trying, on the basis of his brokenness, to envisage himself as not broken, without forfeiting some essential aspect of himself in the process. It releases him from this burden by inserting him, right from the start, into the dramatic dialogue with God, so that God himself may cause him to experience his ultimate definition of man.[75]

---

[74] Hans Urs von Balthasar, *Theo-Drama: Theological Dramatic Theory II: Dramatis Personae: Man in God* (San Francisco: Ignatius Press, 1990), 316. Throughout I am using the following translation of the *Theo-Drama*: Hans Urs von Balthasar, *Theo-Drama: Theological Dramatic Theory* (San Francisco: Ignatius Press, 1988–1998). Hereafter the series will be referred to as *TD*, and this will be followed by the number and title of the volume as it appears in the English translation. In addition, where appropriate in my detailed study of the theology of Balthasar in Chapter 3, I will be quoting from and commenting on the original German, in: Hans urs von Balthasar, *Theodramatik* (Einsiedeln: Johannes Verlag, 1973–1983), which hereafter will be referred to as *TDK*.

[75] *TD II*, 343.

Thus, starting from a firm belief in Christ's immersion in the world, a *Weltanschaung* based on the incarnation and Trinitarian love *ad extra*, Balthasar can weave a picture of a relationship between a broken God and a broken humanity, of humanity's brokenness in relation to God's love. Indeed God draws us to himself as lover through his very victorious brokenness which extended to the point of meeting us in the ugliness of the underworld. The drama of the relationship between God and his creation will be one of an interplay between God's "infinite freedom" in love and humanity's "finite freedom" to respond or not to that love as God in Christ opens us to its possibility. This is what our lives will be about. This is the essence of our humanity. "If we want to ask about man's 'essence', we can do so only in the midst of his dramatic performance of existence. There is no other anthropology but the dramatic. This is why the topic could not even emerge within the framework of the theological aesthetics."[76] Thus it is that when Balthasar turns to the question of the nature of humanity he cannot but find at humanity's core God's image. This image is actually a "finite freedom … it must act as such, that is, it must decide to move toward God – and thus realize the 'likeness' it already possesses – or away from God, so losing this likeness".[77]

So Balthasar, on the one hand, can hold firm to the necessity of understanding the human being's special dignity only in terms of God himself in Christ. Thus we might say that he is following Barth in his perceived return to the Fathers of the Early Church. All the glory is given to God. Any philosophy or anthropology which tries to find a way to God is to be rejected. Yet, at the same time, Balthasar's multi-faceted view wants to allow for some kind of innate human quest for relationship with the infinite. Human beings are opened up to the beauty of the love of God in the Christ who meets them in their sinful state. They can move and ought to respond to the beckoning of Christ to fulfil their desire for the infinite. There is a journey which the human being is on, from finitude back to infinity, to God himself. These latter themes are much more in keeping with the traditional Catholic understanding of grace co-operating with nature. However, Balthasar's aesthetic and dramatic understanding of this is closely tied to a post-Vatican II understanding of the human being's response to grace as actually an incorporation into the life of Christ who has claimed him. Drawn into Christ's company we live out our call not in isolation but in relation to others as we are constituted as Christ's disciples on mission.

It is in the meeting of these strands to his thought that we find in Balthasar a distinctive new ecumenical contribution to the postconciliar understanding of "*imago Dei*". In particular we find in his writings a new evaluation of the Reformed tradition. This aspect of his thought enables him to appreciate the work of Barth and the Reformation whilst developing a fundamentally Catholic postconciliar understanding of the graced dignity and freedom of the human person called into Christ's company and so placed with him on his mission. That is why we shall

---

[76] *TD II*, 335.
[77] *TD II*, 327.

be analysing this aspect of his thought in depth. Before we proceed, however, we introduce our final twentieth-century theologian whose approach to these matters has moved in a different direction.

Jürgen Moltmann

Moltmann was born in the German city of Hamburg in 1926. His upbringing was predominantly secular rather than particularly Christian or religious. However, like Barth and Balthasar before him, he grew up in a world of German intellectualism. It was at the young age of 18 that he was to find himself in the midst of what must have been a horrific experience, drafted into fighting in the German army at the very end of the Second World War. He was only to fight as a soldier for six months until he was taken as a prisoner-of-war. It was his experience as a prisoner in various camps, in Belgium, Scotland and England, that was in fact to change his life.

Here, at first out of boredom, he started to read the Bible. In time he discovered that the Christian message gave him and other prisoners hope in their desperate situation. This experience was to form a lifelong project of preaching faith in Jesus Christ who amid the brokenness of human lives offers hope. When the war was over the young Moltmann began his study of theology at Göttingen where, like Balthasar, he too was strongly influenced by Barth and Reformation theology. Throughout his career his theology has developed and been shaped but it has always been faithful to its original aim. In all of his works Christ is at the centre as the one who gives hope to those who need it most. Proclamation of this truth has for Moltmann been rooted firmly in the Reformed tradition. He is convinced of Luther's doctrine of justification by faith alone and of the importance Barth placed on preaching God's revelation in Jesus Christ. Yet somehow his experience urged him to take this still further.

Moltmann became convinced that the more theology portrays the broken Christ at the centre of suffering humanity the more we are being faithful to the Christ of the Gospels and will make sense of our faith in the world of today. So, in a similar vein to Balthasar in his theology of Holy Saturday, Moltmann sets out to tell the world how the crucified God gives us hope amid suffering because this God is fully immersed in it himself. God does not restore suffering humanity to himself at a distance. Rather he goes the full way into the world of suffering to the extent that God and the world of suffering are intertwined. "God and suffering are no longer contradictions", proclaims Moltmann in his groundbreaking work *The Crucified God*, as "God's being is in suffering and the suffering is in God's being itself, because God is love".[78]

---

[78] Jürgen Moltmann, *The Crucified God* (New York and Evanston: Harper & Row; Minneapolis: Fortress Press, 1974), 227. All of Moltmann's works will be quoted first of all in their English translations, which are now widely available through both North American and British publishers. In addition, however, when I turn to a detailed study of Moltmann's

Thus for Moltmann the key symbol becomes the cross and the key narrative the crucifixion. As with Balthasar's narrative drama of the descent into the underworld so Moltmann's narrative of the cross is retold with a power which aims not merely to interpret but to transform human lives as the human being is opened up to a divine possibility. "Theological concepts", he says, "are engaged in a process of movement, and which call forth practical movement and change".[79] Thus we might say that his aims are so similar to Barth and Balthasar in that he is determined to place Christ at the centre and show his transforming power in people's lives. Yet it is in carrying this through that he parts company with both.

Moltmann's narrative of the cross deserves close attention. In this general introduction, we might point out some initial matters which are very important to understanding the particular direction in which he has taken theology. For Moltmann God's identification with human suffering means that God himself suffers and changes. In the event of the cross there is a rupture in the life of the Trinity as Father and Son are ripped apart, the Son being immersed fully as a man in the suffering of the world. For Moltmann this idea is necessary for a proper understanding of who God is and what God has done for us. The unity of God is only possible through an experience of disunity. Salvation is only possible through God's full immersion in human suffering. These ideas, denying God's immutability and placing human conditions on God's revelation and salvation, divide Moltmann from Barth and Balthasar and from Christian orthodoxy. They also reveal something of the challenges involved in finding a way to express the relationship between God and humanity in a way which gives hope to the contemporary world.

Moltmann goes to great lengths to try to move theology away from a preoccupation with apocalyptic hope, a hope which might to many non-believers seem so distant that it is intangible and expresses last things and endings. He is not at all concerned with a traditional teleological vision of human pilgrimage. Rather he wants to proclaim the immanence of Christ's coming on the earth which promises us new beginnings.[80] Like Barth, Balthasar and postconciliar Catholic theology Moltmann is trying to develop a deeper theological anthropology expressed in the tangibility of the relationship between Jesus Christ and humanity on the earth in a manner which transforms us and can give us true hope. This is an important aim which he shares with the other two theologians.

However, Moltmann's views are different to the other two twentieth-century theologians we are studying in important respects which we shall be examining later in closer detail. His picture of the human being has moved far away from

---

theology in Chapter 4, I will, where appropriate, be quoting and commenting on the original German of most of Moltmann's corpus relevant to this study.

[79] Moltmann, *A Theology of Hope: on the Ground and the Implications of a Christian Eschatology* (New York and Evanston: Harper & Row, 1967), 36.

[80] Cf. Moltmann, *The Coming of God: Christian Eschatology* (London: S.C.M. Press, 1996). Here he develops these themes more fully, as we shall investigate in Chapter 4.

a traditional Christian understanding which includes an explicit account of sin and the Fall. The human being's need of a saviour in the person of Jesus Christ is now characterised in terms of human suffering and death. So there is little room for the concept of sin. God comes to share his life with us and the world and God become intertwined: there is a very clear aim to create a more dialogical, reciprocal understanding of the relationship between God and humanity. Yet in real terms the human response to God's love seems to be an area which is underexplored. The fundamental goodness of the human person in God's eyes shines through Moltmann's writings. The human being is assured of God's love and fellowship. However, as he has shifted the emphasis from sin to suffering, humanity's special dignity does not seem to involve in an obvious way a freedom to fall, to sin, distance ourselves from God, and thus to experience the need of a saviour. So it does not seem to pay great attention to what is the other side of the coin, namely our response to God's love in our life on earth.

In fact we might argue that Moltmann's depiction of the God–human relationship comes to see things in an opposite way. Rather than God's action in the world transforming us the key motif becomes how humanity affects God. This is true both in terms of God's being and God's revelation. God is only truly God when he has met humanity in suffering. He only reveals himself fully as saviour through his immersion in the world of humanity. It seems that Moltmann, through his important project of developing a more dialogical and tangible picture of God's dealings with his creation, has moved away from a fundamental belief in the otherness of God.

This is exactly what Barth was so concerned to avoid. Similarly, Balthasar can help us greatly here as we can note the great care he took when developing his aesthetic and dramatic theology to still retain the necessary balance which gave all the glory to an immutable God. Balthasar's God in Christ was certainly broken-down in the underworld yet never altered in the love he showed to all. Indeed we might note how his seeing the need to retain this balance was extremely important to his view of the whole theological project and thus distances him, as it does Barth, from Moltmann.

For Moltmann his later work has involved more and more the shared and much needed contemporary theological task of constantly turning to the world and naturally to humanity in its suffering to show how in this we find God's image. It is at the intersection of this dialogue between God and the world, between grace and nature, that we find the tension, and the debate in the theological community. Moltmann turns first to the world to construct a view of humanity's special relationship with God. Thus the doctrine of humanity as "*imago Dei*" begins to be seen from the perspective of what is current in culture, be it a political ideology arising from an experience of the need for liberation or a philosophical system which places humanity at the centre of things rather than the Creator.

A general comment of Balthasar's can help us to see the essential difference and the flaw in Moltmann's approach:

as the Son in God is the eternal icon of the Father, he can without contradiction assume in himself the image that is the creation, purify it, and make it enter into the communion of the divine life without dissolving it (in a false mysticism). It is here that one must distinguish nature and grace ... Humanity will prefer to renounce all philosophical questions – in Marxism, or positivism of all stripes, rather than accept a philosophy which finds its final response only in the revelation of Christ. Foreseeing that, Christ sent his believers into the whole world as sheep among wolves.

Before making a pact with the world it is necessary to meditate on that comparison.[81]

For Balthasar much twentieth-century theology strives rightly to make sense of human suffering and to connect God with contemporary experience and the world of culture with God. However we must not lose sight of the otherness of God even in his revelation in the world in the person of his Son. Christ is the perfect image of God who fulfils the human quest for meaning. When constructing a theology of the human person we must turn first and foremost to Christ to work out how we are made in God's image and not be seduced into finding a false image in one ideology or another.

Conclusion

In this opening chapter we have introduced some of the main strands in the history of the understanding of humanity's creation in "*imago Dei*". First of all we must note how in each of these perspectives we find the fundamental narrative inherited from the account in the book of Genesis. Humanity is created in a special relationship with God but falls. The Fall entails humanity's subsequent sinful state and need of a saviour. In the Christian tradition this saviour is Christ.

Theology then interpreted this tradition in varying ways. Augustine is an important primary theological source. He stressed how in the Fall the divine image is distorted through our sin. Thus our reliance on the grace of Christ to restore the image becomes also a very powerful motif. Future theology will tend to place a similar emphasis on our need for a saviour. However the tradition will interpret Augustine in different ways. In very general terms we might conclude that, at first blush, Reformation theology will want to stress human passivity through a firm belief in the absolute inability of humanity to participate in the divine life after the Fall. God's image in us is restored and we simply are to accept that in faith. On the other hand a more Catholic apologetic theology, whilst clearly accepting Augustine's belief in the necessity of grace and condemnation of Pelagianism, will

---

[81] Balthasar, "A Résumé of my Thought", in *Hans Urs von Balthasar: His Life and Work*, David L. Schindler, ed. (San Francisco: Communio Books, Ignatius Press, 1991), 5.

look to Augustine's Platonism, his picture of humanity's pilgrimage back towards a vision of God, actively worked out through a life of virtue.

Both Catholic and Reformed theology, however, will also be influenced by other significant perspectives in the history of the tradition. They will turn not just to Augustine but to the earlier Irenaeus. In rediscovering Irenaeus they will find a complementary vision which distinguishes more sharply between our creation in God's image, which at the Fall is distorted but in some way retained, and our creation in his likeness, which we lose but strive to regain through life. Rather than stress damnation and salvation, Irenaeus sees our imperfection as a necessary aid to our growth. Similarly both Catholic and Reformation theology will respond to Aquinas, who in the medieval period brought a new dimension to the tradition. The Reformation itself was to react strongly to this more philosophical and scientific medieval approach to the doctrine of *"imago Dei"*. The reformers were to reject the move to express human identity in terms of divine possibility and ascent to God.

Thus, in general terms, we might say that the sixteenth-century theological world became something of a battleground between this Reformation emphasis on human passivity in the face of Christ's once-and-for-all restoration of the divine image after the Fall and the Catholic emphasis on our active participation in a relationship with Christ as we worked to achieve our divine destiny in heaven. The Reformation position was laid out especially in Luther's doctrine that we are "justified by faith alone". Calvin went further in teaching that God had already in eternity predestined some for salvation and others for damnation. The Council of Trent, on the other hand, responded to the Reformation, by reaffirming a strong belief in the compatibility of a belief in God's grace in Christ with the more teleological portrayal of the human path back to God. In particular Trent stressed that we co-operate with grace through mortification, putting to death what is earthly in ourselves in order to find our way to heaven.

When we moved into the twentieth century we began to note some of the developments which this thesis will study in more detail. It was the Second Vatican Council, in the documents *Lumen Gentium* and *Gaudium et Spes*, which was to develop a Catholic vision of the human being's creation in *"imago Dei"*. Whilst clearly holding to the Tridentine vision of the compatibility of grace and human nature after the Fall, and rejecting the doctrines taught by the reformers, Vatican II was able to set forth a picture of the vocation of each human being which placed greater emphasis on how through our common baptism we are called to participate here on the earth in the life and mission of Christ in which we have already been constituted as a pilgrim people. Thus a new emphasis was placed on our special dignity here on earth as creatures made in his image. God calls us here and now to build up the Kingdom as a community rather than to work out our own divine destiny in the heavenly Jerusalem.

So we come to the three twentieth-century theologians we are studying. The perspectives of Barth, Balthasar and Moltmann encapsulate many of the tensions in the tradition but it will be my view that their own contributions have cast light on these tensions and can help us to see a way forward. Barth has brought the doctrine back to a firm belief in what God has done for humanity in Christ. The doctrine of election teaches us how we are in a graced position through Christ. All the glory clearly rests not with us but solely with God in Christ. Barth intends to develop a model of *"imago Dei"* which is not merely rooted firmly in Christ but has us called to relationship with him and with our fellow humans. However, his theological system places humanity in a position of passive acceptance of Christ's justification and militates against a more integrated and actively relational model of human dignity.

Balthasar learns much from Barth and the Reformation tradition. Christ is primary and paramount in his thought. Yet he will integrate this into a fundamentally Catholic tapestry of human life drawn into the company of Christ with whom we are placed on mission. The categories of drama and aesthetics will help him to present this perspective and shed light on the tradition he studies in detail. Through these categories, also, and notably his interpretation of Barth, Balthasar will attempt to form a model of *"imago Dei"* which suggests infinite possibility in a dialogical encounter between God and humans. This is more of a vocational model. Christ is still at the apex but calls us to live out our destiny actively as his companions on his mission.

Finally, Moltmann will complete our picture. He too, sharing similar background and similar aims to both Barth and Balthasar, will defend the absolute priority of God's action in Christ. Yet he will also try to develop a relational picture of God's immersion in the world. Here *"imago Dei"* becomes part of a theology which confuses God and humanity to the extent that humanity affects God rather than God transforms humanity. In trying to bring to contemporary theological anthropology the lived quest for meaning, especially on the part of those who suffer, we lose sight of the otherness of God in Christ who is the universal answer to this quest.

Chapter 2
Karl Barth

Understanding of "*Imago Dei*": Objectives and Tensions

In order to understand how Barth construes the teaching that the human being is made in "*imago Dei*" it is vital to examine how Barth himself developed this. He addresses the doctrine more directly in certain sections of *Church Dogmatics III/2*,[1] the volume in which he turns to the nature of humanity in general, but it is in *I/1* in particular where we find how his model will be clearly rooted and fully encapsulated within his doctrine of the Word of God. Barth himself could not possibly discuss the nature of humanity in isolation. In fact for him it would be anathema to do so. Rather his theological system is such that a consideration of how the human being is vis-à-vis God can only be seen in the light of who God is for us. Thus Barth does not treat the understanding of "*imago Dei*" on its own. Rather he comes to his own particular perspective on the doctrine through a series of steps all interwoven within his integrated theological system.

In *III/2* Barth presents Christ as the perfect image of God.[2] It is from the perspective of Christ that he defines the human being's creation in God's image. At the very core of Barth's interwoven theological process is his firm belief in Christ, the incarnate God, that is a God who in Christ is fundamentally *pro nobis*, oriented towards humanity. As we outlined in our general introduction in Chapter 1 the fundamental doctrine of Barth's theological system is that of God's self-election in Jesus Christ. Jesus Christ is the Word of God, the Second Person of the Trinity, incarnate in Jesus Christ, God's revelation to us, and in a profound way expresses God's being for others, God *pro nobis*.

From this standpoint Barth attempts to develop a model of "*imago Dei*" which for me holds together two objectives in ongoing tension. Firstly, he intends to avoid within his theological system a notion that human beings' creation in "*imago Dei*" permits any hint of human similarity to and capacity for relationship with God. Human beings are in one sense irreconcilably apart from him. Christ is the one whose identity is one with God and totally for others. However much we strive to attain this perfect identity as an image of God we cannot. There is in us a tendency to strive for such a relationship with God and to be totally for others, as Christ is, but ultimately, because we are fallen creatures, it will not be possible. Humanity can never attain the perfection of oneness with God which is present in Christ. "[L]et us assume", says Barth,

---

[1] Barth, *CD III/2: The Doctrine of Creation* (1960).
[2] Ibid., 222–50.

that there is in every man at least a serious even if hopeless striving ... The difference between Jesus and ourselves is still indissoluble. It is quite fundamental. For of no other man can we say that from the very outset and in virtue of his existence he is for others ... that he is the Word of God to men (*[N]ehmen wir an, es gäbe hier in jedem Menschen mindestens auch so etwas wie ein ernsthaftes, wenn auch vielleicht aussichtsloses Streben ... Der Unterschied zwischen Jesus und uns bliebe doch unaufhebbar. Er ist grundsätzlich. Denn das ist sicher, daß kein anderer Mensch von Haus aus und kraft seiner Existenz für den Mitmenschen ist ... Kein anderer ist Gottes Wort an den Menschen*).[3]

Thus, as seen already, Barth reacts strongly against a portrayal of the human being by virtue of his own ability encountering God and thus forming a relationship with him.

Yet it would seem that there is a tension at the heart of Barth's project. He also wants to show that a restatement of "*imago Dei*" is somehow necessary if we are to affirm the fact of God's revelation to us in Christ and the likeness we thus have with him. He insists on how our human identity rests in our "relationship" with our fellow humans and how this places us in a position of similarity to Christ. The term "relationship" is used alongside other similar ones such as "encounter" and "mutuality" to express how he intends to construct a relational doctrine of "*imago Dei*". "[A]t the very root of my being", he claims, "and from the very first I am in encounter with the being of the Thou ... the humanity of human being is this total determination as being in encounter with the being of the Thou, as being with the fellow-man, as fellow-humanity".[4] "This is the reach of the likeness in unlikeness, of the correspondence and similarity between the man Jesus and us other men" ("*So weit reicht nämlich die Gleichheit in der Ungleichheit, so weit reicht die Entsprechung und Ähnlichkeit zwischen dem Menschen Jesus und uns anderen Menschen*").[5]

Barth himself states that "it is no accident that ... we have had to make use of terms like image, original, copy, correspondence, analogy, parity, likeness, similarity" when talking about the human being vis-à-vis God.[6] He clearly wants to develop a model of "*imago Dei*" which maintains some correspondence we have with God, especially through the relationship he has with his fellow humans. Yet in doing so the tension with a God who is so far removed from us remains. What lies behind this tension? Let us return briefly to his doctrine of the Word of God in *I/1*.

On the one hand Barth clearly rejects a tradition within both Catholic and Protestant theology up to this point in time which would see in the human person similarity to and capacity for God. For Barth the concept of "*imago Dei*" is "only

---

[3] Barth, *CD III/2*, 222 [Barth, *KD III/2: Die Lehre von der Schöpfung*, 265].
[4] Ibid., 247.
[5] Ibid., 247 [Barth, *KD III/2*, 296].
[6] Ibid., 319.

a hair's breadth from the Roman Catholic doctrine of the *analogia entis* ... our teaching must be very different. We do not construe the analogy, similarity, or conformity to God that is actually to be maintained".[7] Neither can Barth agree with his Protestant contemporary Brunner as he takes "*imago Dei*" to "refer to the humanity and personality which even sinful man retains from creation".[8] For Barth "the humanity and personality of sinful man cannot possibly signify conformity to God, a point of contact for the Word of God".

Yet, despite this apparent reluctance to develop a theology of our real encounter with Christ, Barth appears to be convinced that the doctrine of "*imago Dei*" needs not to be rejected but restated in terms of the relationship Christ has formed with us from his side. For him it seems that this relationship teaches us something more about the dignity of the human person. We are called not just to imitate the perfect image, that is Christ, in being for others. Although Barth's starting point of all theology is unambiguously God, not humanity, it does still seem that humanity's search and need for God was something which clearly fascinated him. Important to this enquiry is his reading of the medieval theologian Anselm.

Barth states that for him the first chapter of Anselm's *Proslogion* is "a particularly instructive document".[9] Barth interprets this section of Anselm leading up to his ontological argument for the existence of God as noteworthy "as regards the epistemological problem" in that it is actually presenting a spiritual treatise which expresses the human being's relationship with God. This clearly involves a very real quest for God which for Barth is worth considering if we are to begin to explain who the human being is vis-à-vis the divine. The quest for God in Anselm's work, however, actually confirms for Barth a very important fact about the human being's situation. Here we come to what I would suggest is at the heart of the Barthian tension.

For Barth we must understand our relationship with God from the perspective of how Christ has placed us in partnership with him, not from the standpoint of our searching for God. Our search for God is always in vain because God in Christ has sought us and made us his partners in an everlasting covenant. "Man is orientated towards that for which he is determined", admits Barth. "Even as a sinner he remains the creature of God and therefore the being whose orientation is to be the covenant-partner of God. He can give himself up for lost. But he cannot escape God, or lose his being as the creature of God."[10]

For Barth the human quest for fulfilment in God reveals an important strand of his theological system which grounds what seems to be a theology of relationship understood as passive. The fallen human being is truly human in that he simply stands before the mystery of the hidden God who in Jesus Christ has reconstituted him in faith. Because the human being is fallen he rejects God. For Barth Anselm's

---

[7] Barth, *CD I/1: The Doctrine of the Word of God*, 2nd edn, 239.
[8] Ibid., 238.
[9] Ibid., 230.
[10] Barth, *CD III/2*, 319.

contribution is misinterpreted when it is taken as a philosophy through which we can find God or some knowledge about the twists and turns of the God–human relationship. Similarly, it is misinterpreted when taken to assume that there is the possibility of our communing with God from our side. There is no "encounter" between us and God in this sense. Rather, Barth interprets Anselm as reflecting a powerful spiritual reality which expresses the core of human relationship with God, that is in point of fact the fallen human being's limitation and inability to enter into a communion with Christ except in the sense that he accepts Christ's taking his sins onto himself. Thus in the final analysis our quest for transcendence in an ongoing relationship with God is in vain. Our being for our fellow humans constitutes our living out our relationship with God.

This is not to say that for Barth the human quest for a relationship with God is not indeed real. Barth veers from a certain resignation that the totality of Christ's work of restoration has been completed back to stressing mutuality as the key to understanding the relationship between God and humanity. However, it is my view that the latter theme needs to be seen in the light of the former inasmuch as it grounds his theology as a whole. In other words his fascination with seeing "*imago Dei*" as above all teaching us about relationship is rightly seen in the light of what on the one hand we might construe as a rather sombre theology of assurance but on the other shows us how the doctrine is to be clearly grounded in Christ and his action in the world.

For Barth himself this tension is necessary within his theological system. The doctrine of "*imago Dei*" can only be properly expressed in terms of our "similarity in dissimilarity". For him it does not amount to a sombre theology of assurance. In fact he states clearly that we retain a "likeness" to God. His view of our relationship to God for him does not represent any tension or impoverishment in the doctrine. Rather it is sufficient to say that "God is in relationship, and so too is the man created by Him. This is his divine likeness. When we view it in this way, the dispute whether it is lost by sin finds a self-evident solution. It is not lost … what man is independent as he is man with the fellow-man, he is in hope of the being and action of the One who is original in this relationship".[11] So for Barth humanity's being made in the "*imago Dei*" involves the quest for relationship with God but always brings us back to God's action in our lives. This takes us to the heart of the Trinity, to the mutuality of relationship between the three persons, but in a particularly central way to the incarnate Word Jesus who is the perfect image of God and in whose humanity we find the essence of relationship with God.

So Barth can define the doctrine of "*imago Dei*" in terms of relationship with God but for him this simply means God's placing us in a particular situation as God's "covenant-partner" in Christ. There is a relational distance between God and humanity because humanity is finite but, despite this distance, we live out our creation in "*imago Dei*" in relationship with our fellow humans. Relationship with Christ does not and cannot involve a similarity with God in terms of our being. We

---

[11] Barth, *CD III/2*, 324.

can in no way participate in the being of God. The relationship is based solely on our faith that Christ is God *pro nobis*. His relationship with us does not beckon us back to share in his divine life. We are not incorporated into his life and onto his mission. It will not be Barth himself but his disciple Balthasar who will develop Barth's Christocentric anthropology into a fuller picture of our communion with Christ. For Barth this view of the mutuality of relationship between Christ and us, however much rooted in Christ's call, is confused. We cannot approach this relationship with Christ from our side. Our being made in the image of God simply places us at a distance from him yet called to be as Christ to our fellow humans.

Thus Barth's doctrine of "*imago Dei*" stops short of developing a theological anthropology which expresses in itself the dignity of each human person. It does not emphasise sufficiently the quest for possible fulfilment in an ongoing relationship with God in Christ lived out in the relationship of humans with each other. He recognises through his reading of Anselm that the human person's personal pilgrimage can be a profound spiritual experience in Christian prayer but believes that we are gravely deluded into thinking that relationship is about participation in the life of God. When the Christian believer prays he might erroneously seek encounter, conformity, oneness with God. He is, however, called back to acknowledge the faith in which he is constituted and which reveals his true situation as a fallen human being now made a covenant partner with Jesus Christ.

All faith's unrest is, in fact, set aside in prayer, but its prayer is its profound unrest. And both as prayer and also as unrest it is expectation, expectation of its object. It lives by its object, at rest or in unrest, having found, seeking, finding again and seeking anew. But this object is the free God who is hidden from man because he is a sinner, who has, of course, put man in the new state of faith in which He can be known by him, but who in this very state – it is indeed that of faith – wills to be sought and found anew and then anew again. For faith, He is and remains enclosed in objectivity, in the externality of the Word of God, in Jesus Christ. He must teach man to seek Him and He must show Himself to him in order that he may find Him. But it is by this external object that Christian faith lives.[12]

In trying to construe the doctrine in terms of a relationship grounded in Christ there remains a relational distance between God and humanity. God's relationship with us simply entails our situation as his covenant partners, not drawing closer to him but living out the relationship through our dealings with our fellow humans. In my view this understanding carries a strength and a weakness. Barth's "relational" model will be so much enclosed within his doctrine of the Word of God that Christ, not humanity, is clearly at its apex. Yet the God–human encounter will lack a more integrated picture of the human being's quest to fulfil his destiny in an ongoing relationship with Christ. Balthasar will be able to integrate his strengths in developing a more rounded model of relationship. In order to understand this it is important to investigate Barth's theological picture further to see how his system could not resolve the inherent tension and, tending towards what I regard

---

[12] Ibid., 231–2.

as a sombre view of the human condition, closed itself to this fuller picture of human dignity. So let us look further in the *Church Dogmatics* at how he really construes this relationship before and after the Fall and how it becomes such an integral part of his theological system. A key factor will be his interpretation of one of the most significant figures in the tradition, Augustine, and the tradition which interpreted him.

The Sources of Barth's Sombre View of Humanity

Interpretation of Augustine and His Tradition

Barth wants to make it very clear that he is firmly in the tradition of Augustine.[13] His own thought process is based in no small way on what he takes to be Augustine's foundational belief that, after the Fall, human beings are incapable of accessing God. In accepting this as the teaching of Augustine he places himself alongside Luther in stating that the Fall places us under the power of Satan and so absolutely incapable of finding our way back to God. For this reason Barth affirms that we need God in Christ to reconstitute us in the special relationship with him we once had but lost through sin.

How, according to Barth, does God in Christ do this? He takes Augustine to mean that "essentially" God "justifies" us in Christ. "*Justificatio*" places us in a new situation of "*rectitudo*" vis-à-vis God in Christ. It does not include any movement on the side of humans through which we have any access to God. According to Barth this is not possible in Augustine's system. He claims that nowhere does Augustine talk in terms of our essential "*deificatio*". Rather "*deificatio*" is part of "*justificatio*". For Barth Augustine's thought certainly does not include as an essential ingredient of our special relationship with God in our finding our way back to him through grace. About this Barth is clear and places himself at one mind with the Reformed tradition going back to Luther.

In defending this picture of how God in Christ reconstitutes us after the Fall "from above, not from below", Barth places his view in the context of his time and so helps us to see how radically he intends to draw the fault lines of this recovered tradition of theological anthropology. We should avoid a false view, he insists, which wants to develop any hint of reciprocity between God and us. At first sight there would seem to be a contradiction between this statement and his development of a model of "*imago Dei*" expressing the mutuality of relationship with God. However, we must consider the doctrinal background here. According to Barth there had been a tendency in the first half of the twentieth century among Lutheran theologians to reinterpret the doctrine of justification by faith alone. This is shown in the scholar Wobbermin's attribution to Luther of the concept of "two-poled relation" and "reciprocity" between God and humanity. For Barth this

---

[13] Ibid., 238ff..

movement was to be resisted. It is not, as Ritschl would have it, "human interest" in God which makes God true God.

Barth now sets out to develop a theological anthropology which resists the tendencies he found in these Lutheran theologians. For him the whole action of reconstitution will now be encapsulated and enclosed in his doctrine of God. The saving action of God in human lives will be expressed through his presentation of a God who in himself is his revelation in the world as Jesus Christ, the Word, God *pro nobis*. The God–human relationship now becomes in its essence an expression of the God who in himself is *pro nobis* in Jesus Christ, the Word. Later in I/1 Barth will confirm this teaching succinctly. "God's Word is God Himself in his revelation" ("*Gottes Wort ist Gott selbst in seiner Offenbarung*").[14] "God's revelation is God's own direct speech" ("*Gottes Offenbarung ist ... Gottes eigenes unmittelbares Reden*").[15]

Barth wants to understand "faith" in a way which rules out any hint of human capacity for encountering God. Here he believes that Augustine himself did not give a sufficiently strict interpretation but that the later Reformed tradition which developed Augustine's thought, and especially Luther, pointed us in the right direction. This tradition is indeed more faithful to scripture. He does not indicate that he is breaking with Augustine. He is clearly at one with him in basing his view on the human being's inability to access God after the Fall. It would seem then that he regards himself as in the tradition of Augustine as brought up-to-date by the reformer Luther to be more in keeping with what is revealed to us in scripture. This is important to recognise. As we will see, Barth's rejection of Roman Catholic theological anthropology is actually aimed at the theology which was to be developed post-Augustine. So when it comes to the key question of how to understand "faith" Barth admits that on this Augustine is not strict enough for him but defers to Luther to develop Augustine's line of thought.

> The older theology ... called faith a gift of God, of the Holy Spirit. This could be meant and said with varying degrees of strictness. We must take it in a more incisive sense than it is stated and understood, e.g., in Augustine. Augustine, of course, taught very explicitly and impressively against the Pelagians that faith is grace. But his *Ut credamus Deus dedit* remained equivocal, for there was always the other saying: *fides in potestate est*, in which *potestas* meant the *facultas faciendi* (*De Spir. et lit.*, 31, 55).[16]

Barth admits that, however seminally Augustine himself taught that faith was a gift, there did remain an aspect of his thought which still left open the possibility of attributing to fallen human beings rather than solely to God the possession of this gift. In Augustine, he says, "there is still the other saying: *Posse habere*

---

[14] Ibid., 295 [Barth, *KD I/1: Die Lehre vom Wort Gottes*, 311].
[15] Ibid., 304 [Barth, *KD I/1*, 320].
[16] Ibid., 245.

fidem naturae est hominum; there is a general human *natura in qua nobis data est possibilitas habendi fidem (De praedest., 5, 10)*".[17] This does not interpret "faith" strictly enough as being out of fallen humanity's reach. Thus he decides to go further, along the lines of Luther and paying closer attention to scripture, in particular Paul's letter to the Galatians.

> Since it is hard to find any basis in man even for this *possibilitas habendi*, let alone a *habere*, it is better to say with Luther: *fidem esse ... simpliciter donum Dei, qui ut creat ita conservat fidem in nobis* (*Comm. On Gal.* 1:12, 1535, W.A., 40:1, p. 130, l.13).[18]

Thus Barth concludes that "faith" is not to be construed primarily in terms of human response but from God's side. For human beings in only the very weakest sense "the possibility of faith" is to be "understood [only] as [one] that is loaned to man by God". Thus Barth will define the human being's creation in God's image not from the perspective of humanity's response to God but in terms of God's self-gift to us. Jesus Christ, the Word of God incarnate, justifies the human being who does not respond so much as "as he really receives God's Word, [man] becomes apt to receive it" (*"indem er das Wort Gottes wirklich vernimmt, dazu geeignet, es zu vernehmen"*).[19] Faith is in fact also enclosed and encapsulated in the understanding of who God is for us. "Faith", affirms Barth clearly, "is not one of the various capacities of man, whether native or acquired. Capacity for the Word of God is not among these native or acquired attributes" (*"Der Glaube fällt ja nicht unter die verschiedenen Kapazitäten des Menschen, weder als angeborene noch als zugewachsene. Unter diesen kommt eine Kapazität für das Wort Gottes allerdings nicht vor"*).[20]

Thus for Barth our post-Fall reconstitution in the special relationship with God which characterizes his notion of *"imago Dei"* involves no hint of mutuality with God. The distance between us and God arises in Barth's thought because he insists on a return to a clear belief that we really do have absolutely no access to God after the Fall. It is his interpretation of the tradition from Augustine through to Luther which has led him to this perspective. It is essentially in the action of *"justificatio"*, not *"deificatio"*, that we are reconstituted in relationship with God. Through this Barth affirms that "man remains man" in "real faith", that is to say the faith which is not ours but understood from God's side.

So who is the newly reconstituted fallen human being vis-à-vis God? Does not Barth also set out to show that there is a point of contact between God and humanity? Importantly Barth believes that the model of *"imago Dei"* he is developing is indeed trying to provide this link. The problem is that he is

---

[17] Ibid., 245.
[18] Ibid., 245.
[19] Ibid., 238 [Barth, *KD I/1*, 251].
[20] Ibid., 238 [Barth, *KD I/1*, 250].

determined to recover a view of fallen humanity which stands before God at a distance inalienable except through the all-encapsulating doctrine of the Word of God. Here in this section of writing he affirms that he still believes that we have to affirm a "point of contact". "There can be no receiving of God's Word", asserts Barth, "unless there is something common to the speaking God and hearing man in this event ... a similarity ... a point of contact between God and man". This is a theme which he will take up later in *III/2*. For him relationship with God is construed in the same way as relationship between humans. It takes both hearing and speaking. This would seem to represent a mutual point of contact between the two. Yet, when we look more closely at what this really means within Barth's theological system we find a diminished sense of mutuality. Barth's model represents not so much the possibility of a union or a communion as would be the case in a Roman Catholic interpretation of the tradition but "in faith there takes place a conformity of man to God ... as he really receives God's Word, man becomes apt to receive it".[21]

Thus we are drawn to the conclusion that Barth is still wanting to express something very important about the dignity of the fallen but reconformed human being who nevertheless, in a state of "*rectitudo*", "righteousness", cannot be said to be in any way like God or have access to him. In acknowledgement of the situation before God in which the human being finds himself, there is a "conformity" to his Creator and saviour. We are covenant partners with him. Our "conformity" to God, however, is by no means the ability to be in any way like God. This is the heart of Barth's difficulty with the Roman Catholic view of the human situation before God in Christ. He is led to reject the Thomist doctrine of "*analogia entis*", that teaching which Barth proclaimed is but a hairbreadth from a traditional understanding of the human person made in "*imago Dei*". Within his system he will reformulate the doctrine of analogy from the perspective of "faith", that vital aspect of the God–human relationship which he has placed inside his doctrine of the Word of God. The human situation before God will be based not on any analogy of being but on what we shall now discover is an analogy of "faith".

Reformulation of the Doctrine of Analogy

"Conformity of man to God" is not an "*analogia entis*" declares Barth.[22] In our introductory chapter we saw that this doctrine was developed especially during the medieval period by Aquinas. We saw that it defined the human being vis-à-vis God as founded on analogy of being and in a way which expressed the possibility of human participation in the very being of God. Let us briefly recall what Aquinas taught.

---

[21] Barth, *CD I/1*, 238.
[22] Barth, *CD I/1*, 239.

As creatures the first question we must ask is regarding our very existence.[23] Aquinas had started his enquiry with the question of God's existence. God, as uncaused cause of all things, is the being from whom all created things receive their existence and so to whom they tend. The very essence of God is to exist. Humanity exists but in a limited way. We discover our existence through our participation in the life of God in whom we find the perfection of existence. We are not just encouraged to participate in the life of God on earth but to set it as our goal. Union to God is the final end of our lives on earth because then we will be one with he in whose image and likeness we were made, the God who is our true identity.

We know too, of course, that Aquinas goes on, in Ia.IIae of the *Summa Theologiae*, to show how we are called to participate in the life of God through the co-operation of our human nature with the grace of Christ. However Barth believes that he needs to reject this concept of "*analogia entis*" forcefully if he is to retain his firm belief in the primacy of grace, in God's sovereignty and, in recovering the true meaning of Augustine, humanity's total incapacity from our side to access God.

Barth tells us exactly why this doctrine of analogy must be rejected. In *CD II/1* he addresses how Roman Catholic theological anthropology has developed in concert with an erroneous understanding of analogy. In particular he sees its influence on the declaration of the First Vatican Council *De Revelatione* that humanity can know God through the light of natural human reason. For Barth this is anathema. Because it exposes a belief system which claims natural human capacity to know God from our side, that is not to see God's revelation for us in Christ, but to try to construct a picture of God and his revelation "*in abstracto*", it shows that Roman Catholicism is "guilty of ... conflict against grace" ("*des Streites gegen die Gnade schuldig*").[24] "Are we really speaking of the real Lord and Creator?", Barth asks rhetorically. "On what ground do we think that we can speak about His knowability in this abstraction?"[25] Rather "we have no analogy on the basis of which the nature and being of God as Creator can be accessible to us".[26]

Moreover for Barth the notion of the "*analogia entis*" suggests that human beings can in a way mirror God as though by analogy we may become what seems to be an "image of the Trinitarian God himself".[27] This, he states in a section of writing towards the end of *I/1*, is the unfortunate end result of what he sees as "a genuine *analogia entis*". The Catholic doctrine assumes wrongly that there is a "*vestigium trinitatis*" in creation distinct from God:

---

[23] I refer here to the following sections in the *Summa Theologiae*: Ia.2–11 in Volume 2, *Existence and Nature of God*, and Ia.75–83 in Volume 11, *Man*.

[24] Barth, *CD II/1*, 85 [Barth, *KD II/1: Die Lehre von Gott*, 93].

[25] Barth, *CD II/1*, 80.

[26] Ibid., 76.

[27] Barth, *CD I/1*, 334ff.

an analogue of the Trinity, of the trinitarian God of Christian revelation, in some creaturely reality distinct from him, a creaturely reality which is not a form assumed by God in His revelation, but which quite apart from God's revelation manifests in its own structure by creation a certain similarity to the structure of the trinitarian God, so that it may be regarded as an image of the trinitarian God himself ... a genuine *analogia* entis.[28]

For Barth the objection is clear. We do not and cannot mirror God. Rather we are conformed to him. We cannot find God through this understanding of analogy as God remains essentially other and inaccessible to us. This is why he declares, in *CD I/1*, 239ff., that any understanding of the human being's relationship vis-à-vis God cannot be one of "*analogia entis*", because we cannot understand it "as an analogy that can be surveyed and perceived ... understood in a synthesis from an onlooker's standpoint". It can only be expressed as an analogy in terms of our acknowledgement of what God in Christ, the Word incarnate, has done in his being for us. This is "inaccessible to any mere theory".

For Barth the analogy we can accept is one of "faith", that is "human decision" to accept how God reveals himself to us. "Our reply to the Roman Catholic doctrine of the *analogia entis*", he claims, "is not ... a denial of the concept of analogy". Truly we need a concept of analogy as "there can be no receiving of God's Word unless there is something common to the speaking God and hearing man ... a similarity ... a point of contact between God and man".[29] However, this is not an "*analogia entis*" but an "*analogia fidei*".

Barth also renders "*analogia fidei*" in the Greek, "αναλογία της πίστεως",[30] that is suggesting he is taking "faith" here to mean an assent, that is an assent to God's revelation in Christ. Our identity can only be that which is expressed in the assent of the human person to God's revelation in Christ because the only analogy of humans to God we can affirm is that of this conforming act of faith. The only likeness to God we can affirm through this analogy is in the God who reveals himself to humanity through the gift of faith loaned to us.

Reflecting on Barth's reformulation of the doctrine of analogy we might ultimately still ask if in his model there is any "point of contact us between God and man", anything "common to the speaking God and hearing man"? The answer Barth has given to us is in this respect a positive one. We need to affirm the positive value of Barth's contribution here. For human beings, fallen yet in faith giving their assent to God's being for them in Christ, their whole lives of faith will radiate the truth of this point of contact with God in Christ. This can be expressed with certain knowledge but only in objective terms, in terms of our "object", God in Christ. In such a way we can say that in fallen human beings there is in this sense

---

[28] Ibid., 334. Emphasis his.
[29] Ibid., 238.
[30] Ibid., 243.

a "likeness" to God: it is "a likeness of the known in the knowing, of the object in thought, of the Word of God in the word that is thought and spoken by man".[31]

Such is the essential content of Barth's view of how the human being is in a special relationship with God. Whilst it places Christ clearly as the "object" of our faith, this Christ remains distant. His dark view of humanity tends to obstruct the more integrated view of the relationship he has at times expressed a desire to construct. The doctrine of "*imago Dei*" remains tied to a reading of Augustine and the Thomist doctrine of analogy from the perspective of a sombre view of humanity. It will be my view that Balthasar's different, decidedly more optimistic, interpretation of the tradition, will enable him to develop the Barthian model into a more integrated perspective. In order to argue this it will be necessary to look still more critically at Barth's own reading of the tradition and his consequent rejection of Roman Catholic teaching which it seems to me disabled him from presenting the fuller picture of human dignity in Christ through the "*imago Dei*" doctrine. So now let us turn to this in a critical analysis of the steps he has taken to arrive at his view.

Critical Analysis: Formulation of Barth's View and Rejection of Roman Catholic Understanding

Augustine and His Tradition

Barth's interpretation of Augustine was the primary factor in his rejection of the Roman Catholic understanding of "*imago Dei*" and explains how his own doctrine is shot through with a rather dark view of the human condition. He has interpreted Augustine in a way which does not give space to the other aspect of the Father's thought which would have allowed him to have emphasised the important aspect of human possibility, the desire for God and transcendence. This is understandable, given Barth's rejection of the notion that human beings have a natural capacity for God, what has traditionally been termed "natural theology". However, Augustine's own understanding of the relationship between God and humanity is much richer than Barth would seem to believe. In Augustine we find a clear doctrine of God's prevenience yet also he expresses how the life of the human being is a pilgrimage of desire and discovery as he comes closer to his divine goal. It is in keeping too slavishly to the interpretation of Augustine favoured by the reformers that Barth has disallowed himself to develop a more positive strand to his thinking about human dignity.

As a result he will be able to speak well of human dignity from the perspective of Christ's descent to us. It is this strand to his thought in particular which Balthasar will express powerfully. However Barth will not be able to develop a narrative of human response to the extent that at times it seems he would like. Instead, for

---
[31] Ibid., 243.

all his attempts to include this, humanity will ultimately be construed as passive. It will be left to Balthasar to hone Barth's radical Christocentrism to give fuller expression to the side of his thinking which remained underdeveloped. One of the primary keys to all this will be the interpretation both thinkers gave to Augustine. So let us turn to Barth's interpretation of Augustine and of his tradition.

Barth has remained attached to a particularly Lutheran interpretation of Augustine. This has had both positive and negative consequences. Through Luther in particular Barth has emphasised a very important and foundational strand in his way of understanding how the human being is created "*imago Dei*" but in so doing he has neglected another which is equally important in Augustine's own thought. There are two important strands in Augustine's teaching. On the one hand there is his fundamental insistence on God's absolute sovereignty and the necessity of grace in the face of post-Fall humanity's distance from the Creator. Barth has stressed this very strongly. We might say that, positively, this represents Barth's emphasis on God's action in human lives yet also betrays his distinctly passive understanding of God's relationship with human beings.

Barth, however, seems to have neglected another important element of Augustine's thought which deserves attention. This element has influenced the development of what we might call a more integrated understanding of the God–human relationship in which humanity is envisaged as engaged on a journey back to God. This latter element reflects a fuller picture of the dignity of the human person created in God's image. Here the human person is involved on a pilgrimage through life at the end of which he can attain, through God's grace, unity with God. It will be an adventure of transcendence and transformation through which the human person not merely accepts how Christ has transformed him even in his sinful state but actively participates in discovering his true destiny with him in eternity.

Regarding the first strand, that which emphasises God's action in human lives, Barth is clearly taking us back to the authentic foundation and core of Augustine's teaching. Let us remind ourselves of how Augustine expresses this in the *Enchiridion on Faith, Hope and Love*:

> Since men are in this state of wrath through original sin – a condition made still graver and more pernicious as they compounded more and worse sins with it – a Mediator was required, that is to say, a Reconciler who by offering a unique sacrifice, of which all the sacrifices of the Law and the Prophets were shadows, should allay that wrath.[32]

The portion of humanity which can be saved, that is the portion which is not damned, can do nothing on its own. Human beings cannot attempt to be saved themselves. They can only be saved by Christ who has paid the ransom for us. "But now, can that part of the human race to whom God hath promised deliverance and a place in the eternal Kingdom be restored through the merits of their own

---

[32] St Augustine, *Enchiridion on Faith, Hope and Love*, VIII.33.

works? Of course not! For what good could a lost soul do...?"³³ We find no freedom in attempting our own salvation. Rather we discover our true freedom in the divine Son, the incarnate Word, Wisdom, the one to whom we are oriented as creatures made according to God's image. Our human nature, despite being made "*ad imaginem Dei*", cannot save us. Our salvation is a free gift, that is what we call grace.

For Barth, however, this strand of Augustine's thought, although it is fundamental, would seem to exclude the possibility of the other fuller, more integrated, view of human dignity in the adventure of transcendence and transformation. Because he insists that we must return to Augustine's teaching that we really do have absolutely no access to God after the Fall, our post-Fall reconstitution in special relationship with God involves no hint of this. It is his interpretation of the tradition from Augustine through to Luther which has led him to this perspective. It is essentially in the action of "*justificatio*", not "*deificatio*", that we are reconstituted. "*Deificatio*", he claims, is not part of Augustine's picture of the God–human relationship but is contained in the fundamental understanding of our "*justificatio*". However, I would argue that we might question such an assumption. In a fuller interpretation of Augustine we may argue that "*deificatio*" is an important strand in his thought which deserves attention.

For Augustine the "*deificatio*" of human beings appears to be not merely part of "*justificatio*", as Barth states, but more expressive of human participation in the return to God. For him "*deificatio*" was an essential process through which humans return to the source to be one with God. In Augustine's work of personal narrative, the *Confessions*, he speaks in terms of the goal of the soul, which is happiness. This is to be found in God: "wherever the human soul turns itself, other than to you, it is fixed in sorrows."³⁴ It is the soul which makes its ascent to God and so the human being made in God's image returns to the source. "What then do I love when I love my God?"³⁵ Augustine asks: "through my soul I will ascend to him", he answers, "I will therefore rise above that natural capacity", that which makes me human, " in a step by step by step ascent to him who made me".³⁶

Thus for Augustine God's "*justificatio*" of post-Fall humanity in Christ's death and resurrection draws us into reciprocal participation. For Augustine we do not, in our "*deificatio*", respond merely in the passive way envisaged by Barth as the classical rendering of Luther. We do not merely respond in "real faith" as "real man" in assent to this once and for all redemptive act. Rather Christ's ransom opens up the possibility of participation in the life of God. Augustine quotes Paul: "'therefore, as the offence of one man led all men to condemnation, so also the

---

[33] Ibid., VIII.30.

[34] I am using the translation by Henry Chadwick: St Augustine, *Confessions* (Oxford: Oxford University Press, 1992), Iv.x (15).

[35] Ibid., X.vii (11).

[36] Ibid., X.viii (12).

righteousness of one man leads all men to the life of justification'".[37] This is the life which leads back to the "*deificatio*" which is our destiny. Our "authentic justification" which is "nothing other than the likeness of the forgiveness of sins"[38] leads to the possibility of our following our exemplar Christ in returning to unity with the source in which lies our happiness, God the Father:

> Whatever was done, therefore, in the crucifixion of Christ, his burial, his resurrection on the third day, his ascension into heaven, being seated at the Father's right hand – all these things were done thus, that they might not only signify their mystical meanings but also serve as a model for the Christian life which we lead here on the earth. Thus, of his crucifixion it was said, "And that they that are Jesus Christ's have crucified their own flesh, with the passions and lusts thereof"; and of his burial, "For we are buried with Christ by baptism into death"; of his resurrection, "Since Christ is dead through the glory of the Father, so we also should walk with him in newness of life"; of his ascension and session at the Father's right hand: "But if you have risen again with Christ, seek the things which are above, where Christ is sitting at the right hand of God. Set your affection on things above, not on things on the earth. For you are dead, and your life is hid with Christ in God."[39]

So rather than our "*deificatio*" being, as it is for Barth, merely a non-essential extra supplementing the once and for all justification which we acknowledge in "real faith", Augustine's picture is of a dynamic process through which we respond to God's grace through this grace working in us as we make our way along the "*via*" back to God. God's grace is primary in this process but the process is more fully participative as we are to be formed in the moral life so we may be new creatures: "God ordereth our lives, that is, formeth and createth us not as men – this he hath already done – but also as good men, which he is now doing by his grace, that we may indeed be new creatures in Christ Jesus."[40]

We will be taking this examination of Barth's interpretation of Augustine further. In the next chapter in particular I will be showing how Balthasar was able to develop this fuller more integrated interpretation of Augustine. Balthasar, seeing also the fundamental value in Barth's emphasis on the first strand of Augustine's thought, with its emphasis on the gratuity of God's action in Christ, is able to express this in tandem with the fuller picture of humanity's pilgrimage back to God and thus give a more rounded interpretation of the tradition. This fuller Augustinian picture of the God–human relationship will be given its meaning by capturing Augustine's sense of humanity's desire of God's beauty in the face of God's revelation.

---

[37] Augustine, *Enchiridion on Faith, Hope, and Love*, XIV.51.
[38] Ibid., XIV.52, 5.
[39] Ibid., XIV.53, 15.
[40] Ibid., IX.31.

However, for the present let us conclude two important points from our closer scrutiny of Barth's particular interpretation of Augustine. We might say that the first is positive, the second negative. Barth has highlighted for us a fundamental aspect of our understanding of how the human being is created in "*imago Dei*". This is the sovereignty of God in the face of human limitation and the primacy of grace in Christ. But he has left another aspect underdeveloped. This is our response to God as creatures on a journey back to the Creator. Because Barth has grounded his thought in this particular tradition of Augustine we may understand how he has also rejected the Roman Catholic understanding of "*imago Dei*" as developed in later theology up to the present time. To this we now turn, bearing in mind both the positive and negative aspects of his position.

*Rejection of Roman Catholic Understanding of "*Imago Dei*"*

Rejection of Thomist Method
In the light of his interpretation of the Augustinian tradition Barth's rejection of Roman Catholic teaching is understandable. For him, rather than developing the strand of Augustine's teaching which emphasises fallen humanity's dependence on Christ, Roman Catholic theology has moved in a wholly unacceptable direction. Aquinas' doctrine of analogy brought a more philosophical and scientific way of approaching the doctrine which expressed a clear belief that our very human identity of its own nature involves a call to fulfil our destiny in participation in the life of God. This has become part of a Roman Catholic view, stressed in particular at Vatican I, which places emphasis on our human ability to find God through using the gifts we are given by him. For Barth this is in fact nothing less serious than "conflict against grace".[41] However, whilst we may argue that this critique, given where Barth stands in the Augustinian tradition, is understandable but flawed, it is worth considering the point of Barth's rejection of Roman Catholic teaching in itself. Furthermore it is important to note that it is not just the Roman Catholic teaching in itself to which he is so vehemently opposed but a whole method of constructing theological anthropology also present in post-Enlightenment Protestantism but with roots in Thomistic methodology.

Barth seems to regard the Thomist project as very influential both within Roman Catholic theology and in recent developments within his own tradition which militate against grounding theological anthropology in the Word of God. For Barth Aquinas expressly set out to construct a "*theologia naturalis*" on the basis of the "*praeambula fidei*". This way of doing theology is one which makes the fatal error, common to both Roman Catholicism and more recent Protestant orthodoxy, of making our *raison d'être* the quest for understanding human identity rather than seeing God's revelation in Jesus Christ for what it is first. In Barth's own terms it is an erroneous method of constructing theology in that it concentrates

---

[41] Barth, *CD II/1*, 80.

on the "subject", the human person, rather than the "object", God, in his revelation in Christ:

> From the very outset Protestant orthodoxy suffered from a surplus rather than a deficit in the regard it paid to the religious subject. Its aim at least – and this was the point of the turn to *scientia practica* – was to understand the Word of God altogether as a word addressed to man. The only trouble was that there was another meaning to the development as well. It is patent that what was also sought and attained with this development was that the object of theology, as scientific consciousness after the Renaissance was increasingly demanding, was transferred from a Beyond genuinely confronting the place of man to the sphere of man himself. Though it did not have to be, this object could now be thought of as one that is embraced and conditioned by the general truths of man. An attempt could thus be made to view it, or the possibility of it, within the sphere of man's self-understanding. The contemporary reconstruction of a *theologia naturalis* as the science of the *praeambula fidei* in the ancient Thomistic sense, the slow but noticeable withdrawal of the doubts the Reformers had regarding the value of this enterprise, shows that there was interest in this incorporation from other angles too.[42]

There are some good reasons for accepting this picture of Thomism. Augustine had defended the Church from the heresy of Pelagianism in reasserting the primacy of grace. Aquinas and his followers, however, were responding to different needs. Aquinas himself was chiefly interested in the more scientific and philosophical question of how we "subjects", human beings, can, from our own perspective, know God. Such a quest led him to the understanding of the human being's "analogy" to God which Barth was to reject so forcefully. God is not simply beyond "the sphere of man", as Barth would have it. Rather human beings can know God inasmuch as there is an "analogy of being" between God and us. In this sense it is true that the Thomistic perspective, whether integrated into Roman Catholicism or post-Enlightenment Protestantism, tries to understand the human being not just from the perspective of the Word of God but from the "sphere of man himself". In *De Veritate* Aquinas himself is clear about his position:

> We cannot say ... that whatever is predicated of God and creature is predicated purely equivocally, since if no real likeness of creature to God existed, his essence would not be the likeness of creatures and then he would not know creatures through knowing his essence. So we must state that the name "knowledge" is predicated of God's Knowledge and of ours neither wholly univocally nor purely equivocally, but by analogy, which merely means according to proportion.[43]

---

[42] Barth, *CD I/1*, 192.
[43] Aquinas, *De Veritate*, in *Opera Omnia Tomus IX* (New York: Musurgia Publishers, 1949), II.1. Here I am following the translation in *An Aquinas Reader*, Mary T. Clark, ed.

It is important to be clear that, although God is far from "beyond", Aquinas also preserves the analogical distinction between creator and creature. He accepts the narrative of the Fall. Because of Adam's sin humanity's likeness to God is coloured by our sin. Nevertheless for Aquinas it is true that he has highlighted likeness to God as our true destiny and identity and so fuller participation in this reality is our true calling. We might indeed say that he had set the stage for the theological community to debate the consequences of an accepted narrative involving belief in a sovereign Creator God whose creatures then fell from some elevated state yet could still, through Christ, attain salvation. If we accept this we naturally ask questions regarding our human identity. Who exactly are we and how do we attain full participation in that for which we were made? As one influenced by the Platonic school of philosophy we have seen that the picture of the human being on pilgrimage back to God was also present in Augustine. However it was indeed Aquinas, recovering Aristotle, who made this line of enquiry his theological starting point.

As creatures the first question we must ask is regarding our very existence. Aquinas had started his enquiry with the question of God's existence. God, as uncaused cause of all things, is the being from whom all created things receive their existence and so to whom they tend. The very essence of God is to exist. Humanity exists but in a limited way. We discover our existence through our participation in the life of God in whom we find the perfection of existence. Thus this is why we are not just encouraged to have faith in the objective truth of God's revelation in Christ but are called to participate in the life of God on earth and to set it as our goal. This is at the core of our human dignity. Union to God is the final end of our lives on earth because then we will be one with he in whose image and likeness we were made.

It is this way of approaching the doctrine of "*imago Dei*", more from the perspective of the human "subject" than the "object" of the Word of God, which Barth was keen to reject. As such he saw himself as reorienting the doctrine in the revelation of God in Christ. This reaction to what he takes to be a far more anthropocentric way of approaching the doctrine is of enormous value. Any understanding of "*imago Dei*" must be rooted in God's action in human lives. However, how fair is his treatment of the Roman Catholic position? The key to evaluating this appears to be his understanding of how Roman Catholicism today understands the dynamic of the God–human relationship as the interplay of grace and knowledge of God natural to human beings through the light of reason.

For Barth Roman Catholicism is not just misguided in starting from an anthropocentric rather than theocentric methodology. It is in fact this methodology which leads to nothing less than a "conflict against grace". We have seen that Barth's preoccupation is to do with methodology, hence his concern about not just Thomism and its influence on Roman Catholic teaching, but also about post-Enlightenment developments in Protestant theology. However, he does seem also to

---

(London: Hodder & Stoughton, 1974), 99.

regard Roman Catholicism in particular as militating against a belief in the primacy of grace. This is as a direct result of its methodology. Precisely because, following Thomist method, it has placed the quest for knowledge about God's being prior to knowledge about God's saving action in Christ, when it comes to defining the situation of human beings before God, we look for our ontological status before we consider what God has done for us. In Barth's terms we erroneously accept an "*analogia entis*" rather than "*analogia fidei*".

For Barth the First Vatican Council, in following the Thomist rather than Augustinian methodology, made this very mistake in affirming that God is indeed knowable through the light of human reason.[44] "What we have said", reiterates Barth in defence of his own position, "is that the accessibility of the nature and being of God as Lord, Creator, Reconciler and Redeemer is not constituted by any analogy which we contribute but only by God Himself". Vatican I, however, "intends to make a provisional division or partition in regard to the knowability of God". Vatican I, according to Barth, speaks of God as "*Dominus noster*" but then defines who God is from the basis of human reasoning as "*rerum omnium principium et finis, creator*". The problem in using the light of reason to address this question is that we come to an incomplete conclusion because we have placed incomplete human reason on a par with the completeness of God's grace.

The only satisfactory thing we can say about God is contained in his revelation to us and not in our reasoning out who he is and thus who we are in relationship to him. "Of course, we too understand by 'God' *principium et finis omnium rerum* and also *creator*. But God is not only this. He is also God the Reconciler and Redeemer." Barth, on the other hand, starts his dogmatics from God's being in himself for us: "in our discussion of the lordship of God we kept in mind the fact that it is the lordship of the Holy One in the world of sinners, and for that reason we affirmed that the lordship of God evades all the analogies that we can bring." Grace itself thus properly defined cannot include any consideration of our natural human ability to know God, even through grace. This would be to destroy the whole Barthian dogmatic system. "Grace is God's good pleasure. And it is precisely in God's good-pleasure that the reality of our being with God and of His being with us consists" ("*Gnade ist Gottes Wohlgefallen. Und eben in Gottes Wohlgefallen besteht die Realität unseres Seins mit Gott, seines Seins mit uns*").[45] Thus Barth does really seem to believe that in Roman Catholic teaching the primacy of grace is threatened:

> Can we ever speak properly of grace and faith if at the very outset we have provided ourselves with a guarantee of our knowledge of God which has nothing to do with grace and faith? Does it not necessarily change and even falsify everything if at this point we are guilty of enmity and conflict against grace?[46]

---

[44] Barth, *CD II/1*, 79–85.
[45] Ibid., 74 [Barth, *KD II/1*, 80].
[46] Ibid., 85.

Despite the important point Barth might be making and his understandable reasons for it, it would seem that this criticism, at least from the Roman Catholic perspective, is unfair. As a result of this Barth's theology leaves underdeveloped the aspect of the God–human relationship which reflects our adventure of transformation. The relational model he intends to construct remains static and passive. It is true that there are times when the more integrated view does seem to emerge. Barth's writing itself here is not always consistent. Despite his clear will not to admit any possibility of our having access to God and his grace courtesy of our own dignity as made in "*imago Dei*", in fact he comes close to conceding this in a later volume of the *Church Dogmatics*. However, for the moment let us return to his specific accusation regarding Roman Catholic teaching. We may argue that throughout the history of Roman Catholic teaching there has in fact been a firm belief both in the primacy of grace whilst allowing necessarily the development of a theology of human participation in this grace–nature relationship.

"Conflict against Grace"
It was the method inherited from Aquinas which Barth was to reject so strongly. However, when we examine the seminal medieval doctor's teaching more closely, we discover that he clearly followed Augustine in insisting on the necessity of grace. In IaIIae.109 he stresses this at length as he raises 10 key questions regarding the primacy of grace in the grace–nature dynamic and responds to them in a way which cannot avoid affirming, with Augustine and scripture, the primacy of grace over the in fact God-given potential to draw closer to him. I will take four articles of this *quaestio* to illustrate my point. Aquinas asks if human beings can know any truth without grace. The answer is clearly no.[47] It is to be granted that here Aquinas wants to admit that human nature truly possesses internally, in the soul, a God-given ability. This he calls "*naturale lumen*", "*natural light*", which "moves the mind to understand and utter the truth". This natural light, however, "is from the Holy Spirit". As such, in terms of the primacy of God's grace, Aquinas affirms that he is at one with Augustine, stressing the need of divine assistance to move the human being to discover the truth.

"Can man merit eternal life without grace?" Aquinas asks. It is true that we are called to respond in carrying out good works but clearly, once again, grace is required.[48] For Aquinas good works are an important aspect of our living out our relationship with Christ. In doing them we are seen to turn from sin and towards Christ but we cannot do this without the assistance of grace. For Aquinas, as for Augustine, we are fallen creatures, and so constantly need to turn away from our fallen human nature and towards our destiny in Christ, but this clearly is impossible without grace. It is true that Aquinas wants to concede rather more to God-given human potential than did Augustine hence he does not claim our nature as creatures

---

[47] In Aquinas, *ST* Ia.IIae.109.1.responsio, Volume 30.
[48] Aquinas, *ST* Ia.IIae.109.6.responsio ad 2, Volume 30.

made for God is totally destroyed. Rather it is "spoiled" ("*corrumpitur*"). But grace is still primary:

> When a nature is intact, it can be restored by itself to what is fitting and proportionate to it; but without external assistance it cannot be restored to what transcends its proportionate scope. Consequently, human nature, dissipated by the act of sin, is no longer intact but spoiled ... and so by itself can be restored neither to the good connatural to it, nor still less to the good of supernatural justice.[49]

Finally, Aquinas asks how we might persevere on our journey back to God. Once again he cannot but declare that grace is needed. But neither will this rule out the need for us to persevere as human creatures, even in our spoiled state after the Fall, co-operating with grace.

> As Augustine says, In his first state man received the gift by means of which he was capable of persevering; but that he should persevere in fact he did not receive. Now, on the other hand, by Christ's grace, many receive the gift of grace by which they are capable of persevering, and further it is given to them that they should in fact persevere.[50] And thus Christ's gift is greater than Adam's crime. All the same, in the state of innocence, in which there was no rebellion of the flesh against the spirit, man could more easily persevere by the gift of grace than we can now, when the restoration due to Christ's grace is not yet brought to completion in the flesh, although it is initiated in the mind. This will come about in our heavenly home, when man will not only be able to persevere, but he will also be unable to sin.[51]

Thus it seems that an analysis of the issue in Aquinas reveals that, whilst we will still hold that Barth is making a very important point in his reorientation of theological anthropology, his accusation that Roman Catholic teaching is "conflict against grace" may be said to be unfair. We may argue that this objection has prevented Barth, for all we may learn from him, from recognising the importance of the Roman Catholic appreciation of the privileged place of the human being within a relationship which is firmly grounded in God's coming to us in Christ, that is grounded in revelation and in grace. When we turn to Vatican documents we see this more clearly.

The declaration on divine revelation of the Second Vatican Council, *Dei Verbum*, clearly wished to assert the primacy of the revelation of Christ. Christ, however, draws humanity into an ongoing relationship. "By thus revealing himself", says the Council, that is in Christ the "God, who is invisible (see Col 1,

---

[49] Aquinas, *ST* Ia.IIae.109.7.responsio ad 3, Volume 30, 95.
[50] *De Corruptione et Gratia* 12. *Patres Latini* 44, 937.
[51] Aquinas, *ST* Ia.IIae.109.10.responsio ad 3, Volume 30, 107.

15; 1 Tim 1, 17), his great love speaks to humankind as friends (see Ex 33,11; Jn in 15, 14–15) and enters into their life (see Bar 3, 38), so as to invite and receive them into relationship with himself".[52] Thus the document clarifies the teaching of the First Vatican Council, the teaching which Barth rejects. It makes clear that the gift of divine revelation, revelation it is granted containing divine treasures which "surpass human understanding", engages the human being in the quest for God who still is "'the first principle and last end of all things'". God's grace is primary but the "natural light" of human reason plays its part in the dynamic between God and his creatures with whom he has initiated this special relationship:

> By divine revelation God has chosen to manifest and communicate both himself and the eternal decrees of his will for the salvation of mankind, "so as to share those divine treasures which totally surpass human understanding".[53] This council reaffirms that "God, the first principle and last end of all things, can be known with certainty from the created order by the natural light of human reason" (See Rm 1, 20). Further, this teaching is to be held about revelation: "in the present condition of the human race, even those truths about God which are not beyond the reach of human reason, require revelation for them to be known by all without great effort, with firm certainty and without error entering in".[54] [55]

For current Roman Catholic teaching, in the light of the Second Vatican Council, it becomes clearer and clearer how the light of human reason has this important part to play whilst it is also clear that this is not separate from but as a consequence of and knitted to God's revelation in Jesus Christ. Rather than "conflict against grace" Roman Catholic teaching would see human natural capacity for God as responding to grace and in a dynamic relationship with it. We do not know how Barth would have responded to the development of Roman Catholic teaching following the Council. However it is in the Encyclical Letter *Fides et Ratio*[56] where we find once more a clear synthesis of Roman Catholic teaching which is consistent with the tradition we have been outlining. Here above all we find a belief in the absolute sovereignty of God's revelation in Christ construed as a treasure for contemporary humanity as people of today are invited to respond to the call to relationship as a privileged race made in "*imago Dei*".

Natural human reason does have an important part to play in the God–human relationship but this is not to be confused with a rational or existential philosophy which operates apart from God's revelation. God's revelation in Jesus Christ is

---

[52] Second Vatican Council, *Dei Verbum*, no. 2.

[53] First Vatican Council, Dogmatic Constitution on the Catholic Faith, *Dei Filius*, ch. 2: Denzinger 1786 (3005).

[54] *Dei Filius*, Denzinger 1785 and 1786 (3004 and 3005).

[55] *Dei Verbum*, no. 6.

[56] Pope John Paul II, *Fides et Ratio* (Vatican City: Libreria Editrice Vaticana, 1998).

presented to contemporary humanity as an eternal truth. The Encyclical finds the Thomistic strand of tradition in the Church to be particularly relevant to this particular project as it enables us to ask key questions about our human existence in the light of the eternal truth of God's revelation in Jesus Christ. However *Fides et Ratio* also turns to Augustine and other Church Fathers, to Vatican I and Vatican II teaching, and to scripture to present what has always been the Church's firm belief in the absolute sovereignty of God who extends to humanity an invitation to find meaning in him as a creature made for him in his image. It is in scripture in particular, the Encyclical says,

> that we learn that what we experience is not absolute: it is neither uncreated nor self-generating. God alone is the Absolute. From the Bible there emerges also a vision of man as *imago Dei*. This vision offers indications regarding man's life, his freedom and the immortality of the human spirit. Since the created world is not self-sufficient, every illusion of autonomy which would deny the essential dependence on God of every creature – the human being included – leads to dramatic situations which subvert the rational search for the harmony and the meaning of human life.[57]

Fides et Ratio thus ties the contemporary Roman Catholic understanding of the human being made in the "*imago Dei*" to a firm belief in God's action in human lives. Thus Barth's claim that Roman Catholicism is "conflict against grace" would seem unfair. His belief that this is the case, however, has led him to reject a view of "*imago Dei*" which associated itself with the Thomist understanding of analogy but also the more integrated strand of Augustine's thought. As a result he will stop short of developing a model of "*imago Dei*" which will give humanity its fuller picture of human dignity through a relationship to God which involves active participation in the pilgrimage of transformation.

Critical Analysis: Karl Barth's Model of "*Imago Dei*" in Itself

Reorientation in God

We have considered critically how Barth has interpreted the tradition. It is time to evaluate critically the model of "*imago Dei*" which he formed. In order to do this let us examine his actual position more closely both from the perspective of the text and the wider theological community. I will divide this analysis into two sections.

Firstly, we consider how Barth, in attempting to reorient the doctrine in God, is making an important contribution to its contemporary understanding. Secondly, however, we see how, on the other hand, the Barthian model in itself lacks sufficient concentration on human response to God. Here, specifically, I shall turn again to

---

[57] Ibid., no. 80.

primary textual analysis to argue that in Barth's work itself his own avoidance of the "subjective" element is at times insecure. In turn this will show how it is a necessary development for a contemporary understanding of humanity's place in the relationship with God.

Firstly, however, I wish to turn to the outstanding contribution Barth has made to the contemporary development of the doctrine. This is his reorientation of the doctrine of "*imago Dei*" in God. The wider theological community, both Catholic and Protestant, has recognised this important contribution. In the Protestant world Barth's reorientation of dogma in God's revelation has been a hallmark of twentieth-century theology. This, however, is not within the scope of this current study. We do return to the Protestant tradition later to examine Moltmann. Here, however, we will discover how, in his attempt to recover the "*imago Dei*" doctrine for contemporary Protestant theology, Moltmann has in fact failed to appreciate the outstanding contribution of Barth and integrate it into his own synthesis. On the other hand Catholic theology, since Vatican II in particular, has learned much from Barth, principally through his interpretation by Balthasar. In the next chapter I will be analysing Balthasar in depth from the perspective of his debt to Barth. In general, however, it is important to note briefly here how the teaching of Vatican II keeps the same standard as Barth in underpinning its teaching in God's revelation in Christ.

As we saw in our section on the Council in Chapter 1 the documents *Lumen Gentium* and *Gaudium et Spes* portray human dignity as rooted in the perfect "*imago*" who is the new man, Christ. God's revelation must be stressed as primary. Only then can we dare to develop a Christian anthropology. Since the Council this has been a keynote of Catholic theology throughout the pontificate of Pope John Paul II. We have seen how, even despite Barth's disagreement with it, the primacy and centrality of Christ's revelation was in fact a consistent theme underpinning the encyclical *Fides et Ratio*. An account of human dignity rooted in Christ is also present in many documents from the pontificate of Pope John Paul II, whether stressing the moral life or Christian vocation in general.[58] Now, however, in order to show the significance of Barth's own particular contribution to postconciliar Catholic theology in this regard, I would like to turn to an important and specific observation in the seminal *Introduction to Christianity*,[59] of Pope Benedict XVI, then Joseph Ratzinger, to show my view more clearly.

Ratzinger wanted to stress that the revelation of God in Jesus Christ is the starting point in the act of faith. He, like Barth, has been dismayed at how

---

[58] The scope of this book does not include a detailed survey of the documents on human dignity of John Paul II, only to show the relevance of the three theologians it studies to contemporary postconciliar Catholic theology. However, for a thorough study of the theme in John Paul II, see the following doctoral thesis: D. Hranić, *L'uomo imagine di Dio nell'insegnamento di Giovanni Paolo II (1978–1988)* (Rome: Gregorian, 1993).

[59] Joseph Cardinal Ratzinger (Pope Benedict XVI), *Introduction to Christianity* (San Francisco: Ignatius Press, 1990).

theology in the first half of the twentieth century moved further and further away from taking as a fundamental starting point the dogmatic truth that Jesus is the Christ revealed for us. For him it is not so much a phenomenological approach post-Schleiermacher but the quest for the historical Jesus, in dividing the Jesus of history and the Christ of faith, which above all has brought theology to this unfortunate position.[60] This trend now needs to be reversed. In the theology of Karl Barth Ratzinger detects a theological ally on the other side of the confessional spectrum and in the history of twentieth-century theology a common aim. Our faith must start from the perspective that Jesus is Christ, from assent to the truth that God has revealed himself to us in the person of Jesus Christ and whose identity is synonymous with his giving himself over for us. Rather than start from the perspective of human enquiry we must start from faith in Jesus Christ whose identity is to give himself to us:

> as faith understood the position, Jesus did not perform a work that could be distinguished from his "I" and depicted separately. On the contrary, to understand him as the Christ means to be convinced that he has put himself into his word. Here there is no "I" (as there is with all of us) which utters words; he has identified himself so closely with his word that "I" and word are indistinguishable: he is word. In the same way, to faith, his work is nothing else than the unreserved way in which he merges himself into his very work; he performs *himself* and gives *himself*; his work is the giving of himself.[61]

In particular Ratzinger sees how in Catholic theology Balthasar has uncovered this specifically Barthian approach to reorient the doctrine of "*imago Dei*" in the revelation of a God who, specifically for Barth, is in Jesus Christ and his being for us. He refers to a passage of Balthasar's *Creator Spirit*[62] in which he quotes Barth:

> Jesus is utterly holder of an office. He is therefore not first man and then in addition holder of this office ... There is no such thing as the neutral humanity of Jesus ... The remarkable statement of Paul in 2 Cor. 5.16, "Even though we once regarded Christ from a human point of view, we regard him thus no longer", could also be uttered in the name of all four evangelists. The latter were quite uninterested in anything that this man might have been or done outside his function as Christ and therefore aside from its fulfilment ... Even when they recount of him that he hungered and thirsted, that he ate and drank, that he grew tired and rested and slept, that he loved, mourned, showed anger and even wept, they are touching on accompanying circumstances which nowhere betrayed

---

[60] Ibid., 141–51.
[61] Ibid., 150. Emphasis his.
[62] Balthasar, *Explorations in Theology Volume III: Creator Spirit* (San Francisco: Ignatius Press, 1993), 76–91.

anything like a personality independent of its work, with definite tendencies, inclinations and emotions peculiar to itself ... His being as man is his work.[63]

Ratzinger's point in following Barth is that profession of faith in the truth that Jesus is the Christ is the only appropriate starting point for "personal faith". It is in these two words, Jesus Christ, in which "faith's decisive statement about Jesus lies". "The person of Jesus *is* his teaching, and his teaching is himself. Christian faith, that is, faith in Jesus as the Christ, is therefore truly 'personal faith'." It is personal in that it takes as its starting point the person of Jesus Christ who is God for us. "What this means can really be understood only from this angle. Such faith is not the acceptance of a system but the acceptance of this person who is his word; of the word as person and of the person as word."[64]

It was Balthasar in particular who was to integrate this perspective into Catholic teaching. In the section of *Creator Spirit* to which Ratzinger refers Balthasar is addressing the need for historical approaches to the study of Jesus. He sees this in a positive light in that it can uncover the central dogmatic truths about Jesus as Son of God and Son of Man and his revelation. All study of Jesus serves this function, to preach what we know to be true before we start to search for it. For this reason Balthasar describes Barth's as "functional Christology", "the interpretation of the existence of Jesus as the substantial mission of the Father".[65] According to Balthasar it is this truth that we need to take as our starting point in dialogue between Christians. Fired by Barth's contribution he claims that "the ecumenical successes lie, not in mutual concessions and flattenings at the periphery, but in the common holding out in the presence of the maximalist claims made by God's love, which makes the maximum gift to us".[66]

The insights which Balthasar and Ratzinger have gleaned from Barth are very important to the future of ecumenical dialogue on human dignity. To understand and to accept Barth's chief contribution to the contemporary debate demands that talk of the human person's dignity is rooted in God's descent to us in Christ. At the same time, once this is understood, it permits us to speak of human dignity in a way which expresses our capacity for and likeness to God without appearing to emphasise human capacity per se. In particular postconciliar Catholic theology has been at pains to emphasise this. As a result theologians on both sides of the Reformation divide are now better able to speak to each other of human dignity from the perspective of the "*imago Dei*" as long as the dialogue is rooted not in a subjective understanding of human potential but in God's action in human lives through the person of Christ.

---

[63] Ibid., 150, quoting Barth, *CD III/2* (Zurich: 1948), 66–9, quoted in Balthasar, *Creator Spirit*, 89ff.

[64] Ibid., 151. Emphasis his.

[65] Ibid., 100.

[66] Ibid., 100–101.

Let us now turn from Barth's influence on contemporary Roman Catholic theology through our consideration of the common emphases we find in Ratzinger in particular. To conclude this first section of evaluation, let us affirm how Barth has succeeded in reorienting the doctrine of *"imago Dei"* in God and so presents to contemporary theology a clear picture of God's direct and transforming action in the world and in the lives of human beings made in his image. Later on, in Chapters 3 and 4, we shall see how this theme will be integrated into the work of Balthasar and Moltmann in different ways.

However, the significance of Barth's positive contribution understood, we must now consider the shortcomings of his theological picture. Whilst he may help us to reorient the doctrine of *"imago Dei"* in God has his overall picture left sufficient scope for the human response to this God in whose image we are made? I would suggest that this is an aspect of Barth's theology which is unclear and leaves scope for further development.

The Human Response

Behind this profound reorientation of the Christian narrative in God in Jesus Christ lies a fundamental problem which forces us to conclude that, while his outstanding contribution can root a contemporary doctrine of *"imago Dei"* in Christ, we must step out of the straightjacket of his own theological system if we are to develop a fuller picture of human dignity. My point here will be that from this weakness in Barth's thought too we can learn much. In effect we learn what we must discard and what to develop in the tradition to open theology to a more forward-looking and positive picture of the human person before God. It is not merely that Barth has brought theology back to God as starting point but that fundamental to his view is the belief in the loss of God's image in human beings. For Barth this seems to be the necessary theological platform for his powerful portrayal of humanity's subsequent total reconstitution through the once-and-for-all action of God in Jesus Christ. In our own analysis of Barth's formulation of his view we focussed on this and saw that this stemmed from his interpretation of Augustine as upholding the total loss of humanity's capacity for God after the Fall. The image of God in human beings is truly destroyed then humanity is reconstituted, that is conformed once more to God. The action of God in Christ is sudden and disruptive. Human beings are completely lost. They are not on a life's pilgrimage, engaged in the gradual process of finding their home in the Creator in whose image they are made. Rather they are lost and then, through the power of God's action in Christ, once-and-for-all, they are found, that is reconstituted, conformed to him. The Barthian scholar George Hunsinger calls this view the "'*Aufhebung*' of Nature" and explains it thus:

> Fallen human creatures are affirmed in so far as they are creatures, negated in so far as they are fallen, and raised again to new life. They are affirmed, negated, and reconstituted on a higher plane, not partially, completely, not gradually through an existential process but once-for-all through a disruptive, eschatological event.[67]

Such a powerful statement of God's action in Christ implies a fundamental belief that the human person is not simply dependent on God's grace but also lacks an essential divine possibility proper to his or her dignity as one made in God's image. The God who bursts into human lives is all-transforming but, because there is no sense of God's image remaining in the human being after the Fall, there is no sense of the *capax Dei* through which to develop a more bipolar sense of the God–human relationship. Thus, whilst we learn from his overall reorientation of the doctrine towards God in Christ, we must admit that Barth's overall picture of the human response to God leaves room for necessary development.

The contemporary need to develop a theology which, whilst learning from Barth's approach and integrating it into the narrative, also finds more scope for human response, is borne out in postconciliar Catholic theology and brought into focus by Balthasar. Barth's inability to develop this himself is of course in turn partly due to the fact that he rejects Catholic theology as "conflict against grace", a view we have already questioned in our analysis of the formulation of Barth's view. However it is here in Balthasar and postconciliar Catholic teaching that we find the link missing in Barth which is necessary to foster a more balanced perspective, clearly rooted in God's sovereignty, yet expressing the deeper search for God in the midst of life.

The human situation before God would seem to involve a necessary element of quest, pilgrimage and reciprocity as human beings place themselves humbly before their Creator. This would seem to correspond to a sense of human dignity as creatures made in God's image and retaining that despite the consequence of the Fall. In order to develop an appropriately reciprocal theology of the God–human relationship Balthasar would hold to a sense of humanity remaining in God's image. Here the work of the Barthian scholar Hunsinger demonstrates to us how this has not always been fully appreciated within the Reformed tradition. His own Barthian reading of "*imago Dei*" seems to miss the difference between Barth and Balthasar here. Hunsinger attributes to Balthasar the Barthian view of "*Aufhebung*" of human nature but this seems to have missed a point which serves to distinguish the two theologians on this question. There is an additional element in Balthasar's thought which represents a necessary correction.

In Balthasar God's image in humanity clearly remains and thus represents divine possibility and ongoing reciprocity between the God in Jesus Christ who saves and the human being made in his image who is drawn into an ongoing

---

[67] George Hunsinger, *Disruptive Grace: Studies in the Theology of Karl Barth* (Grand Rapids: William B. Eerdmans Publishing Company, 2000), 270.

transforming relationship. Indeed in the section of *Creator Spirit* to which we have been referring he includes an important footnote explaining this distinction. Rather than believing in the "*Aufhebung*" of nature Balthasar recognises the problem in Barth, stating that we may not speak of our being in the image of God, "*Gottebenbildlichkeit*", as lost, "*verlust*". As such the possibility of natural theology should remain and Balthasar intends to develop this:

> The great majority of scholars admit that it is not possible to speak in the Old Testament of a loss of man's being in the image of God through sin, and this means in my opinion that Karl Barth's chief polemical position (the denial of any natural theology) cannot any longer be maintained.[68]

Contemporary Catholic theology, reflecting on the human situation, is keen to hold fast to this fundamental belief in humanity's retention of God's image whilst not losing sight of the action of God in Christ. The recent document of the International Theological Commission of the Sacred Congregation for the Doctrine of the Faith[69] represents a very significant development here. The document clearly intends to hold both of these elements together. "For the theological tradition", the Commission affirms, "man affected by sin is always in need of salvation, yet having a natural desire to see God – a *capax Dei* – which, as an image of the divine, constitutes a dynamic orientation to the divine".[70] In order to hold these two ideas in tandem the Commission affirms both the necessity of God's action in Christ, grace, and also the human *capax Dei*, God's image in him disturbed but not totally destroyed. This capacity for God remaining in humanity is an important element in a God–human narrative which speaks still powerfully of the free embrace of God's love for humanity and transformation of human liberty:

> man affected by sin is always in need of salvation, yet having a natural desire to see God – a *capax Dei* – which, as an image of the divine, constitutes a dynamic orientation to the divine. God the saviour addresses an image of himself, disturbed in orientation to him, but nonetheless capable of receiving the saving divine activity. These traditional formulations affirm both the indestructibility of man's orientation to God and the necessity of salvation. The human person, created in the image of God, is ordered by nature to the enjoyment of divine love, but only divine grace makes the free embrace of this love possible and effective. In this

---

[68] Ibid., 92, footnote 13 [Balthasar, *Spiritus Creator* (Einsiedeln: Johannes Verlag, 1967)], 82, footnote 13.

[69] International Theological Commission of the Sacred Congregation for the Doctrine of the Faith, *Communion and Stewardship: Human Persons Created in the Image of God* (Vatican City: Libreria Editrice Vatican, 2002).

[70] Ibid., no. 48.

perspective, grace is not merely a remedy for sin, but a qualitative transformation of human liberty, made possible by Christ, as a freedom freed for the Good.[71]

This document goes on to explore this twin reality, the indestructibility of God's image in human beings and their corresponding orientation to God, and the transforming truth of Christ's death on the cross and resurrection. It concludes that a belief in the power of Christ's saving action on the cross is not about the destruction of the human person but instead offers humanity made in God's image divine possibility, "to participate in the death to sin that leads to life in Christ". The saving work of Christ leads us on a pilgrimage, "the passage that leads to new life".

> The reality of personal sin shows that the image of God is not unambiguously open to God but can close in upon itself. Salvation entails a liberation from this self-glorification through the cross. The paschal mystery, which is originally constituted by the passion, death and resurrection of Christ, makes it possible for each person to participate in the death to sin that leads to life in Christ. The cross entails, not the destruction of the human, but the passage that leads to new life.[72]

It is important to note how important the concerns of the Commission are in the context of the development of Catholic theology since Vatican II. This twin belief in the primacy of grace yet the dignity of the human person called to participate in an ongoing relationship with the God in whose image he is made has become the keynote of how Roman Catholic teaching not simply understands the individual human person but also the community of the Church as the People of God. This had become especially clear in the document *Lumen Gentium*. God has initiated a covenant with his people. Humanity breaks this covenant in sin but Christ has restored us once more to an ongoing relationship with him as a pilgrim people always seeking our fulfilment in him. The Church as God's People can thus be construed as "one complex reality comprising a human and a divine element" (*LG* no. 8). We should not confuse this relationship in thinking that the human and divine are to be separated out to the extent that we take grace and revelation not to involve human possibility of participation in the mystery. The human and the divine are part of a dynamic of human existence which we live out daily in the Church. The human quest for God is inevitable in this world on which God bestows his grace and reveals himself as Lord of history in Jesus Christ:

> Christ, the one mediator, set up his holy church here on earth as a visible structure, a community of faith, hope and love; and he sustains it unceasingly and through it he pours out grace and truth on everyone. This society, however, equipped with hierarchical structures, and the mystical body of Christ, a visible assembly and spiritual community, an earthly church and a church enriched with heavenly

---

[71] Ibid., no. 48.
[72] Ibid., no. 49.

gifts, must not be considered as two things, but as forming one complex reality comprising a human and a divine element.[73]

It would seem that if our theological anthropology is truly to reflect this dimension it becomes difficult to avoid admitting our natural subjective orientation to the divine. In this light Barth's determination to do this appears to be a weakness. I would conclude moreover that, if we may return to the text of the *Church Dogmatics* briefly, this begins to show through in Barth's writing as a whole. It would seem that at times he falls into trying to integrate the subjective dimension himself. However, in summary it will also be clear that this aspect of Barth's thought, while left unresolved and ambiguous, still leaves insufficient scope within his theological framework to develop this aspect of the relationship between God and humanity.

In *II/1*, especially in pages 640–652, Barth employs an important image of the human being in the face of God. First of all Barth proclaims a God who in "glory" is "standing in contrast to all other beings and marked off from them".[74] On the one hand God appears cut off and distant, out of human reach. But this God of contrast to humanity is for Barth also glorious in that at the core of God's freedom as God is the relationship to humanity in the freedom to love. At the core of the very being of God marked off from human beings is also the very seeking and finding of fellowship, "creating and maintaining and controlling it".[75]

It is within God's very freedom to be who God is that we find the God–human relationship, from God to us, monological, as God's Word, but nonetheless relationship as God, revelation *pro nobis*, a God who comes to us and invites us to respond. In that he is glorious, that is that God is who God is *pro nobis* in this way described in this section, he shows his love for humanity.[76] So the relationship between God and humanity involves human response in relationship with him. The relational dynamic here in this section of writing is powerfully reciprocal. As Barth describes it, God's self-radiating light permeates humans so that "God's glory is the answer evoked by Him of the worship offered Him by his creatures" ("*Gottes Herrlichkeit ist die ihm hervorgerufene Antwort des ihm durch seine Kreatur dargebrachten Lobpreises*").[77] At one point in this narrative we might almost construe this image of radiant light to mean that within the human being there resides some spark of the divinity, some special dignity expressing capacity for God. Speaking of the glory that is the God in relationship Barth says: "He is the radiance of light that reaches all other beings and permeates them."[78]

The image of the radiant light is of an omnipotent God whose revelation has its reality and truth within itself both from the standpoint of God in God's self and

---

[73] *LG*, no. 8.
[74] Barth, *CD II/1*, 641ff.
[75] Ibid., 641.
[76] Ibid., 641.
[77] Ibid., 647 [*KD II/1*, 730].
[78] Ibid., 646.

of the human relationship. It has a clearly objective base but it is intended to lead us to a God who in "standing in contrast to all other beings and marked off from them" is not "separated from them by any distance", but, Barth asserts, "changes such distance into proximity".[79] The pertinent question for us is whether Barth has succeeded in developing an adequate theology of human response to God. This image of radiant light is powerful but is still very different to that of Balthasar and postconciliar Catholic teaching on the human being made in "*imago Dei*".

Barth's teaching at root is still that God, rather than draw us into a fuller sense of mutual participation in the God–human reciprocal relationship as human beings made in his image, relates to us inasmuch as God is in God's very self in fellowship with us. There is an intended sense of the proximity of God to us but this is still part of a system which is grounded in what Barth has set out in *I/1* as necessarily "objectively normed and objectively formed dogmatics" to the extent that "God's revelation has its reality and truth wholly and in every respect – both ontically and noetically – within itself".[80] However, Barth does show signs of wanting to develop a theology of human response, what we might call a more "subjective" element to his "objectively normed and objectively formed dogmatics". If now we move to a later section of the *Church Dogmatics* we may note a further move to draw into this system what he defines as a "subjective" element in terms of human response and dignity. The development of this in Barth is still at the same time suggestive of both its pressing need yet in the final analysis its incongruence within his system.

In *Volume IV/1* Barth returns to his discussion of the nature of "faith", that which he had defined earlier in a way thoroughly in keeping with "objectively normed and objectively formed dogmatics" as wholly from God's side, "on loan to man". In *IV/1*, however, he appears not totally satisfied with making faith totally "objective" and looks for a way of expressing how "faith" has an element "subjective" to human beings, specifically so that we can express more of a "relationship" between God and us. These terms "objective" and "subjective", and the term "relationship", appear ambiguous: it is not totally clear what Barth means by them. "Faith", "*der Glaube*", he concludes now, "*d.h. er besteht als menschliche Tätigkeit in der Subjektivierung einer objektiven* res", "that is, as a human activity, it consists in the subjectivisation of an objective *res*".[81] The words "subjectivisation" and "objective" are direct translations of the original and make it clear that he wishes to link these two elements in his understanding of "faith".

What does Barth mean? Here he seems to mean that "faith", although it comes from outside, from God, and is on loan to us, also consists of "*menschliche Tätigkeit*". This is translated as "human activity" but just as easily could suggest more than this, for example human "occupation", "function", or even that in the

---

[79] Ibid., 646.
[80] Barth, *CD I/1*, 304–5.
[81] Barth, *CD IV/1: The Doctrine of Reconciliation* (Edinburgh: T&T Clark, 1956), 742 [Barth, *KD IV/1: Die Lehre von der Versöhnung* (1953), 828].

act of faith human beings are "*tätig*", "busy", or called to "*tätig werden*", "take action" in the act of faith in response to the object. Certainly it seems that in this section Barth wants to stress that, despite his predominantly "objectively" based theology, the human being can be said truly to be in a "relationship" of some active co-operation with the "object". The aspect of faith which involves human "activity" is unable "to be compared with any other in spontaneity and native freedom", but nevertheless "it is in a relationship" ("*Verhältnis*").

In this section Barth is striving to develop space for a narrative of the human response to God in Christ and even an orientation towards relationship with him. "A first thing which characterises" human activity, Barth says, "is the fact that it consists in the orientation of man on Jesus Christ" ("*Ausrichtung auf Jesus Christus*").[82] Indeed Barth seems to believe that the active desire for Jesus Christ, the "object" of faith, is in a sense that which makes the human being Christian and speaks to us of "existence", "essence", "dignity", "significance" and "scope" for the "subject".

Barth wants to stress how in Christ the human situation vis-à-vis God has changed so much for the better. He clearly wants to show that we are oriented to God, in a relationship with him, and that this speaks of special dignity. Further on in this section of *IV/1* he still seems to want to put this over, seeming to step further and further towards a more Catholic belief that the human being does have a special dignity which speaks of capacity for God. It is true that in faith, says Barth, "there takes place ... the constitution of the Christian subject ... a new and particular being of man".[83] This is connected with the passage of our lives in the course of which there is a sense of "being" and "becoming" something which in faith is analogous to God in Christ, a "parallel", even a "likeness". The "life of the Christian – the one who recognises Jesus Christ in faith – will become and be the *analogatum*, the parallel, the likeness ... of His justifying being and activity".[84]

However, in the final analysis we must recognise how this project, by his own definition, becomes circular. Barth's system requires these terms speaking of a special dignity and ability for relationship with Christ not to be attributed to human beings but to be reserved for Christ, the "object" of faith.

> What takes place in faith is simply that in a specific activity, which in this sense it to some extent expects, the objective *res* finds existence and essence and dignity and significance and scope, creating respect for itself and actually being respected in the presence of this activity – but only as it was already the object of this subject, only as it had all these things, existence, essence, dignity, significance and scope even for this subject, and without his activity and faith and respect.[85]

---

[82] Ibid., 743 [*KD IV/1*, 830].
[83] Ibid., 749.
[84] Ibid., 770.
[85] Ibid., 742.

So in the end Barth goes on to say that despite our orientation to Christ, "faith is simply following, following its object. Faith is going a way which is marked out and prepared". It is a "relationship" but only the "normalising of the relationship between man and this object" which already existed. "It is the act in which man does that which the object demands ... the fulfilment of the correspondence to what this object is and means of itself for every man." In fact the Barthian system requires him to state that all is enclosed in the circle which is Christ: "He, the living Christ", affirms Barth, "is the circle enclosing all men ... the circle of divine judgment and divine grace".[86]

In conclusion I would make two observations. On the one hand Barth does seem tantalisingly to want to admit some human subjective capacity for God. Yet on the other hand in the final analysis his theological system requires him to stop short. Therefore in the end, rather than developing the theme of our ongoing orientation to Christ, Barth affirms what he must claim to be objectively true about the human being in the face of God. He has clearly presented an important challenge to include in a theology fundamentally reoriented in God in himself the human orientation to this God. For Barth himself, however, this subjective element remains underdeveloped. Rather he seems to bring us back to exactly where we started. His reorientation of theological anthropology in God for him necessarily involves a wholly objective statement about humanity's orientation to God and fundamental dignity. The truth is that it is an objective fact that we are oriented to God but "man himself is nothing. He is not in control. He simply finds himself in that orientation" ("*der Mensch ganz und gar nicht und nun doch auch ganz und gar bei sich ist, in welchem er sich eben in jener Ausrichtung befindet*").[87]

Conclusion

Our critical analysis of Barth may be said to bring us to an important impasse in the twentieth-century understanding of "*imago Dei*". We might say that this impasse reflects two realities. One we might say is a positive and valuable contribution to the theological community whilst the other helps theology to see what is lacking and in need of development. Firstly, on the one hand, it would seem that Barth has succeeded in reorienting the doctrine of "*imago Dei*" in God's action in Christ. Yet, secondly, because he has done this so forcefully and coherently, it would seem that there is something lacking in the element of human response. He sets out to construct a relational model of "*imago Dei*". The relationship to God is lived out in humanity's relationship with his fellows. However, on closer analysis we concluded that his understanding of this relationship will lack a narrative of human response expressing relationship, dignity, capacity for God. Although these

---

[86] Ibid., 743.
[87] Ibid., 744 [Barth, *KD IV/1*, 831].

themes occasionally come through in sections of his writings, we may argue that this is underdeveloped.

It is important to be aware of and to understand critically these aspects of Barth's model of "*imago Dei*" if we are to understand his significant influence on later interpretations of the doctrine in both Catholic and Protestant thought, and in particular the writings of the two theologians we shall shortly turn to, Balthasar and Moltmann. This has been the point of this chapter. So before we turn to these later writers let us briefly summarise what we have learned here.

Our study has shown that from the outset it is clear that Barth's intention is to reorient the doctrine of "*imago Dei*" in God. Indeed we cannot treat the doctrine of "*imago Dei*" in isolation but only from the perspective of the fundamental core of Barth's theological system, the doctrine of the Word of God. Barth understands the human situation before God from the specific and concrete perspective of how God is revealed to us in the incarnate Word of God, Jesus Christ. He is concerned from the outset to avoid any hint of possibility of human communion with or knowledge of God. Yet he seems to want to stress how, if we reorient the God–human relationship in the concrete reality of God for us, we must still speak of a special relationship between God and humanity. We saw that he was moved through his reading of Anselm to recognise how the human quest for God is real. There must be some point of contact between God and us. Yet in the end this shows him how our own quest for God merely confirms how our quest is pointless. The relationship we have with God is construed as the acceptance of the situation we find ourselves in as fallen but reconstituted "from above" by God in Christ.

Central to the development of Barth's picture of this human relationship with God is his interpretation of Augustine. Here he places himself alongside Luther. Human beings after the Fall have no access to God. There is no pilgrimage back to God, no process of divinisation. Rather we are justified by faith in what God has done in Christ to conform us to him. Even faith is enclosed and encapsulated within the doctrine of the Word of God. It is not a human capacity but on loan to us.

Thus Barth rejects the Roman Catholic doctrine of "*analogia entis*" and proposes a doctrine of "*analogia fidei*". In doing this he underlines his convictions regarding Roman Catholic teaching's conflict against grace and admission of the human capacity for God he wishes to deny is possible. This we found to be Barth's position. However our critical analysis of his interpretation of the tradition raised significant questions. Firstly, we considered his crucial understanding of Augustine. From this study we were able to conclude two important points. We might say that the first is positive, the second negative. Firstly, we concluded that his particular interpretation of Augustine allowed him to highlight a fundamental aspect of our understanding of how the human being is created in "*imago Dei*". This is the sovereignty of God in the face of human limitation and the primacy of grace in Christ. Secondly, however, he has left another aspect underdeveloped. This is our response to God as creatures on a journey back to the Creator. This aspect of Augustine's thought appears to be given insufficient attention by Barth but is important.

Barth's rejection of the Roman Catholic understanding of the doctrine, however, still merited closer attention from the perspective of Thomist methodology and later developments. We concluded that Barth's rejection of Thomist methodology is making an important point. Thomism brought a more philosophical and scientific way of approaching the doctrine which expressed a clear belief that our very human identity of its own nature involves a call to fulfil our destiny in participation in the life of God. This has become part of a Roman Catholic view, stressed in particular at Vatican I, which places emphasis on our human ability to find God through using the gifts we are given by him. This way of doing theology is one which for Barth makes the fatal error, common to both Roman Catholicism and more recent Protestant orthodoxy, of making our *raison d'être* the quest for understanding human identity rather than seeing God's revelation in Jesus Christ for what it is first. In Barth's own terms it is an erroneous method of constructing theology in that it concentrates on the "subject", the human person, rather than the "object", God, in his revelation in Christ.

We recognised that there are good reasons for accepting this picture of Aquinas. He was indeed chiefly interested in the more scientific and philosophical question of how we "subjects", human beings, can, from our own perspective, know God. Such a quest led him to the understanding of the human being's "analogy" to God which Barth was to reject so forcefully. However, Barth takes this further to suggest that Roman Catholicism in particular amounts to "conflict against grace".[88] We considered how fair his treatment of the Roman Catholic position was.

We concluded that rather than conflicting with grace Roman Catholic teaching upholds the necessity of the primacy of grace in a forceful manner whilst also giving the human being a privileged place in the special relationship he has with the Creator. Aquinas clearly followed the teaching of Augustine in insisting on the necessity of grace. When we turn to recent Church teaching we see this dynamic expressed more clearly in *Dei Filius*, *Dei Verbum*, and most recently synthesised in *Fides et Ratio*. We concluded that Barth's objection has prevented him from recognising the importance of the Roman Catholic appreciation of the privileged place of the human being within a relationship which is firmly grounded in God's coming to us in Christ, that is grounded in revelation and in grace.

Thus we proceeded to give a critical evaluation of the model of "*imago Dei*" Barth has left with us. Our evaluation fell under two headings, one we might say was more positive, whilst the other was more negative. Firstly, Barth has clearly reoriented the doctrine in God.

Secondly, however, we concluded that, whilst we may learn much from how Barth reorients the doctrine in God, the element of human response is underdeveloped. This is clear from the perspective both of the wider theological community and also from Barth's writings themselves where he seems at times to want to admit more scope for the element of human subjectivity but stops short because his overall theological system cannot withstand this. Hunsinger shows us

---

[88] Barth, *CD II/1*, 80.

how such a powerful statement of God's action in Christ implies a twin fundamental belief that the human person is not simply dependent on God's grace but also lacks an essential divine possibility proper to his or her dignity as one made in God's image. The God who bursts into human lives is all-transforming but, because there is no sense of God's image remaining in the human being after the Fall, there is no sense of the *capax Dei* through which to develop a more bipolar picture of the God–human relationship. This is essentially different to Catholic teaching about the dignity of the human being before God, fallen yet remaining in what Balthasar calls "*Gottebenbildlichkeit*". Hence we come to the impasse between reorienting the doctrine in God yet still speaking of the subjective element, the dignity of the human being still retaining God's image and seeking union with him.

Thus it is at this point that we must turn to the second of our three twentieth-century theologians to consider this impasse through the eyes of a writer who has learned so much from Barth's reorientation of theology in God in Christ yet wants to develop his thought in such a way as to restore a sense of this human response to the God in Christ who calls us into his company. It is Balthasar, in a direct quotation of Barth, who seems to express and then try to answer the very question Barth leaves with us. "Must we not establish more than just the *factum brutum* of God's glory in his revelation? Must not rather the question be raised: 'To what extent is the light of God's self-revelation really light, and therefore enlightening?'"[89]

---

[89] Balthasar, *The Glory of the Lord: a Theological Aesthetics I* (Edinburgh: T&T Clark, 1982), 53, quoting Barth, *CD II/1*, 732ff.

Chapter 3
Hans Urs von Balthasar

Understanding of "*Imago Dei*"

The Core of His Conviction

In our introduction in Chapter 1 to Balthasar's life and thought in its wider historico-theological context we noted that a summary of his particular understanding of how the human being is made in the "*imago Dei*" is no simple task. Balthasar wrote so much which relates to the doctrine in a manner which leaves us with less of a synthesis than a poetic narrative which in its meanderings presents beautiful and dramatic truths about how the human being finds himself in such a special relationship with God. In order to more fully understand Balthasar's position we need to turn to some of his own words towards the end of his life. Here we have some important clues as to what was at the core of his conviction about who the human being is before God. As we saw with Barth we can only appreciate what Balthasar means if we turn once more to his own initial concerns. In so doing we find, as with Barth, that the underlying point of his thought really was to turn away from a direct analysis of who the human being is qua human being and towards God in Christ in whose image he is made. This is Balthasar's starting point so if we are to do greater justice to his view it needs to be our starting point too.

In fact Balthasar did leave with us a simple résumé of his thought, presented at a conference just before his death in 1988, and published posthumously in *Communio*, which takes us to the very heart of what he believed about God and us.[1] Here he outlines most clearly the direction he has taken. The human being's creation in "*imago Dei*" is to be understood from the perspective of God revealed to us as Jesus Christ, and more concretely from the perspective of two fundamental dogmas expressing this truth, that of the Trinity and of the Incarnation:

> The Christian response is contained in these two fundamental dogmas: that of the Trinity and that of the Incarnation. In the Trinitarian dogma God is one, true and beautiful because he is essentially Love, and Love supposes the one, the other, and their unity. And if it is necessary to suppose the Other, the Word, the

---

[1] Balthasar, "A Résumé of My Thought" (*Communio: International Catholic Review* 15, Winter 1988), reproduced in *Hans Urs Von Balthasar: His Life and Work*, David L. Schindler, ed. (San Francisco: Ignatius Press, 1991), 1–5.

Son, in God, then the otherness of the creation is not a fall, a disgrace, but an image of God, even as it is not God.[2]

So the most important truth about our being made in "*imago Dei*" is not our fall from grace. Rather we are drawn back to a recognition of our being loved by God as creatures made in his image. Because Balthasar accepts this he also accepts that Christ's love transforms creation made in his image through his relationship with it. In concrete terms this represents the transforming action of Christ in human lives. Creatures made in God's image are thus transformed by Christ as he assumes the image that is the creation, purifies it, and, in a way which maintains the distinction between God in Christ and his image in creation, draws that human creation into communion with himself:

> And as the Son in God is the eternal icon of the Father, he can without contradiction assume in himself the image that is the creation, purify it, and make it enter into the communion of the divine life without dissolving it (in a false mysticism). It is here that one must distinguish nature and grace.[3]

Thus we must start from the perspective of this God revealed in Christ within the Trinity and fully God and fully man, the Christ whose goodness, truth and beauty within the Godhead is Love. Only from this perspective can we consider God's image in creation. In so doing Balthasar was clear about the direction in which he wished to take the discussion of the human person and how it was in fact counter-cultural:

> All true solutions offered by the Christian faith hold, therefore, to these two mysteries [the Trinity and the Incarnation], categorically refused by a human reason which makes itself absolute. It is because of this that the true battle between religions begins only after the coming of Christ. Humanity will prefer to renounce all philosophical questions – in Marxism, or positivism of all stripes, rather than accept a philosophy that finds its final response only in the revelation of Christ.[4]

In other words Balthasar presents turning to Christ as the only authentic way of discovering the truth about ourselves. If we are made in the image of God then we discover what this means by looking at who God is in his fullness and unity. Christ represents the very fullness and unity of God. Compared to the world around us God might seem to be invisible to us but in fact we have God in his fullness and unity revealed in the flesh made visible in Christ. Thus it is that Balthasar presents Christ as what he calls the "*Gestalt*", the real "form" of God. The appearance and

---

[2] Ibid., 4.
[3] Ibid., 5.
[4] Ibid., 5.

sight of this "form" of God by human beings transforms who they are as creatures made in God's image. The appearance and sight of the "form" offers us, in a very personal way, an overwhelming perception of the mystery which constitutes the human condition. This is the mystery of how the reciprocal act of love expresses at its deepest level what it is to be human. As we experience the infinite love of God we are called to respond in love as his finite creatures. Thus there is one central truth which we might say captures what Balthasar believes is at the core of the God–human dynamic in Christ, namely the mystery of infinite and finite love played out in the drama of finite and infinite freedom.

In the 1988 résumé of his thought Balthasar returns to a very vivid image of this, first presented more fully in *Glory of the Lord V*,[5] to express what he believes. This is the picture of the infant, as he describes it, "brought to consciousness of himself only by love, by the smile of his mother".[6] It is "in that encounter" that "the horizon of all unlimited being opens itself for him". In other words in this meeting of lover and beloved, of the unity and fullness of love with the one receiving this love, the finite human being intuits for the first time who he really is.

In this very first encounter with infinite love the finite human being discovers he is not just flesh and bones but he is *Geist*. He intuits that through this relationship with another infinitely loving human being, there is infinite possibility. This deeply spiritual intuition of the infinite possibility of the other, of the "thou", is no less than a consciousness on a deep level of our openness to the unity and perfection of all existence, that is God, and for us humans the God revealed in human form, God in Christ. The appearance of God in Christ on the finite horizon awakens us to embark on our earthly pilgrimage towards him who represents the fullness and unity of our existence. Humanity is thus, for Balthasar in its deepest sense, as O'Donnell describes it, "openness to God",[7] an openness which represents the very core of our identity.

At this point, however, we must draw back and entertain a certain caution. We have tried to uncover the very heart of Balthasar's conviction about the human person made in God's image. This is possible and necessary up to a point but we know also that Balthasar's own view is multi-faceted. Above all, however, we can affirm that his view of the human being before God is at root about mystery

---

[5] Balthasar, *The Glory of the Lord: a Theological Aesthetics V, The Realm of Metaphysics in the Modern Age* (San Francisco: Ignatius Press, 1991), 615ff. Throughout I am using the following translation of *The Glory of the Lord*: Hans Urs von Balthasar, *The Glory of the Lord: a Theological Aesthetics* (San Francisco: Ignatius Press, 1982–1989). Hereafter the series will be referred to as *GL*, and this will be followed by the number and title of the volume as it appears in the English translation. In addition, where appropriate, I will be quoting from and commenting on the original German.

[6] Ibid., 3.

[7] John O'Donnell, "Hans Urs Von Balthasar: the Form of His Theology", in *Hans Urs Von Balthasar: His Life and Work*, David L. Schindler, ed. (San Francisco: Ignatius Press, 1991), 207.

and paradox and that the human being is not so much defined as presented as an enigma. In such a way Balthasar presents his picture of this openness to God in Christ, so imaginatively depicted in the mother–infant encounter, as at the heart of our identity. At one and the same time this represents our identity yet reveals humanity as enigma. At one and the same time we find our fulfilment yet paradoxically our frustration as infinite love will throughout this earthly life elude us. We might say that at the heart of the encounter between infinite and finite love is paradox and mystery.

This being said, the very paradoxical nature of Balthasar's thought allows him to have a firm conviction about one thing regarding the search for human identity. Thus it is that through his writings he will always bring us back full circle to where we started. At the apex of this paradoxical relationship between infinite and finite love the answer to all our questions about human identity appears. The constant search for meaning brings us back to the answer to all our searchings, that is the concrete universal Jesus Christ. In the appearing of infinite love on our concrete horizon, the human *Gestalt* of God himself, Jesus Christ, we discover who we really are. In this very profound sense Christ is our identity as creatures made in his image. As O'Donnell puts it "this enigma" of human identity "can only be resolved in Christ, for it is only in Christ that the reality of God is revealed as the mystery of love".[8] Now we have returned to the core of his conviction, namely regarding the person of Christ, we can attempt to lay out briefly some basic strands of the beautiful and dramatic narrative Balthasar recounts.

The Basic Strands of the Narrative

Against this background we might say that Balthasar's theological narrative of the human being as "*imago Dei*" achieves more clarity. We may understand why, after his long excursus on aesthetics, *The Glory of the Lord*, with its narrative of the human search for infinite love and the appearance of its *Gestalt* in Christ, Balthasar declares that he is still unable to define "*imago Dei*". Turning to the doctrine itself in *TD II* he declares that the topic is still "a little premature here".[9]

He is reluctant to give any clear definition because he believes it is Christ's transforming action in human beings' lives that will unlock the true meaning of the doctrine. As, for Balthasar, human beings are indefinable except through reference to Christ, he cannot begin to explore properly how we are created "*imago Dei*" before he begins his treatment of Christology, as it is in Christ that humanity will discover its identity and dignity:

> In a Christian theodramatic theory we have the right to assert that no other, mythical or religio-philosophical anthropology can attain a satisfactory idea of man, an idea that integrates all the elements, but the Christian one. It alone can

---

[8] Ibid., 209.
[9] Balthasar, *TD II*, 316.

release man from the impossible task of trying, on the basis of his brokenness, to envisage himself as not broken, without forfeiting some essential aspect of himself in the process. It releases him from this burden by inserting him, right from the start, into the dramatic dialogue with God, so that God himself may cause him to experience *his* ultimate definition of man.[10]

Thus, starting from a firm belief in Christ's immersion in the world rooted in the incarnation and the Trinity, Balthasar can begin to portray the relationship between God and a broken humanity. This will take shape through his account of the response to God's infinite love made by humanity in its finitude. Crucially, it will be God's infinite love in Christ which will be the keynote of Balthasar's narrative, not humanity's post-Fall status as finite. So the unfolding drama of the relationship between God and his fallen yet loved creation will be expressed in the dialogue between God's "infinite freedom" revealed in Christ's self-gift and humanity's "finite freedom". This is the core of Balthasar's understanding of human identity in Christ:

> if we want to ask about man's "essence", we can do so only in the midst of his dramatic performance of existence. There is no other anthropology but the dramatic. This is why the topic could not even emerge within the framework of the theological aesthetics (*daß wir den Menschen nur mitten im Vollzug seiner dramatischen Existenz nach seinem "Wesen" fragen können. Es gibt keine andere Anthropologie als eine dramatische. Aus diesem Grund konnte das Thema im Rahmen der theologischen Ästhetik noch gar nicht aufscheinen*).[11]

Balthasar will conclude from this that the human being is on a most fundamental level created in the image of God in Christ revealed in his infinite love for us. This image is actually a "finite freedom ... it must act as such, that is, it must decide to move toward God – and thus realize the 'likeness' it already possesses – or away from God, so losing this likeness".[12]

Thus Balthasar, on the one hand, roots the "*imago Dei*" in terms of God himself in Christ. So he follows Barth in his perceived return to the Fathers of the Early Church in giving all the glory to God. Yet, at the same time, Balthasar wants to allow for some kind of innate human quest for relationship with the infinite as we are opened up to the beauty of the love of God in the Christ who meets us in our sinfulness. We are to be led towards Christ, who fulfils all our infinite desires. Human life involves a pilgrimage, a movement towards the infinite reality of union with God himself. As such they reflect much more of a Catholic rather than a Barthian and Reformed perspective on Christian anthropology.

---

[10] Balthasar, *TD II*, 343.

[11] Ibid., 335 [Balthasar, *Theodramatik II/1: Der Mensch in Gott* (Einsiedeln: Johannes Verlag, 1976), 306, hereafter referred to as *TDK*].

[12] Ibid., 327.

However, it is the conviction that it is the person of Christ impacting on and transforming human lives which will give Balthasar's aesthetic and dramatic understanding of the special relationship between God and humanity a very particular appeal. Here we see how he expresses the post-Vatican II understanding of the human beings' response to grace as the answer to a call from Christ to be drawn into his life and mission. So we are called to live out our Christian lives not in an individual way but in relation to others as his disciples on earth.

The basis of our human identity is a dialogue with Christ who draws us outwards towards dialogue with others. Thus our being made in "*imago Dei*" cannot possibly be considered a private matter. Rather it is a communal one. To be in communion with Christ is to be called into communion with others. Scola's exposition of Balthasar's position explains the dialogical and communal nature of our identity thus:

> the fact that man both synthesizes and transcends the cosmos means that ontological discourse takes as its starting point the existential analysis of man, that is, of his enigmatic structure (man is limited but is capable of the entirety of being), in order to go beyond it ... Man is thus the point of departure of meta-anthropology; but if I pose the question of the ontological difference in terms of man I must first recognize that man exists only in dialogue with his fellow man. The horizon of infinite Being in its totality opens to him in dialogue. And in dialogue, correlatively, man gains self-awareness.[13]

O'Donnell makes a similar point in his exposition:

> Man is created with the faculties of intellect and will but he becomes a person only through the dialogical relation. The supreme dialogical partner is God through whom the person receives the mission by which his freedom becomes concrete ... From all eternity God knows each man or woman with a particular love which is realized in a unique mission which no one else can fulfill. In this way the person's own holiness is fulfilled by responding to the mission, and at the same time holiness is never a grace for oneself but is always a gift given for the upbuilding of the Church.[14]

It is in the meeting of all these strands to Balthasar's thought that we find in him a distinctive new ecumenical contribution to the postconciliar understanding of "*imago Dei*". In particular we find in his writings a new evaluation of the Reformed tradition. This aspect of his thought enables him to appreciate the work of Barth and the Reformation whilst developing a fundamentally Catholic postconciliar understanding of the graced dignity and freedom of the human person not just in a

---

[13] Angelo Scola, *Hans Urs von Balthasar: a Theological Style* (Edinburgh: T&T Clark, 1995), 25.

[14] Ibid., 220.

reciprocal relationship with God but actually called into Christ's company and so placed with him on his mission. The richness of Balthasar's position is due to many factors. Among them are the style of his theology, using the media of aesthetics and dramatic narrative. Another is the complex weave of influences on his theology from various traditions, finding their apex in a particular reading of Barth. It is now time to consider and analyse these factors in depth in order to evaluate critically the particular multi-faceted model of "*imago Dei*" Balthasar is presenting.

Critical Analysis: Patristic Sources

The Influence of Irenaeus

Balthasar's reading of Irenaeus brings a particular and permanent colour to the pastiche which was to become his doctrine of "*imago Dei*". It will form a background and basis for his positive and creative vision of the human being's infinite possibility in Christ. From his reading of Irenaeus he will begin to locate the doctrine in the drama, a drama between infinite and finite freedom only made real in the appearance of Christ on the human horizon. In this sense Christ is our origin and our goal. He comes to us in our finitude as human beings, free to respond to him or not, and beckons us to draw closer to him. In drawing closer we move freely towards our goal as finite creatures, that is the freedom Christ represents, that which knows no limits.

In Irenaeus' writings Balthasar finds a basis for a nuanced portrayal of the doctrine which accepts humanity's fallen state yet emphasises its infinite possibility.[15] The key to appreciating this seems to be his conviction about the value of the early Greek Father's distinction between "image", "εικών" (Balthasar quotes the Hebrew "*selem*") and "likeness", "ομοίωσις" (Balthasar quotes the Hebrew "*demut*"). He lays great store by Irenaeus' teaching that in the Fall humanity loses its true "likeness" to God yet retains God's "image". This is significant: he intends to stress through this that humanity retains that possibility of drawing closer to God yet that we need a saviour to draw us to him. It appears, however, that Balthasar is not just saying that we should simply hold to this teaching using the traditional language of "image" and "likeness". Rather the distinction finds its true meaning when we incorporate Irenaeus' emphasis on how it is Christ who restores to humanity what was lost.

For Balthasar the distinction between the lost "likeness" and "image" retained is to be understood in the light of the distinction between the notion of "*imago Dei*" in the Old Testament and that in the New. Paul's statement, expressed in Romans 8:29 and 2 Corinthians 3:18, that we are called to a conformity to the "image" of God, is a call to move towards He who is the express "likeness" of God, that is Christ, as defined in 2 Corinthians 4:4. For Balthasar Irenaeus' teaching

---

[15] Balthasar, *TD II*, 324–34.

emphasises this Christological heart of the "image"–"likeness" distinction and thus allows us to portray humanity in a positive way. In the light of the incarnation, the "*imago Dei*" in humanity is not lost after the Fall: rather Christ assimilates us to Himself so we become once more precious in God's eyes and are restored to that relationship with Him. He quotes Irenaeus as portraying how humanity:

> is perfected according to the image and likeness of God. The truth of this was manifest when the Word of God became man, assimilating himself to man and mankind so that man, becoming like the Son, should become precious in the Father's eyes. In earlier times it was said that man was created in the image of God, but it was not a manifest truth, for the Word according to whose image man was created was invisible, and so the likeness was easily lost. But the Word, becoming flesh, firmly established both: it demonstrated the truth of the image by becoming precisely what its image was and restored the likeness by assimilating man to the invisible Father through the mediation of the now Visible Word.[16]

This statement of belief that humanity's relationship with God is more fully revealed and also restored in Christ and the precise location of the doctrine in the incarnation is clear from this text Balthasar quotes but what exactly does this mean in terms of the actual status of the "image" and the "likeness" in post-Fall and now post-incarnation humanity? It is important to be clear as to how Balthasar is interpreting Irenaeus here because it will have implications. He certainly does not intend to imply that on account of the incarnation humanity is now simply restored to the same status as before and need do nothing more to draw closer to God. Rather he goes on to show how Irenaeus is "more precise" when he says that humanity lost the original "likeness" to God but held on to the "image".

When Irenaeus states that "[what] we lost in Adam, i.e. being in God's image and likeness, we have won back in Christ" this means that, as he says in the concluding sentence of *Adversus Haereses* (V, 36, 3), there is an ongoing assimilation to Christ as we continue to be transformed into the full image and likeness of God. In other words we might take Balthasar as concluding from Irenaeus that through the incarnation we are conformed to the new "image" of the new man, Christ, God made visible, and now move towards the perfection of the "likeness" as we embark on our pilgrimage through life drawing closer to him. So, for Balthasar, the "image" is revealed in Christ, but the "likeness" will involve the drama of our incorporation into Christ's life. Balthasar appears to understand the distinction between "image" and "likeness" in this way. The distinction in itself is less significant than how Balthasar uses it. "Image" and "likeness" have often been used coterminously in the tradition to the extent that distinctions can be ambiguous. Balthasar's particular understanding of Irenaeus' distinction, however, presents new possibilities for his portrayal of the doctrine.

---

[16] Ibid., 324–5, quoting St Irenaeus, *Adversus Haereses*, V, 16, 2.

Through the incarnation an infinite possibility has opened up for fallen humanity. What lies ahead is a road towards a destiny which is the full "likeness" of God. Christ has set us on a pilgrimage which will transform us and assimilate us still more closely to God. It is this picture from Irenaeus which forms the background Balthasar is creating and which begins to give a very particular shape to Balthasar's doctrine of "*imago Dei*". The appearance of Christ on the human horizon does not merely conform humanity to God. Balthasar's distinction between the "image" of God in humanity before Christ and the "image" after, or in the light of, the incarnation, allows him to be much more creative in his depiction of the human condition. The "second image", he says, the "image" in the light of Christ, "not only restores the first but causes it to transcend itself and attain a totally unexpected likeness to God" ("*das erste nicht nur wiederhergestellt, sondern über sich hinaus auf eine unerwartete Ähnlichkeit mit Gott bezogen wird*").[17] It is this potential for transcendence that Balthasar now aims to define in terms of the interplay between infinite and finite freedom.

"Here the possibility emerges", he goes on to say, "of defining the 'image' of God in man as finite freedom". Human beings "must decide to move toward God".[18] The human person now freely sets out on a pilgrimage which must aim at transcending the finitude of this life, to realise the "likeness" of God. In doing so the human person will discover his true identity and destiny in which lies the fullest meaning of his existence. He is free in a finite sense, however, so can and will turn away from God. The "likeness" of God will, on account of his finitude, be elusive. We may turn away from God, "so losing this likeness". Yet in the drama of life as we freely move towards this "likeness", as we search for our true and infinite freedom, that is to say as we live out what it means in its deepest sense to be made in the "*imago Dei*", we realise that through Christ, the transcendence of infinite freedom is attainable.

Balthasar's reading of Irenaeus, however, has not led him to claim in any sense that in aiming at this goal we can somehow attain it through human resources. Being made in the "*imago Dei*" is not understood first and foremost from the side of this human potential but from how Christ gives and realises this possibility. Humanity's moving towards God's "likeness" is in fact, as Tertullian, influenced by Irenaeus, would define it, "realizing the 'likeness' it already possesses".[19] It is the infinite potential Christ has sealed for each human person. Thus, in the light of the incarnation, being made in God's "image" entails this potential for ongoing transformation in Christ. The doctrine of the incarnation entails the notion of an active human response in a reciprocal relationship with Christ as we move towards the realisation of our infinite potential for transcendence.

For Balthasar this altogether optimistic and creative vision which he has taken from Irenaeus becomes an important and permanent aspect of his doctrine of

---

[17] Ibid., 326 [Balthasar, *TDK II/1*, 298].
[18] Ibid., 326.
[19] Ibid., 327, quoting Tertullian, *De baptismo* 5, 6–7.

"*imago Dei*". It is a vision of the new life the human person has, in virtue of the relationship with Christ, which stresses our infinite worth and potential. We are not merely fallen creatures, now passive recipients of Christ's salvation, but actors in a drama in which we have a special role as God's imprint on earth capable of infinite transcendence in virtue of Christ our origin and goal. We shall see how it will be a constant throughout his interpretation of the tradition. Balthasar will interpret Augustine in a particular way which accentuates the human pilgrimage and potential for transcendence despite the Fall. In so doing he will be taking a different interpretation of Augustine to that of some key figures in the Reformation tradition and the tradition of Barth. His more optimistic and teleological view of the human being's creation in the "*imago Dei*" will colour his reading of Barth.

We might conclude that this altogether more optimistic view of post-Fall human nature he has formed would seem on the one hand to be far removed from the view we found to be present in a significant albeit nuanced way in Barth and Barth's own reading of the development of the doctrine of "*imago Dei*". We saw there that, amid the complexity and ambiguity of his thought, he seems to favour the view that our relationship with God was truly lost and, in its restoration, we cannot entertain any thought of moving closer to God, of becoming "like" God. Christ has restored us but, rather than this opening for us infinite possibility for transcendence, we accept our admittedly favourable but, in a profound sense, passive, position before God.

In fact in the section of *Theo-Drama II* to which I have been referring Balthasar seems to see in his work a potential conflict with what he calls "Protestant polemics". In his admission to the retention of the "image" in humanity after the Fall and to the inherent ongoing transformation in post-Fall humanity there appears to be a stance distinguishable from some Protestant apologists. "Irenaeus' distinctions", he states, that is between "image" and "likeness" and "image" of God in humanity before and in the light of Christ, "provide the basis for a more nuanced theology of the 'image'; its elements cannot be dispensed with, despite Protestant polemics".[20] "Protestant polemics" he goes on to define in terms of the rejection of a view which attributes to humanity both a "natural" and a "supernatural" aspect, that is an aspect which would admit some kind of potential for "likeness" to God. For these thinkers this has been seen as an unwelcome facet in a doctrine which should be summed up not in such metaphysical and ontological terms, focussing on humanity, but in terms of the history of salvation through Christ. It is a position which at first sight would seem to be not too far removed from Barth's.

Balthasar refers to Brunner's claim[21] that Irenaeus' teaching has been "falsely overlaid" with the secondary distinction between "natural" and "supernatural". He also refers back to a debate from the pages of *Münchener Theologische Zeitschrift*

---

[20] Ibid., 325.
[21] Emil Brunner, *Dogmatik II: Die Christliche Lehre von Schöpfung und Erlösung* (Zurich: Zwingli-Verlag, 1950), 92.

of 1959 between Stephan Otto and d'Alès and Ratzinger,[22] in which Otto, he says, "attempts to play off the 'salvation-historical' development (from paradise to man's final state) against the 'categorical-analytical distinction made between a "natural" and a "supernatural" element in man'".[23] In other words Otto would not accept that one could talk of Christ as saviour in unequivocal terms whilst at the same time accepting that human beings had a natural capacity for God. The objection to Otto in this article was based on a contemporary view which had come through strongly in Ratzinger's 1954 doctoral thesis *Volk und Haus Gottes in Augustins Lehre von der Kirche*.[24] This had seen in the development of Patristic theology, particularly in the West, an understanding of the Church as People and House of God both in terms of the history of salvation and the personal call to holiness on the part of the believer. The point is that, following the Fathers, we may talk of Christ as saviour yet also speak of human capacity for God. Christocentrism can be coupled with what has been termed "natural theology". Thus we may say that in Christ we are conformed to God's "image" and, through Christ, we are then called forth into a closer incorporation into his "likeness". For Balthasar the attack from "Protestant polemics" which intends to divide the two categories is invalid as in Irenaeus and other Fathers in both the East and the West we do have this understanding of the call to personal holiness, with an attribution of "natural" and "supernatural" to humanity, but this is clearly placed in the context of salvation history.

The two motifs are present and, it would seem Balthasar is saying, need to be in our contemporary understanding of "*imago Dei*". It would seem to me that in its simplest form he seems to be saying that we must see the doctrine clearly in terms of Christ and salvation but at the same time allow space for a creative vision of the potential of the human being for transcendence. Balthasar will set out to combine the two and so distance himself from what he terms "Protestant polemics". We might think that in so doing he would also be in disagreement with Barth. Such might be our initial conclusion from this section of *Theo-Drama II* to which I have been referring.

However, as we move on in this analysis of the formulation of Balthasar's position, we shall discover that there will be much more colour and many shades of colour to add to his picture. It will turn out that his dismissal of what here he has termed "Protestant polemics" in favour of the "nuanced" optimistic picture in Irenaeus will not preclude his deep appreciation of other aspects of the tradition, both Catholic and Protestant. In point of fact we shall discover that Barth in particular, and the form of Protestant thought he develops, despite its apparent leaning to a nuanced but overridingly sombre view of the human condition, differs from the polemics from which he has distanced himself. Rather it is the richness

---

[22] Stefan Otto, "Der Mensch als Bild Gottes bei Tertullian" (*Münchener Theologische Zeitschrift* 10, 1959), 276–82.

[23] Ibid., 325, footnote 33.

[24] Joseph Ratzinger, *Volk und Haus Gottes in Augustins Lehre von der Kirche*, in *Münchener Theologische Studien* II.7 (Munich: Karl Zink Verlag, 1954).

and subtlety of this at first sight incongruous dialogue partner which brings a new layer of paint to Balthasar's portrait.

Balthasar, building on the layer he has been forming, will appreciate Barth's approach more fully, bring it into closer relief and transform it as he attempts to combine Christocentrism with a creative vision of the human being's infinite potential for transcendence. In order to understand how he comes to approach Barth we need first to turn to the Latin Father Augustine, who far more than Irenaeus was the source of different interpretations in different traditions. Balthasar will interpret Augustine in a particular way which gives shape to his understanding of Barth and in turn to his doctrine of "*imago Dei*".

The Influence of Augustine

Balthasar seems to believe that Augustine's understanding of "*imago Dei*" also holds together in a comprehensible dynamic the two dimensions we concluded were present in Irenaeus. For him Augustine affirms the gratuity of God's action in Christ as the prototype of the "*imago*" whilst also stressing the human movement back towards God's likeness. Thus Balthasar places Augustine in an unbroken line of theological teaching which holds these two movements, that is what he terms the "descending" and the "ascending", in an unbroken chain.

This view is important to my overall argument as we will recall how Barth regarded Augustine's doctrine differently. For Barth Augustine signalled a clear break in the tradition. The "*imago*" in humanity is totally lost so there is no possibility of ascent to God. The "*imago Dei*" can only be understood in terms of the descendant. It is only understood in terms of the prototype Christ, who through his incarnation and salvific action has made us partners in his covenant with us. In the next section, in which I turn to the influence Barth had on Balthasar, I will be arguing that Balthasar was able to integrate this Christocentric aspect of the Barthian interpretation of Augustine into his own, whilst, through his altogether different reading of the Latin Father, shape this into a more integrated, creative, doctrine, which reaffirms human dignity and potential for transcendence.

In *Theo-Drama II*[25] Balthasar states that for Augustine the "*imago*" is not lost in humanity but rather that through sin, it is placed in jeopardy. It is, in Balthasar's words, "a slackening of the movement toward God, which obscures the image, covers it over and attacks it".[26] Thus Balthasar can still affirm that for Augustine the human being can ascend towards God, and so agree with Gregory of Nyssa, that the image can be assumed into the likeness. Having read Augustine in this way Balthasar will now construct an interpretation of him in his own terms. This interpretation will be expressed as a dynamic of finite and infinite freedom and will place Augustine alongside other Church Fathers and the medieval theologian Bernard.

---

[25] Balthasar, *TD II*, 329–30.
[26] Ibid., 329.

"If we look from finite freedom to infinite, that is, in an 'ascending' manner", says Balthasar, "the actual 'image' in finite freedom persists as it transcends itself toward finite freedom, in what Gregory of Nyssa calls '*epektasis*' and the medieval theologians call '*excessus*'".[27] For Augustine this entails not simply being covenant partners restored in Christ as Barth had maintained. Rather it entails turning to God, conscious of the "*imago*" still present in us, and following a path ascending towards God. "Augustine, together with Gregory of Nyssa", affirms Balthasar, "tirelessly recommends the inward path as the prime way of seeking God in our own soul-spirit and beholding him as in a mirror; not so that we should come to a full stop with ourselves ('*transcende te ipsum!*') but should rather throw ourselves entirely into the movement toward God".[28]

If we go deeper into the background of Balthasar's interpretation of Augustine we uncover some of the bases for this particular reading of Augustine which would enable him to develop and expand his doctrine of "*imago Dei*" in a different and fuller manner than was evident in Barth. In his interpretation of the history of theology Balthasar seemed to regard the Pelagian controversy as vital to this particular understanding of Augustine. In what amounts to a short summary of his views on the debate towards the end of *Theo-Drama IV*[29] he stresses the importance of preserving in Augustine the two important aspects of the God–human dynamic mentioned earlier, that is the "descending" and "ascending", both the aspect which stresses the descent of Christ to earth bringing through him God's restoration of his image in us, and that which represents our capacity to ascend to God and in some way to become like him.

In this section of *Theo-Drama* Balthasar examines the writings of Pelagius and Augustine within the wider perspective of Patristic thinking. He starts by arguing that it would be misguided to see Augustine as the first in the history of theology to distinguish nature and grace. It is true, he says, that there is a "decisive struggle" between Augustine and Pelagius on this very question and that Augustine asserts the priority of God's action before human response. However, Balthasar would appear to be saying that, if we consider the background to the debate more closely, we must be careful not to assume that Augustine's apology for the priority of grace amounts to a rejection of the concept of the human "*capax Dei*" as presented in earlier Patristic theology. Rather both aspects of the God–human dynamic, the "descendant" and the "ascendant", are present, in a coherent theology already carefully distinguishing grace and nature.

Already in Tertullian we have both aspects expressed in terms of God's grace and our free response. In the Greek Fathers, he says, the idea of "divinisation" "is always the result of a grace that is rigorously distinguished from nature, a grace that elevates us to a super-natural dignity".[30] Thus Augustine's contribution

---

[27] Ibid., 329.
[28] Ibid., 329.
[29] Balthasar, *TD IV, The Action* (San Francisco: Ignatius Press, 1994), 373–83.
[30] Ibid., 374–5.

in asserting the clear distinction between grace and nature over against Pelagius is not to deny the idea of potential "divinisation" in humanity. Rather "the distinction insisted upon by Augustine is thoroughly traditional".[31] Instead Augustine retains the idea that humanity, created in God's image, is summoned by Christ, that is summoned through the power of what now becomes known in the tradition as grace, to become more like him. The key assertion is that for human nature this process of transformation is not possible without God's grace, without placing Christ who works that transformation at its origin and its end. However this is not to say that the ascent to God is simply not possible. On the contrary it is vital to the life of the disciple to progressively draw closer and closer to God in Christ.

Balthasar's reading of Augustine here is vital to the development of his doctrine of "*imago Dei*" and in particular his reading of Barth. A closer look at the Pelagian controversy seems to convince him that the key distinction between Augustine and Pelagius was not about the human capacity for becoming like God but of how this is construed as either fundamentally "anthropocentric" or fundamentally "Christocentric". Thus we will see how he will appreciate Barth's Christocentrism, but will want to shape this into a view of the human being which emphasises, in the light of Christ, a capacity for transcendence. Balthasar asserts that Pelagius is right to say that humanity's endowment with the freedom which constitutes his being made in the "*imago Dei*" "is the same presupposition that forms the basis for man's development toward 'likeness' with God".[32] Pelagius' error was not to place this in the context of God's love for us, in the Trinity, grounded in the incarnation. For Pelagius all forms of grace are traced back to a single form, "God's gift of finite freedom and his maintenance of it".[33] This, according to Balthasar's view of the controversy, serves to ground Pelagius' view of the God–human dynamic not in God or in Christ but in humanity per se. Augustine, in line with Irenaeus and other Church Fathers, teaches us the importance of grounding the doctrine in Christ. The doctrine, however, still necessarily proposes the God-given capacity for humans to draw closer to him.

As Balthasar sees it, Pelagius regards "primal grace" as "the original gift of freedom to man, whereby God hands man over to himself".[34] Thus, although he calls this original gift of freedom "primal grace", and so would seem to intend to ground his notion of humanity in God's action, in fact it is our fundamental independence from God which defines us. Thus Pelagius in fact taught that "it is precisely in his autonomy that man is an 'image of God'".[35] Balthasar's reading of Pelagius here relies heavily on the work of one recent scholar of his theology,

---

[31] Ibid., 375.
[32] Ibid., 380.
[33] Ibid., 378.
[34] Ibid., 376.
[35] Ibid., 376.

Gisbert Greshake,[36] whose work he finds informative and enlightening although his view of Pelagius he rejects strongly. Greshake went some way to defend Pelagius from his critics, stressing that dependence on a concept of human nature which emphasised freedom as potential for self-realisation, allowed him to avoid an overly mystical view of God's action in human lives which overpowered subjectivity. Balthasar is quick to reject such an apology for Pelagius as "complacency"[37] as it belies what Greshake admits is at the heart of the matter, namely that "'Pelagius' whole theology is grounded in the theology of creation'", not of God in Christ.[38]

It is this admission about Pelagius which shows us how he has moved the doctrine of "*imago Dei*" from a grounding in God in Christ as our origin and goal to a grounding in humanity striving for self-realisation. Balthasar is showing us here how Pelagius' place in the history of the doctrine does not provoke Augustine and later theology to block out the notion of the "ascendant", humanity's finite freedom yearning for self-fulfilment. Rather it leads Augustine to ground the doctrine not in the anthropocentric but in the Christocentric. In Pelagius:

> [t]he specifically Christian grace is always given solely in order to reestablish and strengthen man's original freedom – which is, of course, a religious freedom. In other words, all Pelagius' Christian spirituality is decidedly anthropocentric. God comes to fallen man's aid with the *correctorium* of the law, holding up a mirror to him, as it were, in which man can see his true essence and so strive for it anew;[39] in this context, Pelagius is thinking less of God's covenant with Israel, in which God reveals his essence, than of a means whereby man can return to himself and find himself.[40]

Balthasar will now develop a view of Augustine which sees in his response to Pelagius the assertion that the relationship between God and humanity must be grounded not in humanity's own finite freedom but in the infinite freedom which in Christ summons us to ascend to him. Augustine's point is that our ascending to God must be grounded in God's descent to us. The doctrine of the "*imago Dei*" will relate to both poles, the "ascendant" and the "descendant", but it must be rooted in the One who descended to us, Christ. Thus for Balthasar the movement of the two freedoms, finite and infinite, are grounded in the mystery of the giver, that is Christ. Thus humanity's finite freedom as representing God's image is beckoned by Christ to transcend itself in becoming like him. "Infinite freedom summons finite freedom to go beyond itself and share in the former." "There is a distinction between the ineradicable nondivinity of the creaturely 'image' and its vocation

---

[36] Gisbert Greshake, *Gnade als konkreten Freiheit. Eine Untersuchung zur Gnadenlehre des Pelagius* (Mainz: Matthias-Grünewald), 1972.

[37] Balthasar, *TD IV*, 379, footnote 43.

[38] Ibid., 376, quoting Greshake, *Gnade als konkreten Freiheit*, 130.

[39] Texts in Greshake, *Gnade als konkreten Freiheit*, 96, footnote 13.

[40] Balthasar, *TD IV*, 376–7.

to participate in the divine prototype ('likeness')" but the human vocation is to become more like God in Christ.[41]

Balthasar's conclusion from his study of the Pelagian controversy is two-fold. Firstly, "we can speak concretely of *theosis*". Secondly, however, we can do this "only in the context of Christology" ("*[V]on 'Theosis' kann deshalb konkret nur innerhalb des Raumes der Christologie gehandelt werden*").[42] Thus Balthasar sees the contribution of Augustine in a different way to Barth and this will affect his own understanding of his ecumenical partner's theology and his integration of Barth's perspective into his own. For Balthasar Augustine should, firstly, not lead us to reject with Barth an understanding of "*imago Dei*" which sees in human beings the "*capax Dei*". Secondly, however, Augustine's contribution leads us to ground the doctrine in Christ's descent. On this he will find himself agreeing fundamentally with Barth.

From this perspective he will insist on a thoroughly Christocentric understanding of the human vocation, with Christ as our origin and our goal. In shaping such a theology he will consider himself also in line with Patristic theology, especially as we have seen, Irenaeus and Augustine, but on his interpretation of the latter, he will incorporate the second element we have shown Barth to have rejected, namely that of our "ascent" to God, that is our progressive transformation into the likeness of Christ whose image we are on earth. So now we turn to Balthasar's interpretation of Barth in itself, tracing how his reading of Augustine now draws him to an appreciation of the move in Barth's thought to place Christ at the centre, a theme itself rooted in the Reformation and its own understanding of Augustine, and to what might at first sight be an unexpected appreciation of Barth's overall contribution to the development of the doctrine of "*imago Dei*".

Critical Analysis: The Barthian Contribution

In our study of the development of Barth's own understanding of the doctrine of "*imago Dei*" we touched briefly on how Balthasar responded to Barth's views. Then, in this chapter so far, as we have begun to trace the influences on Balthasar's own perspective on the doctrine, firstly in Irenaeus, and then in Augustine, we have been referring back to Barth and his different interpretation of the tradition. Until now this has been our basic argument. Balthasar's different interpretation of the tradition led him to develop an understanding of the human person's creation in the "*imago Dei*" which places Christ, not humanity, at its centre. Yet at the same time Balthasar wants to develop an understanding of the human person's infinite possibility of transcendence in virtue of Christ. Thus Balthasar will integrate the former aspect, which is clearly present in Barth –

---

[41] Ibid., 380.
[42] Ibid., 380–381 (Balthasar, *TDK III: Die Handlung*, 355).

what we might call the Christocentric or the "descendant" pole – into his own theology. However, he will shape Barth's Christocentrism into an understanding of the doctrine which also expresses what Barth appears to have rejected, that is the "ascendant", the human potential for self-fulfilment in Christ.

If we turn to Balthasar's early and seminal work, *The Theology of Karl Barth*,[43] we find a chapter dedicated to an appreciation of what he calls Barth's "Christocentrism". Here he defends Barth's general direction to make Christ, not humanity, what he calls "the ground of creation". This idea of Barth's, claims Balthasar, has become a concern of twentieth-century theology and is also rooted in the Catholic tradition.[44] At the same time, Balthasar argues, "one can be as radically Christocentric as Barth is without having to go down his 'dead end'". Balthasar clearly regards Barth's "radical Christocentrism" as vital but flawed and intends to develop it to include the notion of a human quest for God. Regarding this proposed development, at least at first sight in this early work, he is equally clear. "The Incarnation", he argues, "demands that there be a relatively solid content of meaning that cannot be totally robbed of its substance when we provisionally abstract from our supernatural goal ... out of respect for human nature, human freedom and decisions (a respect that God himself shows), the eschatological climax must remain an open question".[45]

Thus, in his interpretation of Barth, Balthasar sets out from this basic perspective. Barth can teach us the importance of grounding the doctrine of "*imago Dei*" in Christ, but we need to develop a different Christocentric doctrine which leaves room for humanity's free response to move closer to our supernatural goal. In other words he sets out to try to reconcile Barth's "radical Christocentrism" with the tradition of "natural theology". Clearly this is an important aim for him. When he meets criticism for suggesting the real possibility of such a reconciliation of perceived opposites he is quick to defend his conviction. When he is criticised by Engelbert Gutwenger, following the publication of *The Theology of Karl Barth*, for pursuing this line in his theology, he quickly responds in an article[46] which confirms that his appreciation of Barth's Christ-centred approach is to be coupled with a fully developed "natural theology". This robust response was later restated in a postscript he was to write to the book in 1961. Gutwenger had seen in his work too much reliance on the idea of human initiative in the God–human dynamic, on philosophical approaches to theology which clouded

---

[43] Balthasar, *The Theology of Karl Barth* (San Francisco: Ignatius Press, 1992), 326–63.

[44] Ibid., 333. Here he is indebted to one author who traced the idea throughout the history of Catholic theology, namely Emile Mersch, *La Théologie du Corps mystique* (Paris: Desclée de Brouwer; Brussells: Edition Universelle, 1946).

[45] Balthasar, *The Theology of Karl Barth*, 362–3.

[46] Balthasar, "Der Begriff der Natur in der Theologie" (*Zeitschrift für Katholischen Theologie* 75, 1953), 453–61.

the gratuity of God's action in Christ. In reply Balthasar insists on the need to underline humanity's capacity for transcendence as a "natural" gift.[47]

Thus, for the development of his doctrine of the "*imago Dei*", his application of Barth's radical Christocentrism is qualified in very specific terms. Barth's placing Christ at the centre does not require us to state that the image in humanity is lost:

> The great majority of scholars admit that it is not possible to speak in the Old Testament of a loss of man's being in the image of God through sin, and this means in my opinion that Karl Barth's chief polemical position (the denial of any natural theology) cannot any longer be maintained.[48]

Rather, in virtue of Christ's descent, humanity's "ascent" as enduring "natural" capacity for God must be expressed as fully as possible. In pursuing this, at first sight, clear line of thinking, Balthasar will interpret Barth in a particular way. However, we will also see how, in insisting on and developing a thorough natural theology in line with this Christocentrism, a paradoxical character to Balthasar's approach takes shape.

This is important. Here we see a new dimension to Balthasar's theology which would enable him to make a very significant ecumenical contribution. It is my contention that in his subtle interpretation of Barth – at times seeming to place a Catholic construct on his theology but at times finding in it a clear desire to learn from natural theology – Balthasar truly takes on board the complexity of Barth's position. Why is this significant? In short it seems that Balthasar understands how Barth stands at the crossroads of ecumenical dialogue on human dignity, at one and the same time looking back to the Reformation's renewed emphasis on the centrality of Christ, yet looking forward to a new more positive vision of the human being's quest for transcendence and witness as Christ's presence on earth.

It is this particular interpretation of Barth's contribution which will enable Balthasar not just to root his own doctrine of "*imago Dei*" in Christ but to engage in a new way with the challenge of contemporary ecumenical dialogue. We will see how his appreciation of Barth will enable him to marry the ascendant and the descendant in a way which from the Catholic side does greater justice to the Reformation position. Thus he makes a lasting contribution not just to Catholic but to ecumenical theology, and so, as we will conclude, shows us a way forward for a contemporary ecumenical understanding of the doctrine as part of a fuller theological picture of human dignity for the twenty-first century.

Balthasar's interpretation of Barth becomes more and more nuanced, as we see how, in painting his more positive picture of the possibility of transcendence within human nature, he tries to read into Barth an element alien to Barth's line of

---

[47] It should be noted that Balthasar was influenced here by the work of his teacher at Lyon-Fourvière, Henri de Lubac, through his particular work on grace, nature and supernature.

[48] Balthasar, *Creator Spirit*, 92, footnote 13.

thought. Through this Balthasar will present a more integrated doctrine of *"imago Dei"* as he is able to develop a fuller picture of human dignity, transformation and vocation in Christ. The paradox in Balthasar's interpretation of Barth is at root of an ecumenical nature. He desires to integrate as fully as possible a theological outlook rooted in the Reformation into a thoroughly Catholic theology. As we have now seen in tracing the influences in the history of theology on the two theologians, both have taken, as a key source, Augustine, yet they interpret him in different ways. How can Balthasar integrate fully what is truly "radical" about Barth's Christocentric understanding of the doctrine, namely that he believes that to be truly Christocentric entails a reading of Augustine which claims that there is nothing the human being, in whom the *"imago"* is lost at the Fall, can do naturally to ascend to God? How can Balthasar do this when he still insists on the *"imago"* in humanity in terms of natural theology, finding in Augustine a picture of humanity's ongoing transformation?

As we concluded at the end of the last section Balthasar sees Augustine's contribution to be in line with this view of our ongoing transformation in Christ he wishes to develop. Yet for Barth Augustine's contribution is more radical, requiring us not simply to place Christ, rather than humanity, at the centre, but to understand his "Christocentrism" as eliminating the possibility of a progressive transformation through which fallen human nature can still move towards God in Christ. Barth thus places Augustine not in line with Irenaeus and Catholic theology but with Luther and Reformation theology. "Radical Christocentrism" here seems to mean something different. It means to reject the possibility of human *"deificatio"* which Balthasar sees as so important to his own Christocentric picture.

We will recall how we looked more closely at how Barth was linked to this Lutheran understanding of Augustine. For Barth, this strand of Augustine's thought would seem to exclude the possibility of the fuller, more integrated, view of human dignity in the adventure of transcendence and transformation. Because he insists that we must return to Augustine's teaching that we really do have absolutely no access to God after the Fall, our post-Fall reconstitution in a special relationship with God involves no hint of this. It is his interpretation of the tradition from Augustine through to Luther which has led him to this perspective. It is essentially in the action of *"justificatio"*, not *"deificatio"*, that we are reconstituted. *"Deificatio"*, he claims, is not part of Augustine's picture but is contained in the fundamental understanding of our *"justificatio"*.

I then argued that we might question such an assumption and look for a fuller interpretation of Augustine. We found that Balthasar was disposed to this more integrated understanding. However, when it comes to analysing how Balthasar intended to integrate Barth's Christocentrism into his own view, we need to go back again in the tradition to see how he really understood it. In now returning to the roots of Barthian Christocentrism in the Reformation we come closer to the heart of Balthasar's at first sight paradoxical but ultimately ecumenical contribution. We see how Balthasar attempts to appreciate the radical nature of Barth's Christocentrism from the side of Barth's own perspective within his own tradition rooted in the Reformation. As he does this we find his model of *"imago Dei"*, through the paradox and ambiguity which is part of the attempt to understand from a totally different perspective, to take shape, and in this ultimately we can begin to see potential for true ecumenical significance. The key figure who will serve here as an ecumenical bridge will be Luther.

Understanding of Luther

When Balthasar set out to present Barth's theology in his book of that title, he was already looking for, as he himself put it in the final chapter, "prospects for rapprochement", between Protestant and Catholic theology. In the penultimate chapter of the book he turns to the relationship between Barth and Luther. Here we find some clues as to how he understood what was key to Barth's contribution. In short Balthasar seems to see in Barth a more developed interpretation of Luther which opens up new possibilities.

Balthasar suggests that Barth is moving away from what he calls an "exaggerated eschatologism" (*"übertriebenen Eschatologismus"*) which "ascribes justification to man only as a hope and not also as a present reality" (*"die Gerechrigkeit dem Menschen nur als Hoffnung, nicht auch in gegenwärtiger Wahrheit zugesprochen wird"*).[49] For the Catholic understanding Luther's doctrine of justification in itself is unacceptable in that it becomes distorted by this overly eschatological interpretation which places Christ's gift of justification solely in the future rather than within the present reality of human life. On this interpretation, justification "can never become a real, intrinsic part of man".[50] Barth however, so Balthasar argues, is not thinking in terms of this overly eschatological interpretation. On the contrary Barth is highlighting "the real occurrence, the genuine history, of God with the sinner".[51] What does this interpretation mean for Balthasar and the direction in which he wishes to develop a radically Christocentric doctrine of *"imago Dei"*?

For Barth Luther's *"simul iustus et peccator"*, the doctrine that we are, after the Fall, at one and the same time sinners yet justified, propels us not to look to ourselves as sinners nor look to some future hope. Rather than focussing on humanity's past sin and the loss of the *"imago"*, or on humanity's future glory in oneness with God, Barth is focussing on Christ in the midst of human lives in the present. It is Christ who gives our lives meaning as we stop thinking of the balancing out of past sin and future glory but find precisely in Christ the "'abolition of balancing'".[52]

---

[49] Balthasar, *The Theology of Karl Barth*, 370 [Balthasar, *Karl Barth: Darstellung und Deutung Seiner Theologie* (Cologne: Verlag Jakob Hegner, 1951, 1962), 379.

[50] Ibid., 370.

[51] Ibid., 370. Here Barth is referring in particular to sections of *Die christliche Lehre nach dem Heidelberger Katechismus* (1948).

[52] Balthasar, *The Theology of Karl Barth*, 371, quoting *Heidelberger Katechismus*, no. 30–41.

Thus Balthasar seems to see in Barth the possibility of understanding Christ's presence within the human person in a more dynamic way than might have been possible before. Christ and the human being will not be disengaged but in some kind of relationship with one another. This is an attractive strand to Barth's thought because it lends itself to a view of the human person's identity in Christ which gives a fuller meaning to what it is to be human. On this reading of Barth, Luther's doctrine of justification need not place Christ outside of human experience but can serve to place him at its centre. Ultimately Balthasar will develop this into a Christocentrism of his own which can speak powerfully of the vocation of each human being made in God's image, called to be progressively transformed into Christ and placed with him on his mission.

These first stirrings of an interpretation of Barth's Christocentrism as representing a new attractive strand in Protestant thought are significant. Nevertheless, before we progress, we must pause to point out some of the ambiguities and the paradoxes already evident at this stage of our argument. Although this more attractive interpretation of Luther is something Balthasar appears to pursue, he too is aware of problems in Barth's thought. Barth's emphasis on the present reality of Christ in human lives is placed, paradoxically it might seem, within the context of eternity. "Too much in Barth", says Balthasar, "gives the impression that nothing much really *happens* in his theology of event and history, because everything has already happened in eternity".[53] As such we are left with a Christocentrism which, while moving in the right direction, is inadequate in itself, unable to "make for a real and vibrant history of man with his redeeming Lord and God".[54]

In order to do this Balthasar admits that he will learn from both Luther and from Barth, but, in order to speak more directly of the notion of our justification by Christ not merely "*in spe*", but also "*in re*", the "ontological meaning of grace as a real participation in God's nature already in this life" ("*der seinshaften Deutung der Gnade als realer Teilnahme an der göttlichen Natur schon in diesem Leben*"), "the Catholic must sharpen these paradoxes of Luther and Barth by going beyond them" ("*wird der Katholik, das Paradox über Luther und Barth hinaus noch verschärfend*").[55] It seems that Balthasar here is admitting that he must learn from Barth and Luther but still supplement them with a more explicit understanding of how the human person is involved in this relationship with Christ in ontological terms.

Nevertheless Balthasar, while seeing the limitations in Barth's thought, does still seem to see in him new possibilities for developing his vocational model of human identity in Christ. So we must begin to ask critical questions about his interpretation of Barth and use of his thought, some of which will become clearer later in this chapter. For the present it suffices to raise the question as to what extent Balthasar is interpreting Barth from the perspective of his own theological

---

[53] Ibid., 371. Emphasis his.
[54] Ibid., 371.
[55] Ibid., 372 [Balthasar, *Karl Barth*, 381].

tradition and to what extent he is placing a Catholic construct on him and his interpretation of Luther.

We have already seen, in our study of Barth's understanding of "*imago Dei*" itself, that he intended to place himself alongside Luther and Augustine, in insisting on a rather sombre view of the human person after the Fall. We concluded that Christ was at the centre but that he understood the relationship between post-Fall humanity and Christ in terms of a doctrine of restoration as justification, rather than developing a model of an ongoing relationship between humanity and Christ through which humanity finds its ongoing ontological meaning and vocation. However, we also saw that Barth did show signs of trying to develop a more relational model and so, at this point, must keep an open mind on how Balthasar himself will read and use Barth.

Above all, at this point, it is important to register Barth's own response to Balthasar's early appreciation and proposed development of his Christocentrism. Is Balthasar trying to read into Barth's Christocentrism the idea of humanity's innate capacity for ongoing transformation in relationship with Christ? On reading Balthasar's book on him, Barth was clearly concerned about this. In his reply Barth makes this observation. It is in the context of Roman Catholicism in general, and its emphasis on the Mass and the saints, both of which he believed obscured Christ from view, however hard Roman Catholic theologians intended to follow his own theological project in placing Christ at the centre. However, this observation of Barth's is important in the context of Barth's understanding of Luther we have been considering, as he does seem to regard Balthasar to have partially misunderstood him.

Whilst Barth praises the move to develop a Christocentric perspective he does not agree with how Balthasar seems to be going about it:

> In modern Roman Catholic theology, there is a promising but, of course, unofficial movement that is apparently aiming in the direction of what we might call a Christological renaissance ... this promising new beginning in Roman Catholic theology is in danger of returning to (or maybe it has never left) the well-worn track on which the doctrine of justification is absorbed into that of sanctification – understood as the pious work of self-sanctification that man can undertake and accomplish on his own strength. My concern is whether this is perhaps the case ... If only we were agreed ... that the ultimate and penultimate things, the redemptive act *of God* and that which passes for *our* response, *are not the same*. Everything is jeopardized if there is confusion in this respect.[56]

Barth himself is here being critical of a perceived move to understand the human being's response to God and God's redemptive act in Christ in a dynamic through which humanity is understood to work out its own way to God. Barth's own view

---

[56] Barth, *CD IV/1*, 768, quoted in Balthasar, *The Theology of Karl Barth*, 398–9, footnote 14. Italics Barth's.

cannot withstand this as the act of justification is once and for all and cannot be confused with sanctification.

We may tentatively conclude from this response what I have been presenting throughout as the more authentic reading of Barth. Ultimately Barth places himself alongside Luther, interpreting Augustine to mean that in the Fall the "*imago*" is entirely lost, thus rendering humanity incapable of accessing God. It is restored in Christ in an act of justification. This does not lead to our ongoing sanctification in relationship with Christ but we simply live as justified covenant partners in Christ. In concluding this we might also observe from this study thus far that Balthasar may have been looking to develop Barth's reading of Luther in a way which Barth himself would not have seen possible or desirable from the perspective of his own tradition rooted in Reformation theology. Edward Oakes, the editor of the English translation of Balthasar's book on Barth, who included Barth's response in his edition, raises a similar question. "This quotation", says Oakes, "shows, perhaps more than any other, how deeply Protestant Barth's thinking really is, and how deeply Catholic are the presuppositions that von Balthasar brings to his objections to Barth".[57] In other words Barth is firmly in the tradition of the Reformation but Balthasar reads him from a Catholic mindset on it. As we move forward in Balthasar's work to *The Glory of the Lord I*, this becomes clearer still.

Here Balthasar goes further behind Barth's own thought to investigate his debt to Luther. Turning to Luther's *Lecture on the Letter to the Romans* Balthasar clarifies how he sees the unhelpful movement in Protestant theology since the Reformation, which now Barth will begin to reverse. Here he develops the theme of Christ's presence in the midst of human life, which he believes Barth is restoring to Protestant theology. He states that it was Luther's idea of the "hiddenness" of God "*sub contrario specie*", which "'under a form which contradicts our thought and comprehension' (on 8.26), transforms God, even in his mercy, into the hidden God which Calvin then radicalizes into the God of double predestination, the God of whom we can have absolutely no image or vision".[58] The "hidden" God has thus become a "hypostasized image of election" which excludes the possibility of "contemplation" on the part of humanity. This notion in classical Protestantism, that is what is taken as the authentic interpretation of Luther and Calvin, excludes any possibility of participation in the event of Christ's election from the human side. From this, says Balthasar, rather than placing Christ and the human being in an ongoing relationship it merely "allows the believer something like a 'contemplative' state in which he can rest".[59]

Balthasar thus appears here to be defining a classically Lutheran and Calvinist view of the human person's inaccessibility to God after the Fall as that which Barth was to reject. However, we concluded that Barth would, in general, be in agreement with such a view as a Reformation understanding of Augustine.

---

[57] Balthasar, *The Theology of Karl Barth*, 399, footnote 14.
[58] Balthasar, *GL I*, 57.
[59] Ibid., 57.

The "*imago*" in humanity is lost and Christ restores it, but we remain passive recipients of justification. For Balthasar Barth's place within his own tradition is different. This is key to his understanding of Barth's real contribution. The image of Christ's saving action on the cross as one of the Lutheran "hidden" God of Calvin's double predestination had up to this point laid the ground for Protestantism's rejecting entirely any notion of human participation in an ongoing transformative relationship with Christ expressed in the terms "contemplation", "glory" and "aesthetic". However, it was this restricted view of the Protestant tradition, emanating from Luther, which Balthasar believes Barth was partially to expose and reject. Balthasar maintains that the exclusion of these aspects of the theology of the human person "is contradictory", "and, as Karl Barth has strikingly shown, it is wholly foreign to Biblical revelation".[60]

"Thus it was only logical", he concludes,

> that Protestantism should exclude the genuinely contemplative and aesthetic books of scripture from its canon, even though the exclusion was not radical enough. From among the remaining books, the Protestant instinct focussed on those which are particularly actualistic, such as Galatians and Romans, while the Pauline contemplation of the letters from captivity has always been suspected of being in some way inauthentic. Only the *theologia crucis* – the theology of God's mercy under the "alien form" of the most merciless of judgments was seen by Luther to be acceptable in the present age. And he over-hastily identified the *theologia gloriae* with the theology of the coming age and its vision – as if the concept of *doxa* (*kâbôd, gloria*) were not, already in this age, a fundamental concept of the economy of both the Old and the New Testaments.[61]

Here Balthasar is developing his original view on Barth to suggest that he not only teaches us to place Christ in the midst of human life but to develop a Christocentrism which, breaking with the "actualism" of Luther and Calvin, restores the notion of "glory" to theology. By this he understands the human being not as looking to a future glory but to the glory already present in our midst. Balthasar will develop this through his own notion of Christ's appearing as "*Gestalt*", calling us to be transformed more closely into his presence and so be co-workers on his mission. Then later, in *Theo-Drama*, Balthasar will show how significant this is to a fuller, more dynamic and dramatic understanding of the identity of the human person in Christ, which had been lost through a static, passive, anti-contemplative, interpretation of Luther's "hidden God" of justification:

> The high drama of Luther's reduction in fact suppresses that *other* drama, which presupposes the existence of persons, with their proper being and constitution. We can no longer tell whether man, who is both a sinner and righteous, is one

---

[60] Ibid., 57.
[61] Ibid., 57–8.

or two; we can no longer tell whether he is a subject enjoying continuity ... It is only faith that lays hold of justification; love is only involved in the works of "second righteousness". Consequently, there is no place for the primary love of the redeemed for the person of the Redeemer. Artificially, but very deliberately, the unity of grace – which justifies and sanctifies – is torn asunder. Finally, in reducing theology to the *pro nobis* between Christ and sinners, Luther obscures the entire horizon of God's self-disclosure in Christ, everything the Fathers understood by *oikonomia* and the "divinization" of man through the grace of participation.[62]

From this quotation we may conclude that Balthasar rejects Luther's notion of justification in as clear terms as possible. Luther obscures his own preferred understanding of the human person's "proper being and constitution", the possibility of real participation in an ongoing transformative relationship with Christ which includes the possibility of "divinisation". For his own altogether more participative and vocational model of "*imago Dei*" he will turn to other authors and work from within his own more Catholic understanding of the tradition. He will use the medium of both aesthetics and drama to develop this model. However, it is my conviction that also so crucial to the development of his model will be what we are now beginning to see is a particularly nuanced picture of Barth's radical Christocentrism.

In conclusion we might say that Barth stands at a crossroads for him as a Protestant steeped in the Christocentrism of the Reformation whom he also regarded as looking, in some way which is beset with ambiguities, to restore a sense of "glory" and "aesthetics" to Protestant theology. This notion is ambiguous because, firstly, in general but, also, following our detailed study of Barth, in reasonably conclusive terms, Barth's radical Christocentrism appears to militate against these themes. Instead we concluded that Barth wished to present the event of salvation as final and humanity's role in accepting this or not as passive and static. There would appear to be little room to develop an aesthetically grounded theological anthropology which found in the appearance of Christ in glory something beautiful which evoked an ongoing human response in relationship with the divine. Furthermore, Balthasar's exact meaning is, at first sight, ambiguous, since he also regards Barth's theology as presenting, ultimately, a "dead end" with the relationship between God and humanity, ultimately, played out in eternity. Thus we have seen in this chapter that Balthasar is not blind to the limitations in Barth. However, this does not prevent him from finding glimpses of possibilities which will form his nuanced understanding of Barth's radical Christocentrism, which in turn will shape his own more integrated, participative, model of humanity's identity as the "*imago Dei*" rooted firmly in Christ's call.

These perceived glimpses of the more creative dimension in Barth we have been considering in this foregoing section through our study of the Lutheran

---

[62] Balthasar, *TD IV*, 290. Emphasis his.

background will be important as he will develop this for himself into a model of the human person made in the "*imago Dei*" rooted in Christ in whose very appearing on the human stage constitutes the vocation in Christ intrinsic to each one of us. Here Balthasar will see in Barth some possibilities for speaking of the doctrine in radically Christocentric terms, not just in terms of how Christ has restored the "*imago*" in us, but in a fuller way still of the meaning Christ gives to the human being made in his image. In short we might say that both the "descendant", that is the Christocentric, and the "ascendant" pole, through which human beings participate in the drama which unfolds with Christ's appearing, will be present in one integrated dynamic. So now we turn to Balthasar's interpretation of Barth in the pages of *The Glory of the Lord* which follow to show how he develops this and to see in this both critical questions about his interpretation of Barth's place in the tradition yet how, ultimately, Balthasar forms a more integrated and truly ecumenical doctrine of "*imago Dei*".

Balthasar's Barth: Christ-centred Theological Aesthetic

Before I proceed with my line of argument, let me clarify an important point. Balthasar's view that Barth's theology ultimately arrives at a "dead end", with insufficient scope for the active human response to Christ, is not in dispute. The conclusion I myself made from my study of Barth was the same. However, just as we saw in our detailed study of Barth that there are ambiguities and nuances in his thought, so Balthasar's understanding of him will highlight these and work with them. In one way in particular Balthasar's reading of Barth's place in his own Reformation tradition suggests to him an important idea which will be significant to his use of Barth to develop a more relational Christocentric doctrine of "*imago Dei*" than Barth actually could himself.

Balthasar argues that for Barth the aesthetic aspect of theology is an indispensable auxiliary concept. "Barth arrives at the content of 'beauty'", he claims, "by contemplating the data of Scripture, especially God's 'glory' [*Herrlichkeit*], for whose interpretation 'beauty' appears to him indispensable as 'auxiliary concept'".[63] This particular interpretation of Barth attributes to him a key underlying idea, "an intention and manner of presentation", which "both justifies and logically compels Barth … to restore to God the attribute of 'beauty' for the first time in the history of Protestant theology".[64] Such a move will place new emphasis on the relationship between God and his creation made in his image. Barth's theology will be solidly grounded in Christ but also suggestive of the possibility of the human response to the God who appears in human form. It is, affirms Balthasar, an "objectively normed and objectively formed dogmatics" to which "he gave as its content the personal faith-relationship … between the

---

[63] Balthasar, *GL I*, 53.
[64] Ibid., 53.

revealed creator and redeemer God and man, both as he turns away from God and as he re-turns to him".[65]

Starting from the premise that Barth has broken with Luther, Balthasar finds a significant relational dimension in his theology. Balthasar believes that Barth has rejected a Lutheran theology of "*exaiphnes*" or "lightning-flash" which, in proclaiming that human beings are rendered just "*simul iustus et peccator*", has God hidden, "the God of whom we can have absolutely no image or vision".[66] In rejecting this Barth has opened up the possibility of incorporating into a new theological aesthetic certain elements which Luther rejected. He will be able to restate "those elements of Patristic and Scholastic thought which can be justified from revelation itself and which, accordingly, are not suspect of any undue Platonizing".[67] Thus Balthasar might be able to see in Barth a new Christocentric picture of the human person in relationship in which he will "turn away from" and "re-turn to" God, which will not be presented in an overly Platonic way as had been done in the past in the Catholic tradition.

Balthasar argues that "it was perhaps necessary to let the first stage of Barth's thought die away – a phase whose inner form lay in the overpowering and uncompromising rhetoric of Luther and the Reformation ... in order to await the second stage, which as interior form attained the tranquil, attentive contemplation (*theoria*) of revelation".[68] Thus it seems from this section of writing that Balthasar is interpreting Barth in a very particular way. Barth is understood to have broken with Luther and the Reformation perspective which seemed to close the door to developing a doctrine of the human person which stressed how Christ's beauty found its response in our inner longing to return to God. Barth had to make this break, Balthasar seems to believe, because "it appeared to Luther that the Death-and-Resurrection dialectic of the Christ-event had been replaced by the non-dialectical schemata of Neo-Platonic aesthetic metaphysics", and Luther had wrongly concluded that this led to the Reformation view that "such 'aesthetic' theologising saw the world merely as the 'appearance' of the 'non-appearing God'" ("*als 'Erscheinung' des 'nichterscheinenden' Gottes*").[69] Barth's return to what Balthasar will term theological aesthetics, however, would be clearly and objectively rooted in Christ. Thus in Barth Balthasar seems to believe that we may see at one and the same time emphasis on God's glorious appearing in Christ and on the intrinsic nature of the call of Christ this provokes in human beings made in his image.

---

[65] Ibid., 53.
[66] Ibid., 57.
[67] Ibid., 56.
[68] Ibid., 56.
[69] Ibid., 45 [Balthasar, *Herrlichkeit: Eine Theologische Ästhetik I: Schau der Gestalt*, Einsiedeln: Johannes Verlag, 1961, 42] [hereafter referred to as *HK*].

The Mutuality of "Gestalt" and "Bild"

This interpretation of Barth will now have important consequences for Balthasar's own understanding of the human person created in the "*imago Dei*". It is in *Glory of the Lord VI*[70] that Balthasar approaches the doctrine from the perspective of aesthetics and, in particular, the notion of the glorious appearance of God on the human stage and what this means for God's image in creation. This section of Balthasar's writings is of its nature undeveloped as he is presenting his understanding of the doctrine from the perspective of the Old Testament. We will recall that, in his excursus on the doctrine in *Theo-Drama II*, that even there, as he is about to unfold the narrative of the dramatic encounter between Christ and humanity, he regards his treatment of the doctrine as premature. The doctrine has its full meaning only in the appearance of Christ, the "*Gestalt*", and we find the narrative which expresses this unfolded only later in the concluding parts of the *Theo-Drama*.

Yet here in this section of his preliminary work of theological aesthetics we can detect how such a Christocentric statement of the doctrine will be rooted in the very kind of motif he notices in Barth's own Christ-centred theological aesthetic. It will be based on an understanding of the mutual relationship between the one who appears in glory, Christ, the "*Gestalt*", and human persons made in his image, "*Bild*", and the corresponding mutuality between the "image" in humanity and the "covenant" through which humanity is fashioned and transformed. Balthasar discovers these motifs in Barth's account of the doctrine of "*imago Dei*" in *Church Dogmatics III/2* and integrates them into his own. In emphasising this strand in Balthasar's interpretation of Barth I am presenting a different interpretation to that which is more classically accepted. It is the popular view, epitomised for example in O'Donnell's introduction to Balthasar,[71] that Balthasar followed Barth in placing Christ at the very heart of his theology, but then developed around this a more Catholic picture of the ongoing mutual relationship between Christ and us. I, however, am arguing that Balthasar also found within Barth's Christocentrism hints of this more integrated theology of ongoing mutual relationship, and developed this still further in a way which Barth himself could not.

Balthasar takes from Barth the formula that, as Balthasar himself puts it, "creation (and with it, God's image in man) is the outward ground of the covenant and the covenant, in turn, is the inner ground of creation".[72] From this Balthasar seems to conclude that, whereas we must, with Barth, start from the perspective of Christ and his appearance on the human stage, we must also give creation, and in particular humanity made in God's image, a certain "autonomy" in its relationship with him. It is not sufficient to say that God has established a covenant with creation which places humanity in a graced relationship. In this part of Balthasar's work it

---

[70] Balthasar, *GL VI: The Old Covenant* (San Francisco: Ignatius Press, 1991), 87–143.
[71] John O'Donnell, *Hans Urs von Balthasar* (London: Geoffrey Chapman, 1992).
[72] Balthasar, *GL VI*, 88.

seems to me that he is far from a classically Calvinist interpretation of Barth: it is not in the human person's eternal election that he is rendered, passively, saved or not. Rather Balthasar is seeing in Barth's understanding of the human being as the covenant's outward ground the seeds of a theology he wishes to develop himself. This theology will stress distinctive human identity, a freedom to move towards God, and the possibility of transformation.

The "descendant" pole in Barth is fundamental, primary and indispensable. Balthasar is clear about this. Only in the appearance and descent of Christ does the "image" in humanity cease to be "in suspension". Balthasar seems to have integrated this aspect of Barth's radical Christocentrism into his thinking. Humanity's creation in God's "image" is totally meaningless if we do not stress Christ at the centre. Barth is right to highlight through this human nature's inability to realise itself except through Christ. So the "suspension" of the "image" is "proper to the creature as such ... the creature has absolutely no possibility of taking a position over against God".[73]

Yet it appears to me that Balthasar finds in Barth's Christocentrism something more than a statement of the fundamental priority of the descendant pole. He finds suggestions in Barth of a much richer Christocentric anthropology searching for a more dynamic reciprocal relationship between God and us. For Balthasar Barth's Christocentrism suggests the offer of a mutual relationship between God and his human creation in which humanity has a certain "sphere of autonomy over against God" (a "*Gottgegenübersein*"), "a certain space to be at home within itself before God" ("*ein Raum des Insichseins vor Gott*"),[74] and the possibility of a "special relationship of man to God – a proximity and an immediacy of kinship" ("*eine besondere Beziehung des Menschen zu Gott: eine Nähe und Unmittelbarkeit des Abkünftigseins*") proper to his special ontological status as made in God's image.[75]

This particular interpretation of Barth leads Balthasar to unite the "descendant" and the "ascendant" poles in one integrated dynamic. The pre-eminence of the "*Gestalt*" makes as clear as possible that it is God's appearance in human form which expresses at the deepest and most fundamental level human beings' creation in the "*imago Dei*". Yet, precisely through the very presence of Christ at the centre of human lives, and in no way giving any less priority to this fundamental truth, Balthasar highlights further this presence of Christ in the world through expressing in it the mutual relationship between God and his human creation and the special ontological status present in it in God's "image". Balthasar's interpretation

---

[73] Ibid., 88.

[74] Ibid., 88 [Balthasar, *HK III/2/2: Alter Bund*, 81].

[75] Ibid., 91 [Balthasar, *HK III/2/2*, 84]. Balthasar here cites various Old Testament works from the Protestant tradition to defend his view, notably: F. Horst, *Face to Face: the Biblical Doctrine of the Image of God* (Munich: Kaiser Verlag, 1950), G. von Rad in various works, and T.C. Vriezen, *Theologie des Alten Testaments in Grundzügen* (Wageningen: Veenman und Zonen, 1956).

of Barth's Christocentrism has led him to develop a doctrine grounded in the "establishment of a mutual priority between 'image' and 'covenant'",[76] a true mutuality of the "descendant" and "ascendant", "*Gestalt*" and "*Bild*".

In highlighting Barth's quest for the restatement of the doctrine of the "*imago Dei*" in terms of relationship with Christ, Balthasar has found a way to go beyond Barth's "dead end". He will not lose sight of the fundamental importance of placing Christ at the centre of the dynamic of the human relationship. Yet he will unite in one integrated dynamic Christocentrism and human capacity for transformation in Christ. He is able to develop this strand of Barth's thought in a way which Barth simply could not have done within his own tradition. For Balthasar the human being has a special ontological status which gives him a God-given capacity to be progressively transformed through the ongoing relationship he has with Christ. Yet, ultimately, because, in the process of working with Barth, Balthasar integrates and makes dominant in his own thinking the absolute priority of Christ's appearance in descent, he presents a relational and vocational model of "*imago Dei*" which is also truly Christocentric.

However, while this is my own view, it may also, at the same time, be argued, with some justification, that Balthasar seems to impose his own system onto his Protestant colleague. Within Balthasar's own thinking he will certainly see more than many would take to be present in Barth's view of the relationship. Firstly, let us return to the idea of relationship in Barth which we examined in some depth in Chapter 2.

It seems to me that Balthasar's instinct is right. There is no doubt that Barth wished to reclaim a doctrine of "*imago Dei*" which emphasised relationship. We saw, however, that, for Barth, human beings express their relationship to God through their relationship to each other. God and Christ were still somewhat distant from God's image in creation. Balthasar's other instinct, that this presented a "dead end" in maintaining the distance between God and humanity, also seems right. On closer analysis we concluded that the understanding of relationship in Barth lacked that narrative of human response expressing relationship, dignity, capacity for God. We concluded that these themes occasionally came through in sections of his writings but that they remained underdeveloped.

Barth's real contribution, however, was to understand the human relationship to God from the specific and concrete perspective of how God is revealed to us in the incarnate Word of God, Jesus Christ. Balthasar will integrate this Christocentric picture. We concluded from our study of Barth that he also seemed to want to emphasise how, if we reorient the God–human relationship in the concrete reality of God for us in Christ, we must still speak of a special relationship between God and humanity. In short we found within the Barthian ambiguities a certain desire to develop a doctrine which made more of the real contact between God and us. Yet in the end we ourselves concluded that within the Barthian Christocentric system our own desire for God merely confirms how our own quest for a relationship

---

[76] Ibid., 88.

with God is pointless. God cannot be the goal of human desire as humanity does not have natural capacity for a relationship with him. The relationship we have with God is for Barth expressed through our conversion as we accept the graced situation we find ourselves in. We then live out our Christian vocation as creatures made in his image in our relationship with others. All we can ultimately say about human identity specifically vis-à-vis God is that we are fallen but reconstituted by Christ. God himself remains to some extent distant and elusive.

Balthasar, on the other hand, is able to bridge this gap between the Christocentric and the relational because he starts from a totally different perspective, which is fundamentally beyond Barth's system. Thus we may see how Balthasar may be accused of placing a construct on Barth's thought, but more significantly for me he may also develop it into the more integrated relational model Barth showed signs of working towards himself. For Balthasar we are not merely reconstituted in a relationship with God after the Fall because the "*imago Dei*" was never totally lost. In *Theo-Drama II*[77] we saw how Balthasar's interpretation of Augustine has the "*imago*" not lost but, through sin, placed in jeopardy. In our study of Barth we saw that he had taken a view of Augustine which stated that the "*imago*" was lost then restored in a once and for all action of restitution by Christ. Balthasar, affirming the strand in Augustine which stresses the human being's longing for God and continued graced capacity to ascend towards him, and agreeing with Irenaeus and Gregory of Nyssa, that the image can be assumed into the likeness, has now constructed an interpretation of Barth somewhat in his own terms.

Balthasar, it must be ventured, may not have seen these distinctions between his own theological system and that of his Protestant colleague so clearly. What do I mean by this? I am not claiming that Balthasar misinterpreted Barth or that he placed a construct on Barth's radical Christocentrism. Rather, despite the apparent inconsistency between what I have been claiming is Barth's own overridingly sombre view of the human condition and Balthasar's more creative interpretation of his view of relationality, the end result in Balthasar will be the more fully developed doctrine we find the seeds of in the ambiguities of Barth's writings. It seems that Balthasar's ability to do this resulted from what comes through at times as what I would call a particular interpretation of Barth which highlights to the full the more creative attempts to develop a relational model.

This seems evident to me from his use of Barth in *Glory of the Lord I* and in *Glory of the Lord VI*. Having claimed, in Volume I, that Barth had restored the idea of a theological aesthetics to Protestant theology which involves a fuller picture of the mutual relationship between God and humanity, he now uses Barth to develop his more integrated relational model of the doctrine. This now involves the mutuality of the appearance and descent of Christ with humanity's ascent, the mutuality of "*Gestalt*" and "*Bild*" in humanity. Because he sees Barth through this lens it is not surprising that he should interpret him in a particular way which will help his own thought to develop. In particular it is not surprising that he

---

[77] Balthasar, *TD II*, 329–30.

finds appealing the ambiguous strand of Barth's thought which suggests that the "*imago*" may not be totally lost but is in a state of suspension.

The reason Balthasar does this is not because he has misinterpreted Barth but because Barth's statements themselves are at times contradictory and suggestive of further development. We have placed them in the wider context of a theological picture which seems to lack some optimism about the human condition but, at the same time, we saw how they do in fact suggest the kind of orientation towards a more integrated picture Balthasar himself sought to develop. Let us take, for example, the section of *Church Dogmatics II/1*[78] we studied in Chapter 2, in which Barth presents his picture of Christ as the "radiant light" of humanity. Here we see suggestions, within a clearly defined Christocentrism, of what Barth might be taken to mean about how Christ's appearance, expressed in unambiguous terms as the only point of reference in the God–human relationship, claims a response from humanity. This does not cloud the appearance of Christ as the dominant theme but, precisely through placing Christ's appearance at the apex, humanity is taken up by Christ himself into a mutual relationship of transformation.

Here Barth is clearly striving for a fuller expression of the mutual relationship between God and humanity. There is no evidence that Balthasar was thinking of this section when he was forming what I am taking to be his more nuanced interpretation of his theology than is usually presented. However, I would argue that the section itself gives some credence to Balthasar's view that hints of a richer, more dynamic, reciprocal picture of the Christ–human relationship, are suggested within Barth's radical Christocentrism. In this section God's self-radiating light permeates humans so that "God's glory is the answer evoked by Him of the worship offered Him by his creatures".[79] Barth expresses his own particular sense of what we might legitimately call mutuality through the lens of God's glory as the radiant light of Christ: "He is the radiance of light that reaches all other beings and permeates them",[80] he states. The omnipotent God, the source of light and light in itself, has, as it is a part of who God is "*pro nobis*", the radiance of light.

So Barth's was not in simplistic terms a grounding in a distant God whose "otherness" was without any reciprocal element. Rather there is a powerful sense of how God is not just "*pro nobis*" but always "*cum nobis*" as the radiant light which permeates us. Balthasar is taking this insight of Barth's, suggestive of a more reciprocal understanding of the relationship with Christ, clearly not just restoring the lost "*imago*" in humanity but actually always present in human lives and relationships, and pushing it further to develop a more fully participative sense of this mutual relationship.

It seems evident to me that Balthasar himself certainly seems to regard Barth's radical Christocentrism as open to this kind of development. It suggests a fundamentally Christocentric but also relational model of "*imago Dei*" in which

---

[78] Barth, *CD II/1*, 640–652.
[79] Ibid., 647.
[80] Ibid., 646.

some potential for transformation remains in humanity after the Fall as it awaits the appearance of Christ. Thus Balthasar quotes Barth: "'...the dispute whether man lost his likeness to God by sin finds a self-evident solution. It is not lost'" ("*[D]er Streit darüber, ob sie [die Gottebenbildlichkeit] dem Menschen durch die Sünde verlorengegangen sei, ist ... selbstverständlich dahin zu entscheiden: sie ist ihm nicht verlorengegangen*'").[81] Moreover, this interpretation of Barth is not just here, but is carried through in Balthasar's section on "*imago Dei*" from the perspective of the New Covenant in Christ, in *Theo-Drama II*, where he makes clear that in his Protestant colleague he finds scope for developing a doctrine rooted in Christ as the perfect image yet seeing in humanity some residue of special dignity which awaits its realisation in the appearance and descent of this Christ. Here too he defends the retention of the "*imago*" after the Fall, stating that "[M]ost dogmatic theologians are of the same opinion (including Karl Barth)".[82]

From this discussion of how Balthasar uses Barth's theology to shape his doctrine of "*imago Dei*" into his own, I would like, at this point in my argument, to affirm that I am concluding three basic points. Firstly, on a basic level, Balthasar is right to observe the desire to develop a relational model rooted in Christ. We examined more closely the ambiguities in Barth in Chapter 2 but concluded that this relational strand of his thought was clearly evident. Secondly, it seems to me that Balthasar has seen potential in Barth which could easily be overlooked. As restorer of theological aesthetics in Protestant theology Barth is seen as suggesting and sowing the seeds of a radically Christocentric doctrine which at the same time stresses human dignity and potential for transcendence in a mutual relationship with Christ who calls us to be transformed. Balthasar will develop this in a way which Barth himself, from the perspective of what I take to be his own fundamentally sombre view of the human condition, in my view could not. In Barth the ambiguities remain and he could not himself state the real possibility of communion with God from the human side as creatures not merely restored after the Fall but actively involved in this relationship.

Thirdly, and most importantly, in developing this relational model, Balthasar grounds his fuller account of the doctrine in Christ. On one level this would seem to be a simple point I am making. However, from the perspective of what I have been arguing, and turning to the meaning of radical Christocentrism in this light, I am not merely stating what would seem, independent of a more detailed study, basic and obvious. I am not concluding that Balthasar has simply seen in Barth's thought the centrality of Christ and then developed elements of his own tradition, expressing the dignity of the human being despite the Fall, the possibility of a mutual and transforming relationship with Christ, and at the apex of that relationship the appearance of Christ in beauty and truth whose dramatic descent into the world of humanity gives humanity its meaning. Rather I am taking the

---

[81] Balthasar, *GL VI*, 91, footnote 14, quoting Barth, *CD III/2*, 324 [Balthasar, *HK III/2/2*, 85, footnote 14, quoting Barth, *KD III/2*, 391]. Emphasis Barth's.

[82] Balthasar, *TD II*, 321, footnote 20.

view that Balthasar saw in this complex theologian real creative possibilities and, in working with them, he came to a fuller account of a Christocentric doctrine of "*imago Dei*". Working with Barth's own quest for a more relational doctrine of "*imago Dei*" helped Balthasar to find the scope, precisely through following Barth in grounding the doctrine in Christ's appearance and descent, to develop the other pole in a dynamic of mutuality, the one which speaks of ascent to God, longing for mutual relationship, and recognition of a special character of human dignity.

In short the end result of Balthasar's use of Barth will now be a new relational model which will take fully on board the "descendant" pole in working from the perspective of Christ's appearance and descent, but will, specifically through stating the absolute priority of this, portray a mutual dynamic in which the "*Gestalt*" meets the "*Bild*" in humanity to transform it more closely into him. Through his transformation of Barth's radical Christocentrism into this mutual dynamic of relationship between God and his human image, I am taking the view that Balthasar thus succeeds in marrying in one integrated mutual dynamic the "descendant" and the "ascendant" poles. In so doing, Balthasar expresses a doctrine of "*imago Dei*" which places the incarnation, with Christ as the perfect image, at the centre, but gives to human beings a greater sense of participation in the relationship with him as actors playing out a vocational role as Christ's presence on earth.

To show this more fully, it is necessary to turn to another motif which Balthasar used. Balthasar has incorporated into his own theological picture the dogmatic heart of Barth's contribution, that in the incarnation we discover our identity. Balthasar's theological aesthetics, a motif he saw present also in Barth, helps him to do this, as through this we have a vision of our own glory and a recognition of the human longing for a relationship with Christ who, in his appearing, shows us this. However, theological aesthetics itself leaves the "*imago Dei*" in what Balthasar admits is a state of "suspension".

Balthasar will only succeed in presenting the full picture he has been developing through the medium of drama. As Christ appears on the human stage he does so in dramatic fashion. It is this appearance, and Christ's descent into the world of humanity, which draws humanity back towards their glory in him who appears in perfect glory, thus showing human beings their true identity and meaning as participating actors in this God–human drama. Creation in the "*imago Dei*" means that each human being has a role in this drama, a vocation from Christ intrinsic to him or her. It is in this dramatic way that the marriage of the "descendant" and "ascendant" in one mutual dynamic is realised as Balthasar transforms Barth's dogmatic truth about radical Christocentrism into a dynamic drama of mutual relationship and vocation.

From Dogma to Drama

The medium of drama brings to its fulfilment Balthasar's transformation of Barth's radically Christocentric doctrine of "*imago Dei*" into a narrative which speaks of human identity and vocation in a meaningful way. Balthasar has been drawn towards affirming with Barth a fundamental theological truth, that it is in Christ that we discover what it means to be created in the "*imago Dei*". He has found in Barth's own writing on "*imago Dei*" a certain scope which can develop a new dramatic account of the transformative nature of the relationship God's image has with Christ through which God's image in creation begins to be seen as Christ's presence on earth.

Now Balthasar will develop what he will call a narrative of Theo-drama in which Christ is placed in the midst of the dramatic action calling us, as we perceive his glory, out of our longing for him, and forward to action. We have seen that there are signs of this coming through in Barth but ultimately for him Christ seems not quite extended into the drama of the world's longing for the relationship with him which shows us our glory and our vocation. Balthasar will fill this gap.

We turn back first of all to *Glory of the Lord VI*.[83] In the light of Christ's dramatic appearance in human form, the relationship of human beings with each other is no longer simply *an* earthly image of the mutual relationship between God and humanity which ultimately cannot be realised by us. Rather, through God becoming one of us, the mutual relationship with him is seen in the fullest possible sense as humanity's highest calling and is being played out on the human stage. In the dramatic light of Christ's appearance we are invited onto that stage to live out our vocation in "the incarnate relationship between Christ as Bridegroom and the Church as Bride". Humanity's creation in the "*imago Dei*" understood in terms of the most mutual of all relationships between human beings, that is in marriage, finds its fullest expression in its "eschatological sense". In the drama played out in Christ's passion, death and resurrection, the relationship now "transcends itself to become the virginal and Eucharistic reciprocity between Christ as the Man and the Church as the Woman".[84]

Balthasar is now presenting the view that, as Christ appears in dramatic form on the human stage, he beckons humanity to live out his vocation, in which he will discover his own glory which is a reflection of the glory present in Christ. In doing so he is stressing, with Barth, the pre-eminence of the descendant pole. Christ appears on the human stage. This appearance, however, is so glorious, so beautiful and true, that it evokes response. The answer to Christ's call may not be immediate, and in the Gospels and New Testament in general vocation is portrayed in differing ways. Nevertheless the appearance of Christ in beauty and truth brings forth an active human response which reflects Christ's glory which has been revealed to us. In living out this response humanity discovers how it is now Christ's presence in the world and so called to show Christ in relationship with others.

As for Barth our creation in the "*imago Dei*" is a doctrine which begins, ends and has its very heart in Christ. There is nothing humanity can do to discover its own identity and vocation, to attain glory or draw closer to God, on its own. Our own glory as God's image becomes truly resplendent in the dramatic appearance

---

[83] Balthasar, *GL VI*, 99–100.
[84] Ibid., 100.

of Christ, the "*Gestalt*". But the "*Gestalt*" is not simply the model for living our lives as Christians in relationship with each other. Rather the "*Gestalt*" invites our response as we gaze on its beauty and see in the appearance of Christ our own intrinsic beauty as those who will reveal Christ's glory in the world. In this sense it is the drama of God's becoming man which gives the "*Bild*", the "image", in which we are all made, its full meaning, and its full perfection, as Christ draws us into the transforming mutual relationship with him which reveals to us our vocation as disciples on his mission.

Thus the "descendant" pole, Christ's immersion in the reality of human life, becomes a dramatic reality as Christ draws humanity into the action. This will be expressed in not so much of an "ascent" but a progressive transformation into the glory Christ has come to show us is at the core of our identity and vocation. "Everything", says Balthasar, "is summed up in the final suspension between Adam and Christ: Adam's glory as God's image is truly resplendent and becomes legible as form only with reference to the Christ who is to come".[85] So Balthasar's drama will reflect this. In so doing it will marry the "descendant" and the "ascendant" in Christ's meeting humanity at the deepest core of its longing.

Thus it is in Balthasar's work of *Theo-Drama*, summarised later in the narrative of *Mysterium Paschale*, that we find the fruits of his work. It is in his narrative drama of the Descent into Hell in which Balthasar portrays Christ as the one whom he states earlier on in the first volume of the theological aesthetics will call us to "glory" "out of the profanity of a worldly life to a new 'pneumatic' existence".[86] In Christ God immerses himself in his human image in creation so that his human creation may discover how its vocation is to be his presence. Humanity has turned away from God, and so rejected its true calling to be his image. However, precisely in the descent of Christ into the underworld of this negativity, the beauty and truth of Christ's love for his image, confronts us to the extent that we discover it anew in the transformative relationship we have with him.

Balthasar has found in Barth's insistence on the priority of Christ's descent scope for a drama which expresses Christ's immersion in his image in creation. Christ now takes on all which appears lost, which rejects the call to its true destiny and happiness in him, and transforms it. In "going to the dead" Christ is in "ultimate solidarity"[87] with us. Through the "obedience of a corpse"[88] to "the Father's mission in all its amplitude", "the Son *made man*"[89] is one with humanity in humanity's rejection of its own vocation to glory. "By it [the descent into Hell] Christ takes the existential measure of everything that is sheerly contrary to God"[90] and so, only then, when Balthasar has constructed from Barth this dramatic picture

---

[85] Ibid., 102.
[86] Balthasar, *GL I*, 124.
[87] Balthasar, *MP*, 164.
[88] Ibid., 174. Balthasar attributes the phrase to St Francis of Assisi.
[89] Ibid., 175. Emphasis his.
[90] Ibid., 174.

of God truly immersed in creation, can we define the human condition and vocation in the fullest possible sense in terms of Christ's love for us.

"The Son", he states, "must 'take in with his own eyes what in the realm of creation is imperfect, unformed, chaotic', so as to make it pass over into his own domain as the Redeemer".[91] The drama of God's love for us played out in the appearance and descent of Christ thus grounds our identity and draws us out of our longing for meaning into a relationship of love which will now define us. It is in this encounter that the "*eros*" of our longing for the meaning of our earthly existence as God's image is echoed in the "*agape*" of the perfect image in the Christ who meets us.

In such a way, as Christ makes his dramatic descent to meet us in our longing for him, Balthasar is able to present an understanding of human identity which gives to each human person an active role in God's plan. Yet he roots this understanding of identity not in the quest for human meaning in itself as we look towards our glory but in the descent of Christ to us which he has learned from Barth must be at the heart of the dramatic action. Reflecting on what it means to be made in the "*imago Dei*" thus draws us into the drama of an active relationship with Christ which will place us on his mission. This is as his presence on the earth. It is not in our ascent to him but in Christ's descent to us that we define our vocation as his disciples. In such a way I would argue that, in dramatising Barth's Christocentrism, Balthasar has thus married the "descendant" and the "ascendant" poles in a way which gives a fuller picture of human dignity and vocation but still ensures that the doctrine is not fundamentally about the "ego" but about Christ who calls us forward towards others.

Above all Balthasar's new dramatic picture of human identity is vocational. To be created in God's image is expressed above all in Christ's call to each one of us. As a model of "*imago Dei*" highlighting relationship Balthasar has built on Barth's Christocentrism to develop a picture of human identity in Christ which is much more dynamic, active and participative.

It is a doctrine which above all shows our own solidarity in our real incorporation into the life of Christ who has claimed us. Drawn into Christ's company we live out our call not in isolation as we move closer towards our glory in the beatific vision. It is true that oneness with God is our destiny and our life is an ascent to God. However our centre of gravity is shifted from our own longing for God to Christ who is the perfect image of God. Balthasar's model of "*imago Dei*", through its dramatisation of the radical Christocentrism in Barth, has been able to express this idea in a way which captures this emphasis on Christ and which in turn shows us our special dignity and above all vocation, in portraying how it is in Christ's appearance and descent that we are called as Christ's disciples on mission.

---

[91] Ibid., 175.

Hans Urs von Balthasar's Model of *"Imago Dei"* in Itself

Reorientation in God

We have now completed our study of how Balthasar has interpreted the tradition, and in particular Barth. At the end of the previous chapter, devoted to a study of Barth, I offered a concluding evaluation of his doctrine of *"imago Dei"*. This was in two parts, considering respectively two key motifs which have been running through our study. Firstly, Barth's major contribution had been to reorient the doctrine in God. In emphasising the downward movement from God to humanity this represents what we have been calling the "descendant" pole. Secondly, I concluded that Barth had left ambiguous and underdeveloped the picture of human response to God. Here we were referring to the "ascendant" pole, the movement from us to God.

Now I offer my concluding view of Balthasar's contribution. It is in three parts. The first two echo my evaluation of Barth. Firstly, Balthasar, in particular through the influence Barth had on him, has also succeeded in reorienting the doctrine in God. He has integrated the "descendant" pole into his understanding of the doctrine. Secondly, and through his appreciation of the nuances in Barth in particular, he has found scope to develop that which Barth left ambiguous and underdeveloped, that is a picture of the human response to God. Through such a development Balthasar gives us an understanding of the *"imago Dei"* which is rooted in Christ's call yet also proclaims the special dignity, vocation and mission of each human person. In other words I regard Balthasar as marrying the "descendant" and "ascendant" poles. Thus, in the third part of this evaluation, I turn to this achievement itself and suggest that, through his particular interpretation of Barth and his tradition, Balthasar has also made a contribution which has ecumenical significance. Firstly, however, let us turn to what is the fundamental aspect of Balthasar's contribution, that he has reoriented the doctrine in God.

Like Barth, Balthasar challenges contemporary theology to place Christ at the heart of our understanding of human identity. Subjective understandings of the human being cloud this reality as they cannot express what is most central to him. As the recent International Theological Commission document *Communion and Stewardship: Human Persons Created in the Image of God*[92] points out, this has led to a complete disregard or undermining of the doctrine of *"imago Dei"* itself.

The document points out how twentieth-century thinkers tried to marry subjective criteria, regarding the study of humanity's existence per se, to theology. In so doing twentieth-century theology started to sever the indispensable and permanent link between an objective reference in God and the identity of the human being. Existential theology, "with its stress on the event of the encounter with God, undermined the notion of a stable or permanent relationship with God". Secularisation theology "rejected the notion of an objective reference in

---

[92] *Communion and Stewardship*, no. 18–19.

the world locating man with respect to God". Also, "[in] political theology, with its overriding concern for orthopraxis, the theme of the *imago Dei* receded from view". In response to these developments there is a need to restore to theology a clear understanding of how for the Christian human identity is rooted in God's revelation in Christ.

This is the essence of Balthasar's challenge, and that which he shares with Barth. This is also expressed through recent Church teaching, echoing as it does the restatement of the doctrine of "*imago Dei*" in terms of Christ as the perfect image of God in the Vatican II document *Gaudium et Spes*, which proclaims that, if we are to understand humanity's place in the modern world, we must ground our identity in Christ. "Revealed by God who created man in his image, it is the Son who gives man the answers to his questions about the meaning of life and death."[93] The International Theological Commission document expresses the same aim. "Between the origins of man and his absolute future lies the present existential situation of the human race whose full meaning is ... to be found only in Christ."[94] Thus we may see how Balthasar is united in a contemporary challenge to theology and secularism alike. This aims to turn from a focus on subjective or excessively anthropocentric criteria to restate a firm belief in how an understanding of the human person must be rooted in the objective truth of God's revelation in Christ.

However, it is my view that Balthasar develops this theme further. In reorienting the doctrine of "*imago Dei*" in God he not merely exposes other contemporary methods of thought but also finds a way to express the doctrine in a way which communicates to humanity at a deeply personal level the significance of grounding it in God's revelation. When we introduced Balthasar's understanding of the doctrine in the opening section of this chapter we cited a statement he had made which seemed to capture the essence of his thought for our contemporary situation. In the résumé of his thought, presented at a conference just before his death in 1988, and published posthumously in *Communio*, he outlines this most clearly:

> The Christian response is contained in these two fundamental dogmas: that of the Trinity and that of the Incarnation. In the Trinitarian dogma God is one, true and beautiful because he is essentially Love, and Love supposes the one, the other, and their unity. And if it is necessary to suppose the Other, the Word, the Son, in God, then the otherness of the creation is not a fall, a disgrace, but an image of God, even as it is not God.[95]

Focussing on what we believe about God, rather than starting from the subjective perspective of humanity's desire for him, roots an understanding of the human being's creation in God's image as an encounter with God's love for us revealed in Jesus Christ. We have now seen how Balthasar's doctrine, while rooted like Barth's

---

[93] *GS*, no. 41.
[94] *Communion and Stewardship*, no. 55.
[95] Balthasar, "A Résumé of My Thought", 4.

in his doctrine of the incarnation, is not static. Rather Christ's appearance and descent expresses his total love for us and so draws us into a dramatic encounter with that love. So Balthasar's doctrine grounds a spirituality which does not focus on the human being's potential and deficiency, his achievements, or his fall from grace. Rather the deeper contribution here is to model a spirituality whose reference point is more fundamental – the experience of enduring love.

Thus the reorientation of the doctrine in God presents to the human being this way of love Christ shows us as that quality which is at the heart of human identity. Balthasar has found through his theological method a way to speak of humanity's identity in a powerful way which exposes the limitation of methods of anthropological enquiry which start from the subjectivity of the human person. In such a way he succeeds in not merely showing why it is fundamental to reorient the doctrine of "*imago Dei*" in God but also in presenting a dynamic picture of human identity and vocation in response to God.

The Human Response

At the end of the last chapter, we concluded that Barth, in reorienting the doctrine in God, had made a major contribution which was to influence Balthasar and postconciliar Catholic theology to do the same. When we turned to an evaluation of Barth's understanding of the human response, however, we concluded that in his thought this was ambiguous and underdeveloped. It has been my argument throughout this current chapter that Balthasar filled this gap in Barth's doctrine in providing a fuller picture of the human response. Yet I have been arguing that Balthasar did more than merely fill an empty gap. I have not simply been taking the more classical view that Balthasar borrowed from Barth the idea that Christ should be at the centre of the doctrine, then developed his own more Catholic picture of the response to Christ in his creation.

The outstanding achievement of Balthasar was to see specifically in Barth's grounding the doctrine in the "descendant" pole, that is in Christ's appearance and descent, at least the desire to develop a fuller picture of the immediacy and centrality of Christ to human life. We saw how Balthasar traced this desire in Barth through his reference to contemplation and aesthetics as a new strand in Protestant thought. My conclusion, as already stated, is that Barth himself does leave the element of human response in need of development, and that it is Balthasar who fills this gap. However, it is Balthasar's appreciation of the glimpses of development in Barth's own thinking as his own doctrine's firm grounding in Christ shows signs of reaching to new horizons, which leads Balthasar towards his own integrated picture.

Balthasar's recognition, in particular, of how Barth had shown signs of taking a different course to Luther, was crucial. In ensuring that theological anthropology not focus unnecessarily on our sinfulness or our future hope, but on how Christ and the human being are engaged in some kind of relationship, we can now link Christology to theological anthropology in a more dynamic way. It was this potential for a relational model in Barth, coupled with a different understanding of the Fathers Irenaeus and Augustine, which led Balthasar to communicate the dynamism of vocation as relationship in and with Christ in a way which can speak to contemporary humanity of its response through the central motif of love.

So the motif of Christ's love speaks of human identity in a new powerful way as it seals the dramatic encounter which in turn identifies us as human beings. The infinite love of Christ draws humanity, even in its finitude as sinners sometimes in despair, into a dramatic encounter with the Christ, who in going to the tomb has given himself for us in a total act of love. Drawn to love in return we are placed with him in an intimate encounter as we play out our response as his disciples on his mission called to love others. In such a way Balthasar has integrated into his own picture Barth's understanding of our conformity to Christ as his presence on earth, and so married the "descendant" and "ascendant" poles in a new Christocentric doctrine of "*imago Dei*" which finds full expression in the mutuality of the loving relationship between God and his image in creation.

Balthasar's contribution has been to enable theology to speak more coherently and dynamically about the human being's special dignity, vocation and mission from the perspective of Christ's infinite love for each individual. Each human being, precisely through their being loved by God in Christ, has a special dignity and is also given the responsibility to live out a personal vocation as a disciple on mission. Balthasar thus expresses through the motif of Christ's love how the human being's creation in the "*imago Dei*" involves a responsibility to participate in the project of love in creation. Our creation in the "*imago Dei*" speaks of the infinite love of Christ which draws us to reciprocate by loving him and our fellow humans who represent his image in creation. Balthasar seems to express through this dramatic motif what the International Theological Commission document also highlights as essential to the postconciliar restatement of the doctrine from the perspective of the human being's missionary responsibility as his image in creation, sharing in his work:

> Created in the image of God to share in the communion of Trinitarian love, human beings occupy a unique place in the universe according to the divine plan: they enjoy the privilege of sharing in the divine governance of visible creation. This privilege is granted to them by the Creator who allows the creature made in his image to participate in his work, in his project of love and salvation, indeed in his own lordship over the universe.[96]

Balthasar has given us a dramatic narrative which invites us to appreciate more fully the special dignity and thus responsibility that our personal vocation in Christ entails. Through the Barthian influence in particular, he has found a positive way to speak of the human being in a way which answers fundamental questions of human identity. Human beings are understood in a profound way as possessing a

---

[96] *Communion and Stewardship*, no. 57.

special dignity, a personal vocation, and with that a responsibility for others. The key to answering the existential questions, however, is not strictly anthropological but Christological. It is in the person of Christ that we discover what it is to be human. In particular it is in the experience of Christ's infinite love that we find the human response to God in our search for meaning. So we find at the heart of the appeal of Balthasar's Theo-drama the experience of reciprocal love which speaks most deeply of our creation in God's image.

The Ecumenical Contribution

Before I conclude this chapter I must devote one section to the particularly ecumenical significance of Balthasar's synthesis. My critical appreciation of Balthasar's approach to the doctrine of "*imago Dei*" understands him to have made an especially significant ecumenical contribution. He has married two perspectives which have during the modern period often represented an ecumenical divide. The descendant perspective, emphasising Christ's salvific action, has often been taken to characterise Protestant thought. The ascendant perspective, emphasising the active desire, capacity for and human response to God as we progress towards the beatific vision, has often been taken to characterise Catholic thought. Rather than seeing these two perspectives as mutually exclusive poles, Balthasar has portrayed them as part of one integrated dynamic of the relationship between God and his image in creation, and dramatised this in a way which speaks of the essential interplay of divine and human love.

Balthasar's ecumenical achievement stems from his fresh reading of Barth. It is his deeper appreciation of the nuances in Barth's insight in stressing the turn to the descendant pole which has shaped his own doctrine. Balthasar's chief insight is to recognise in Barth not merely the importance of stressing the descendant pole over the ascendant, that is not merely to find in Barth's thought a return to emphasising the priority of Christ. It is not simply that Balthasar finds in the Barthian tradition Christocentrism and then builds around this a more Catholic theological anthropology stressing humanity's desire for and ascent to God. Rather Balthasar finds in Barth's Christocentrism a move away from what he calls Luther's "exaggerated eschatologism" which "ascribes justification to man only as a hope and not also as a present reality".[97]

Balthasar saw Barth to have understood Luther's "*simul iustus et peccator*" in a creative way which will lead us towards the integration of the two poles in a more intimate understanding of the loving relationship between God and his image in creation. We concluded that Balthasar's full interpretation of Barth and the tradition which formed him was ambiguous and at times questionable. Furthermore Balthasar realises that Barth himself still cannot integrate the descendant and the ascendant because of the limits of his own system. In short we concluded that for Barth our response to Christ as his covenant partners is still

---

[97] Balthasar, *The Theology of Karl Barth*, 370.

passive. Barth has clearly rejected the notion that humanity can ascend to God in the sense that it has the capacity to do so. Nevertheless it is my view that Balthasar has found in Barth's radical Christocentrism a key insight which shapes the focus of his ecumenically integrated understanding of the doctrine.

The fact that we are sinners should not compel us to focus on our condition as sinners in whom the "*imago*" has been lost. Neither should it simply invite us to focus on some future hope of deification and ascent to God. Rather than focussing on humanity's past sin and the loss of the "*imago*", or on humanity's future glory in oneness with God, Balthasar understands Barth to have turned us towards the Christ whose descent places him in the midst of human life in the present. In a profound way Christ's appearance and descent to earth gives human life its ultimate meaning here in the present. For Balthasar this will represent that which is at the very heart of the experience of being human, the experience of being loved. This will then be seen to draw the human person to love in return and so enter into relationship. Balthasar wishes to incorporate the Barthian insight which invites us to appreciate the full power of Christ in human life and integrate it into his synthesis. Thus he will succeed in transferring into his own doctrine what, at least in Barth, the Protestant tradition stemming from Luther wished to communicate about the fuller significance of the descendant pole.

Balthasar, however, also finds that Barth's theology represents an understanding of the move Protestantism itself was making towards integrating what would be associated with the ascendant pole, with the human person's yearning for God. He sees how Barth was moving towards the restoration of aesthetics to Protestant theology. This observation of Balthasar's, however, is part of the same hermeneutical dynamic we have been outlining. This view stemmed precisely from his positive appreciation of the full power of the emphasis Barth and his tradition places on the descendant pole, on the impact of Christ's presence on human life.

Balthasar has taken to heart how Barth's Christocentrism is focusing on the descendant pole so significant in Reformation theology, that is that Christ is our saviour and restores us to his image. Working from this mindset Balthasar now observes how Barth is also beginning to think of Christ as beautiful, and how on this understanding Christ inspires us to enter into a relationship which contemplates the glory he so fully and powerfully has revealed to us. For Balthasar these strands of Barthian thought will be shaped more fully into a drama in which Christ's appearance and descent, precisely because Christ's love is so beautiful, glorious and transforming, will evoke our response, and thus place the descendant and ascendant poles within the mutual interplay between infinite and finite love.

Precisely through the Barthian stress on the descendant pole thus understood, on the power of Christ's presence in human life here and now, the human being is called to ascend to God, to enter into an intimate relationship with him. Because Christ's presence is so powerful Christ and the human being cannot be disengaged but in relationship with one another. Now for Balthasar the Protestant stress on Christ's power to save is integrated and developed into a drama in which humanity also has an active role. Balthasar now places Christ at the centre of his drama, calling us to fulfil our vocation. Our ascent is now properly understood as a response to Christ's love drawing us to participate in his vocation as his disciples on mission. Thus Balthasar has integrated the powerful insights of radical Christocentrism in the Protestant tradition into a fresh understanding of the human person. The descendant and ascendant poles have met in a dynamic encounter played out between Christ and his image in creation.

Conclusion

At the end of the last chapter, on the doctrine in Barth's thought, I concluded that we had arrived at an impasse in the contemporary understanding of the "*imago Dei*". This impasse was between two important aspects of the doctrine, namely its grounding in God, and the idea of the dignity of the human being retaining God's image and seeking union with him. The two aspects represent what I have been calling the two poles, the descendant focussing on God's action in human life, and the ascendant, focussing on our orientation towards God. Now we have completed our examination of Balthasar's understanding of the doctrine and placed it in the context of his own interpretation of the tradition and in particular against its Barthian background. We have now seen how in Balthasar's thought the gulf separating these two aspects of a contemporary understanding of "*imago Dei*" has begun to recede as he has married these two in one integrated dynamic. Thus Balthasar represents an important achievement in the twentieth-century development of the doctrine.

Barth had himself made a considerable contribution. He had insisted that the doctrine should be retained but rather than focus on human potential reflection on our creation in God's image should turn us towards God who gave himself for us in Christ. Barth had thus changed the point of reference for a restatement of the doctrine in the twentieth century. He had helped to transfer the centre of gravity from humanity to God. As such he had made a lasting contribution to the development of the doctrine. We have now seen how Balthasar has found great potential in this movement in Barth for a contemporary restatement of the doctrine.

Balthasar has thus managed to use and shape Barth's insights in particular to remodel the doctrine in such a way that a foundation in Christ's love for humanity flowers into a dynamic understanding of each human person's dignity, vocation and mission. I closed the last chapter with a quote from Balthasar which amounted to a question he posed of himself regarding his reception of Barth's theology. "Must we not establish more than just the *factum brutum* of God's glory in his revelation? Must not rather the question be raised: 'To what extent is the light of God's self-revelation really light, and therefore enlightening?'"[98] Balthasar had posed himself a challenge, to look beyond the Christological foundations of Barth's theology to

---

[98] Balthasar, *GL I*, 53, quoting Barth, *CD II/1*, 732ff.

find a way in which he could develop the other pole which found in humanity the presence of Christ on his mission in the world. In short my conclusion at this point is that Balthasar has found this way.

This chapter, however, arrives at this conclusion, aware of ambiguities we encountered in our study of the development of Balthasar's thinking. It is evident that Balthasar's own interpretation of Barth does not always seem to match Barth's own views. We raised questions here. At times it seemed that Balthasar was placing a Catholic construct on Barth's Protestant system. Also, Balthasar is not merely influenced by Barth but by sources in the tradition whom he interpreted in a different way to Barth. He understood Augustine very differently, focussing on the Latin Father's more relational and teleological strands of thought rather than those which stressed humanity's inability to be saved. In the tradition we saw that Barth tended to agree with a Lutheran interpretation of Augustine emphasising justification by faith. Balthasar emphasised Augustine's idea of the human way back to God and our eventual "*deificatio*". Furthermore we saw how Irenaeus also was a particularly significant influence on Balthasar, leading him to his picture of human capacity for God which was, whilst rooted in Christ's "*recapitulatio*", much more teleological, participative and relational.

Yet as we proceeded to trace the development of Balthasar's doctrine through his particular reading of Barth, we found that he had appreciated nuances in his thought which suggested possibilities which pushed him in the particular direction he chose to go. His appreciation of Barth's efforts to express a more relational understanding of "*imago Dei*" rooted in radical Christocentrism leads him to develop this in a way which he realises Barth, given the limits of his own theological system, would not. For Balthasar Barth represents a new movement in Protestant theology from which we can glean much. It is a movement which refocuses Lutheran Christocentrism on Christ's presence in human life and searches for a new Christocentric theological aesthetic expressing human identity in terms of relationship. Through this, and in a powerful way through the medium of drama, Balthasar finds a way to place Christ's appearance, the "*Gestalt*", and his image in creation, the "*Bild*", in one dramatic encounter expressed in the dynamic of love.

Balthasar's understanding of the doctrine thus represents a significant contribution as it speaks in a new powerful way of human identity in terms of dignity, vocation and mission. It shows the enduring importance of the doctrine. This is echoed in the postconciliar interest in restating the doctrine in a way which focuses clearly on Christ yet speaks of the human vocation in an exalted way. Balthasar's work also represents a significant ecumenical contribution, as his work broke through the two poles, descendant and ascendant, often perceived in the tradition as highlighting a divide between Catholic and Protestant thought. Thus I would claim that Balthasar shows us a way forward for the contemporary development of the doctrine.

This way forward will be examined in the closing chapter. Firstly, it is necessary to place both Barth and Balthasar directly in the context of contemporary theology, to show how the development of the doctrine I have been tracing in these two seminal thinkers raises important questions about future directions in the understanding of "*imago Dei*" now at the start of the twenty-first century. At this time we find not just renewed interest in the doctrine in Catholic theology, as expressed notably in the International Theological Commission document we have been studying, but also in Protestant theology.

So we now turn to the last of the three writers in our study, the notable Protestant theologian, Jürgen Moltmann, as it is in his work that we find similar questions and directions to those we have found in Barth and Balthasar. Moltmann's desire to restate the doctrine, while it is not always so explicit, is still evident. Yet his thinking moves in a different direction to Balthasar's, and paradoxically for him as a Protestant theologian, it will be his lack of attention to the lessons learnt from Barth's radical Christocentrism, which will show at one and the same time, the challenges a contemporary statement of the doctrine present, and the problems inherent in the particular direction in which he wishes to take it.

Chapter 4
Jürgen Moltmann

Understanding of "*Imago Dei*": Themes and New Directions

In the opening chapter we considered some of the central themes in Moltmann's theology, and how they placed him vis-à-vis Barth and Balthasar. In particular we noted how, in a similar way to Barth and Balthasar, Moltmann has sought to place Christ at the centre of his thought. Like them he sets out to develop a narrative of Christ's intimate relationship with humanity. Above all he intends that this relationship with Christ will have a transforming effect on his readers. It is this intimate relationship with Christ which can give people of today hope and a sense of human dignity. "Theological concepts", he says, "are engaged in a process of movement, and which call forth practical movement and change".[1]

So he develops a narrative of God's saving power in human life encapsulated in the person of the crucified and risen Christ. In doing this, like Barth and Balthasar before him, he has placed the primary emphasis on Christ rather than on ourselves. Like them his anthropology is Christocentric. The saving power of God in the person of Christ is fundamental in a contemporary understanding of the human being as God's image on earth. In stressing Christ's coming to earth, his death and resurrection, as our only hope, rather than our own natural desire for God, Moltmann may be said to emphasise the descendant rather than the ascendant pole.

However, whilst Moltmann's Christocentrism is fundamental to his understanding of the doctrine, this is tied to an important strand in his thinking which corresponds to the other pole, that we have termed the ascendant. His desire to develop a theology which expresses the closeness of our relationship with God, and above all to show how this gives human beings hope amid suffering, leads him in new directions. He will make a fresh attempt to develop a relational model of "*imago Dei*" which, in a new way especially for a Protestant theologian, will try to express Christian hope through an understanding of the human capacity for a relationship with God. Moltmann's understanding of "*imago Dei*" is still rooted in God's coming to humanity first. "Likeness to God", he states, "means God's relationship to human beings first of all, and only then, and as a consequence of that, the human being's relationship to God" ("*Gottebenbildlichkeit bezeichnet zuerst das* Menschenverhältnis Gottes *und erst dann und daraufhin das* Gottesverhältnis

---

[1] Jürgen Moltmann, *A Theology of Hope: on the Ground and the Implications of a Christian Eschatology* (New York and Evanston: Harper & Row, 1967), 36.

des Menschen").[2] However, in a profound way, Moltmann will also focus on the human condition in itself in order to proclaim the dignity of God's presence inherent in creation.

We saw how Barth had shown signs of wanting to develop a notion of human desire for God but ultimately had rejected strongly any suggestion of the human being's natural capacity for transcendence. Moltmann, however, does not appear to be confined by Barth's way of thinking. Rather he intends to examine, from the perspective of the creation as a whole, how human dignity is so closely intertwined with the revelation of God that humanity may be said to represent God's presence on the earth. This signals a new departure in its interest in creation as a powerful presence of God in itself. It will be part of a larger theme which begins a new chapter in the history of the doctrine of "*imago Dei*". Moltmann's understanding of the human person's divine dignity and intimate relationship with God is part of his broader attempt to portray God and his creation as much more closely interconnected than had been stressed before in Protestant theology. Turning to creation in itself, Moltmann sees God's presence above all in the environment and, as part of this but in a way par excellence, in human beings. Thus Moltmann approaches the doctrine from a different angle to that of Barth and Balthasar before him. His development of a relational model of "*imago Dei*" not merely brings the ascendant pole into play within a thoroughly Christocentric doctrine.

Rather his place in our study of the doctrine takes on special significance on account of how he develops this strand in his thinking. From the perspective of our study of Barth and Balthasar we can detect similar aims. Like them, in their different ways, he is trying to express the human need of God. Like Balthasar he finds himself trying to portray humanity in more positive light, emphasising not the Fall and sin, but salvation and human dignity. We have seen how Barth showed signs of wanting to incorporate a fuller picture of capacity for God into his model of "*imago Dei*" but was restricted by his sombre view of the human condition. Then we saw how Balthasar had been able to develop themes implicit in Barth to speak of human beings' infinite possibility of communion with the divine through the relationship they have with Christ.

Moltmann is part of this movement which tries to reclaim an understanding of the dignity of the human person through a more relational doctrine of "*imago Dei*". He will be unequivocal about God's presence in humanity. Yet, because it is this fundamental belief in God's presence within creation which informs his theology, he will develop the doctrine in a different way to his predecessors. Now the ascendant pole, emphasising not so much Christ's saving work, but the human capacity to reflect Christ's image itself, comes to the fore in Protestant theology. This places Moltmann at the apex of this movement to recover for contemporary theology a belief in the power of God within his creation. He himself seems to

---

[2] Jürgen Moltmann, *God in Creation: an Ecological Doctrine of Creation* (London: S.C.M. Press, 1985), 220 [Moltmann, *Gott in der Schöpfung: ökologische Schöpfungslehre* (Munich: Chr. Kaiser Verlag, 1985), 226. Emphasis his].

see this as a new direction for theology which responds to the needs of a different culture to that of the earlier generation.

It is in his seminal work *God in Creation* that he presents this new model within an overall doctrine of the created order. In his preface to the book Moltmann states that he desires to match what he calls "[t]he salutary 'christological concentration' in Protestant theology" with "an extension of theology's horizon to cosmic breadth, so that it takes in the whole of God's creation" (*"Der heilsamen 'christologischen Konzentration' in der evangelischen Theologie damals muß heute die kosmische Horizonterweiterung der Theologie auf die ganze Schöpfung Gottes entsprechen"*).[3] Here he lays out in principle a theological manifesto. Moltmann's project is not simply to show the impact of Christ on human life. His Christocentrism will be tinged with a new perspective. His aim is above all to show God's presence within creation, in both human life and in our environment. A restatement of the doctrine of "*imago Dei*" is thus necessary to see in human life itself the presence of God.

As he sees it this theme is now paramount in a way that it was not for the earlier generation. In German Protestant theology in particular, according to Moltmann, there has been in the past a dichotomy between what he terms "*natürliche Theologie*", "natural theology", and "*Offenbarungstheologie*", "revealed theology". It was "natural theology" ("*natürliche Theologie*"), Moltmann claims,

> which thought that God's order could be discovered in the natural conditions of nation and race, and that his will could be seen in the event of Hitler's seizure of power (*die Gottes Ordnung aus der natürlichen Gegebenheiten von Volk und Rasse Gottes Willen aus der Geschichte der Machtergreifung Hitlers erkennen zu können meint*).[4]

In other words he seems to be making a link between the term "natural theology" and the Nazi belief that, courtesy of their very nature as a people, the Aryans had a God-given right to power. It seems here that Moltmann is suggesting that the belief in humanity's natural capacity for God could be twisted to refer to one particular race of people even to the extent of the abuse of power as witnessed in the Nazi regime. It must be ventured that the link Moltmann makes between "natural theology" and the Nazi regime is rather convoluted and particular. He has linked "natural theology", the belief that humanity has natural capacity for God, to a movement in history proclaiming the supremacy of one part of the human race. However, for him it was this fear of Nazi ideology which, in the German theological climate of the first half of the twentieth century, led to the fear of "natural theology", that it puts so much store in God's will in creation as to make a god of humanity itself.

For Moltmann this fear was understandable during the Nazi era, and seems, according to his account, to have played a significant part in the German Protestant

---

[3] Ibid., xii [Moltmann, *Gott in der Schöpfung*, 12].
[4] Ibid., xii [Moltmann, *Gott in der Schöpfung*, 11].

predilection for what he terms "'revealed theology'", which hears and holds fast to Jesus Christ as "'the one Word of God'".[5] Moltmann is referring here to the Barmen Theological Declaration of 1934 which proclaimed the thesis that Jesus Christ as "'the one Word of God'" placed "revealed theology" over against "natural theology". His overriding point here is that, the Nazi era now over, the fear of the consequences of "natural theology" has now given way to new contemporary concerns. Whilst modern fears and horizons in no way undermine or supersede the perceived need to proclaim a "revealed theology", we must nevertheless reappraise how we present Christian theology in order to meet these contemporary challenges. Thus, it seems to me, Moltmann realises something important. He sees how we cannot any more shy away from a narrative which expresses humanity's ability to mirror God. In fact, on the contrary, today's concerns require us to speak of this not merely from the perspective of God, vertically, but also, horizontally, from the perspective of humanity's place in the whole of creation through which we are called to find God's presence on the earth.

"Faced as we are with the progressive industrial exploitation of nature and its irreparable destruction", asks Moltmann, "what does it mean to say that we believe in God the Creator, and in this world as his creation?"[6] Our cultural points of reference have shifted in a way that requires us to revise our criteria for developing theological models. The world's "crisis" for him is not the same as it was for the generation of Karl Barth. The problem today is not mere "knowledge of God" ("*Erkenntnis Gottes*"). Rather it is "the nihilism practiced in our dealings with nature" ("*der praktizierte Nihilismus im Umgang mit der Natur*").[7] The challenge today is thus not so much to restate God's descent into the world in Christ. The concerns of Barth, and then Balthasar in developing Barthian themes, are not as valid as they were. Rather we need a positive account of our ascent. Moltmann wants to bring us to appreciate the goodness of the creation as a dimension in itself. Then we will be able to see how human beings made in his image reflect the presence of God on earth as part of the ecological picture as a whole.

On the one hand this seems to be a very valuable new horizon for the doctrine of the "*imago Dei*". Moltmann's theology speaks to us of the need to examine our consciences about how we treat the environment. It is a timely reminder of how, in damaging the ozone layer, humanity is damaging God's good creation, and, conversely how, the more we respect the environment in which we live, the more we allow God's presence to shine forth. Such is a positive reading of Moltmann's basic contribution we have been outlining. It will be my view, however, that this new dimension takes over to the extent that, ultimately, it will cloud the distinction necessary between the God revealed in Christ and his human creation in need of salvation from sin. Moltmann's renewed emphasis on the goodness of God's creation will in our judgment endanger the emphasis necessary on God's saving

---

[5] Ibid., xi.

[6] Ibid., xi.

[7] Ibid., xi [Moltmann, *Gott in der Schöpfung*, 11].

action in Christ. This said, let us be clear what Moltmann himself would seem to believe. For him the recapturing of God's presence in creation does not in any way suggest that we can dispense with or dilute a clear Christocentric approach to theology.

His narrative theology of the cross will, on a fundamental level, show Christ's solidarity with the human race as the revelation of God. Moltmann's point is not exactly to make human beings rather than God the subject. This is clear from the following passage, which we might argue, at first sight, amounts to a definition of his approach to the doctrine. Here we might conclude that Moltmann is merely stating the fundamental points in a more positive relational doctrine as Barth and Balthasar had tried to. God is truly present in his image, and through that human beings have a certain responsibility for others.

> The God who creates for himself his image on earth finds his correspondence in that image. So human likeness to God consists in the fact that human beings, for their part, correspond to God. The God who allows his glory to light up his image on earth and to shine forth from that image, is reflected in human beings as in a mirror ... The God who allows himself to be represented on earth by his image also appears in that image; and the image becomes an indirect revelation of his divine Being in earthly form. So as God's image and appearance on earth, human beings are involved in three fundamental relationships: they rule over other earthly creatures as God's *representatives* ("*Stellvertreter*") and in his name; they are God's *counterpart* ("*Gegenüber*") on earth, the counterpart to whom he wants to talk, and who is intended to respond to him; and they are the *appearance* ("*Erscheinung*") of God's splendour, and his glory on earth.[8]

However, it will be my view that his stated preference for responding to contemporary culture in turning to nature first, will show an important and distinctive strand in the development of his relational doctrine of "*imago Dei*". This is not so immediately clear in this passage in *God in Creation*, but because it undergirds his theological mission as a whole, it will become so later in his other works. At first sight we might see Moltmann as the fulfilment of the theological movement begun in Barth but revised in Balthasar. Moltmann has recognised that a more hopeful account of creation reveals Christ's presence. Yet in the interpretation of this insight lies the more subtle distinction I am making between his approach to the doctrine and that of Balthasar.

For Balthasar it is also true that a more positive account of creation reveals God's presence – avoiding the sombre view of humanity present in Barth and aspects of the Augustinian tradition he succeeds in presenting this. However Balthasar also follows the Barthian insistence that we start from the Word of God revealed in Christ. So his fundamental aim will be not only to state in a more positive way the goodness of creation which reveals God's presence, but first and foremost to

---

[8] Ibid., 220–21 [Moltmann, *Gott in der Schöpfung*, 226–7].

state who God is as revealed in Christ as it is above all he who reveals himself in the goodness of creation in each human being. Moltmann sees in God's plan a relationship between God and his human creation which suggests that we may look to humanity first and see the presence of God dwelling there. As a model of "*imago Dei*", therefore, I would claim that Moltmann is fundamentally anthropocentric in stressing from the outset the human capacity to reflect God. This becomes clearer when we turn to what will be an important theme in the development of this new model of "*imago Dei*", namely the Trinitarian dimension.

Moltmann will present a narrative of Christ's transforming relationship through his crucifixion and resurrection. This is important. Yet for his understanding of the human person there is another aspect of the Trinitarian dimension which is equally important. Moltmann will emphasise in a new way the role of the Holy Spirit within the Trinity, and it is more specifically the presence of the Holy Spirit, rather than as for Barth and Balthasar Christ, which constitutes the presence of God in all created beings. Thus, unlike Barth and Balthasar, Moltmann is not just concerned with portraying the intimate relationship humanity has with God within a Christocentric doctrine of "*imago Dei*". Rather he turns to the presence of the Spirit present in creation to develop a new paradigm of the God–world relationship.

Incorporating the Spirit, he regards his model as more fully Trinitarian and so more fully relational through its reflection of the relationships between the persons of the Trinity. Through this he is able to express more fully how God is so closely intertwined with creation that he is *in* his created order. "If we understand the Creator, his creation, and the goal of creation in a trinitarian sense", he says, "then the Creator, through his Spirit, *dwells in* ('*wohnt … ein*') his creation as a whole, and in every individual created being, by virtue of his Spirit holding them together and keeping them in life".[9]

This new way of looking at the doctrine is influenced by another different perspective. Moltmann is open to draw on theological sources from both East and West, from Protestant, Catholic and Orthodox authors. Attempting, as had Balthasar, to cut through perceived ecumenical distinctions, he is not confined, as Barth had been, by the system of what he has termed "revealed theology", with its overly exclusive Christological concentration. In order to develop a theology expressing more fully the intimate relationship between God and the world he finds himself open to ways of portraying this, especially in Orthodox theology, which point first of all to humanity's capacity and goal to find and reflect God.

The theologies of Irenaeus and Gregory of Nazianzus have a significant place, as they speak of humanity's natural ability to reach and reflect God. He is led to appreciate and model the theology of the Eastern Fathers as one which, as Balthasar also has seen, finds in human nature the presence of God. It leads him towards such a positive doctrine of human nature which is present also in Balthasar but which, through his particular understanding of Augustine, eluded

---

[9] Ibid., xii [Moltmann, *Gott in der Schöpfung*, 12].

Barth. Moltmann clearly realises this. "Orthodox theology", claims Moltmann, "has preserved a creation wisdom which was pushed aside and lost in the West ... It is the earliest traditions of Christian theology which frequently offer the most pregnant ideas for the revolution in our attitude to nature which is so vitally necessary today".[10]

However, as we now turn to study these particular influences in more depth, we will see how Moltmann integrates them into his doctrine in a different way to Balthasar. As such we will see also how this highlights some of the key problems inherent in Moltmann's model. Whilst we will find that he goes some way to fulfilling his aim of developing a more intimate picture of the God–human relationship, which can speak to contemporary humanity of hope and transformation, we will also discover that God and God's presence in the world become so closely intertwined that we lose sight of the otherness of God. Because Moltmann has moved away from the "revealed theology" of Karl Barth, to stress the closeness of God within creation, he has left insufficient room for a concept of God's transcendence.

Rather, as we shall go on to see, Moltmann is so concerned to avoid all talk of God as sovereign and humanity as subordinate that, in his later work *The Spirit of Life*,[11] he defines the presence of God above all as friendship. Friendship, he seems to believe, is a more appropriately intimate way to define God's presence in creation, than the more traditional ones stressing Lordship over creation. Thus Moltmann's God seems at times almost to be reduced to something of a benign force within the cosmos. "Friendship is simply something we have to discover", he states at one point. "It is 'the sympathy of the world' – the gentle power of attraction and participation, which holds together everybody and everything that lives. It is a vulnerable atmosphere of life."[12]

Furthermore, as we trace Moltmann's narrative of God's dealings with the world, and in particular his Trinitarian narrative of the crucified God, we will see that his picture of the human being has moved away from a traditional Christian anthropology giving an adequate account of sin and the Fall. In emphasising humanity's dignity reflecting the indwelling divine spirit, he stresses salvation rather than sin, but with the negative aspect in humanity as not our turning away from God but our suffering, in which we become one with God who suffers with the world on the cross. Thus we will find that Moltmann's God is so closely involved in human experience that there is insufficient room to express the human need of a saviour.

In this way the relationship between the world and God becomes so blurred that humanity affects God. Hence I will argue that the fundamentally different

---

[10] Ibid., xii.

[11] Moltmann, *The Spirit of Life: a Universal Affirmation* (Minneapolis: Fortress Press, 1993) [Moltmann, *Der Geist des Lebens: Eine ganzheitliche Pneumotalogie* (Munich: Kaiser Verlag, 1991)].

[12] Ibid., 255.

starting point in creation which Moltmann has taken in the final analysis came back on itself and disabled him from starting from an adequate doctrine of God. As such we see in closer relief the value of Balthasar's approach, and of the lessons he learned in Barth's radical Christocentrism. We shall thus see how Balthasar may be seen in contrast to Moltmann to have developed a model of human dignity in a mutual relationship with God but how, as it is more firmly rooted in Christ, it still speaks of God's presence in creation without confusing it with the Creator.

Now, against the background of these central themes in his thought, we must consider how Moltmann proceeded in his aim to portray a more fully intimate relational model of *"imago Dei"*. What more precisely does Moltmann mean by the relationship between God and his creation? Addressing this question will shed further light on Moltmann's ideological aims and also on the problems inherent in his approach. To address this question we must turn to the work which followed *God in Creation*, which sets out his use of the doctrine of the Trinity within his overall theological project, namely *The Trinity and the Kingdom of God*.

The Quest for a Relational Model

Moltmann believes strongly that the key to understanding humanity's relationship with God lies first in a revision of the doctrine of the Trinity. In the history of theology he claims that a monarchical understanding of the Trinity prevalent in the tradition has adversely affected our portrayal of the relationship between God and his creation. Our understanding of the relationship God has with his human creation has thus been expressed in terms of God's divine rule and humanity's abject servitude. If we are to succeed in portraying the human being's intimate relationship with the Creator and God's presence in his human creation, we must reverse this trend. A new paradigm of Trinity is required which defines the Trinity not in terms of a single divine ruler but in terms of the divine life of the three persons Father, Son and Holy Spirit, present in the earthly Kingdom.[13]

Moltmann believes that Barth had interpreted the Trinity in an unhelpful way which prevented theology from a freer portrayal of God's presence within the creation. "Is the doctrine of the Trinity the appropriate interpretation of the one divine lordship (Barth's view)", he asks, "or does the history of the kingdom of God reveal the divine life of the Father, the Son and the Spirit?"[14] Our own study of Barth concluded that he had emphasised the Lordship of God in history, expressed in particular in the Son's incarnation, saving death and resurrection. For Barth this is a once-and-for-all event which restores humanity to oneness with God as his image in the earthly Kingdom. This saving action, in which God reveals himself

---

[13] Moltmann, *The Trinity and the Kingdom of God: the Doctrine of God* (London: S.C.M. Press, 1981), 191 [Moltmann, *Trinität und Reich Gottes: zur Gotteslehre* (München: Kaiser Verlag, 1980)].

[14] Ibid., 191.

fully as Father, Son and Holy Spirit, has a cosmic effect on creation as the "*imago Dei*" is thus restored, but it is construed outside of time and space.

To me Moltmann's instinct appears right. Barth had left insufficient space for portraying the saving presence of God within history. Barth tries but, precisely because his doctrine of "*imago Dei*" is tied to a static understanding of revelation, he stops far short of giving an adequate account of the mutual relationship between God and humanity. In such a way we can see the wisdom in trying to develop a model of the Trinity which shows God not outside of creation but always in reciprocal relationship with it. It was an aim also, as we have seen, of Balthasar, who, through a narrative based on aesthetics and drama, bridged a gap between the God of revelation and the response of his image on earth. For Balthasar this would be expressed in the "nontime" of Christ's descent into the underworld. Moltmann, however, intends to place the narrative of God's saving presence within history. "At the centre of Christian theology", he argues:

> stands the eternal history which the triune God expresses in himself. Every narrative needs *time*. For the narrative in which he praises the triune God, man needs his time too (*Im Zentrum der christlichen Theologie steht die ewige Geschichte, die der dreieinige Gott in sich selbst erfährt. Jede Erzählung braucht Zeit. Für die rühmende Erzählung des dreieinigen Gottes braucht der Mensch seine Zeit*).[15]

In order to do this Moltmann finds himself making a more far-reaching claim than Balthasar, which will eventually take him in a different and dangerous direction. He believes that Barth has construed the Trinity not simply too much from the perspective of the Trinity's immanence, so we would need to emphasise God's presence in the economy. Rather Moltmann believes that, deep within the tradition, the doctrine of the Trinity's undivided unity is closely linked to the notion of God's Lordship and humanity's subjection. As Moltmann sees it, in order to present a narrative expressing the true intimacy of the relationship between God and his image on earth, we need to broaden our understanding of the Trinity to stress far more the relationship between the three persons. The more we express this model of relationship the more we move away from what he regards as a monotheism prevalent within the tradition which amounts to a monarchical and so unequal view of the God–human relationship, in which human beings are slaves to a dominant Lord of history.

Moltmann's quest for a relational model of "*imago Dei*" thus takes us into new theological territory which relies on what he himself terms a new social model of Trinity. It is true that in much of the tradition the relationship between the persons of the Trinity has been an important theme which has served to form a perspective on the doctrine of the Trinity stressing God as relational. Barth's and Balthasar's theological narrative is keen to continue this. Moltmann, therefore, is developing

---

[15] Ibid., 190 [Moltmann, *Trinität und Reich Gottes*, 206]. Emphasis his.

the theme of the relationship between the three persons. However, it seems that he himself believes that, in following a social model, he is also breaking with a significant aspect of the tradition. Above all he believes that he is abandoning a model of God's presence in the world as monarchical. The doctrine of the Trinity, he claims, "must ... also overcome this monarchism, which legitimates dependency, helplessness and servitude". Instead it must be developed "as the true theological doctrine of freedom".[16] It must not point towards a monotheistic God who is "'the Lord of the world'". Rather there is a clear distinction for Moltmann between this model showing how it is "the monarchy of a ruler that corresponds to the triune God" and that which sees in the persons of the Trinity "the community of men and women, without privileges and without subjugation" ("*die Gemeinschaft von Menschen ohne Privilegien und Unterwerfungen*").[17]

For Moltmann an appropriately relational understanding of the doctrine of "*imago Dei*" rests on a rejection of the understanding of God as monarchical Lord of history and a revival of the notion of God as a community of persons. This emphasis on "*perichoresis*" between the persons of the Trinity has been lost in Western theology. We need to reclaim the model of Trinity as "family" favoured in Eastern theology. The mutual relationship between persons suggests to us the more relational understanding of the human being's creation in the "*imago Dei*" for which we are searching. The analogy of the Trinity to a family of persons is "not just arbitrary", argues Moltmann. Rather it is the key to unlock a truly social understanding of the human person's creation in God's image. The "Triunity" of persons, rather than the monotheistic monarchism favoured by Western theology:

> means ... that people are made in the image of God. But the divine image is not the individual; it is person with person ... the image of God must not merely be sought for in human individuality; we must look for it with equal earnestness in human sociality.[18]

In his later work concentrating specifically on human identity, *The Spirit of Life*, Moltmann clarifies how far-reaching his claim is for an understanding of "*imago Dei*". In this work he lays out in more detail the view that it is the tradition's consistent emphasis on monotheism that has prevented theology from expressing a balanced understanding of the human person. In its place we need a new social model which expresses how humanity's creation in God's image challenges the human person to be responsible for others. Such an understanding of the relationship between the persons of the Trinity means that to reflect God's presence on earth is to discover one's personhood not in mastery or subjugation but in relationship with others.

---

[16] Moltmann, *The Trinity and the Kingdom of God*, 192.
[17] Ibid., 198 [Moltmann, *Trinität und Reich Gottes*, 215].
[18] Ibid., 199.

Thus Moltmann's recasting the doctrine of *"imago Dei"* around a social doctrine of God is the necessary foundation for his understanding of the human person's uniqueness, dignity and capacity for God as an individual. Humanity's distinctive individuality, with the Spirit of God residing in us, is discovered above all in our relationship with others. According to Moltmann in our postmodern society the dignity of the individual must be expressed in these terms rather than those reflecting a monarchical view of our relationship with God which stems from such a doctrine of the Trinity.

At first sight this seems a very positive way of approaching the doctrine, especially when considered against the background of contemporary needs and the movement to restate the doctrine of which Moltmann's project is a part. For him the doctrine of *"imago Dei"*, if construed against this background and in these terms, is theologically fundamental in preserving a sense of the dignity of the human individual from total abolition in our contemporary relativistic, industrial and mechanistic postmodern society. "It is understandable", he says, "that – following the modern age, with its atomization of nature and its subjectivization of human beings – people should now seek for the 'New Age' of a cosmic feeling of community and a 'self' rich in relation. But this 'new age' would become a velvet-gloved conspiracy", he argues, "for the abolition of the human being if the inward experiences of human autonomy and personal initiative were to be condemned".[19] The doctrine of the *"imago Dei"*, if construed in the context of a God who calls us to relationship, gives us an appropriate sense of the dignity of each individual human person. It is an altruistic Christian identity which, whilst recognising the uniqueness of each human being, looks outwards towards the community rather than simply inwards towards the self's autonomy.

We should express our own special individual dignity as God's image, in relationship, with God and, because God himself is a community of persons, with others. "People experience themselves", says Moltmann, "in the relationships of society, and society is made up of independent people".[20] It is the Spirit of life present in each human individual which expresses God's presence. This presence is the essence of social relationship between persons, that is above all the experience of love. "The Spirit of life is the Spirit of love. Love unites what is separated, and separates what is united, and in this rhythm gives life its movement."[21]

In several important ways the direction in which Moltmann is going is part of a whole twentieth-century theological movement which has distinct advantages. It will for him ultimately lead to a narrative theology of salvation which will place much more emphasis on the theological understanding of the human person as relational. It will stress the community of humanity, and human responsibility to be his earthly image. Moving away from an emphasis on "ego" as solely individual, it will try to express the human person's divine dignity within the community of

---

[19] Ibid., 254.
[20] Ibid., 254.
[21] Ibid., 254.

persons in the earthly Kingdom. He will thus be able to communicate what Barth and Balthasar also intended, that the doctrine of "*imago Dei*" expresses the mutual relationship of love between God and humanity, which is also expressed in the love we have as a community of persons on the earth. When humanity reflects God's presence it reflects love. Moltmann's new social model of the Trinity makes this clear.[22] "What he *is* is not almighty power", he states; "what he *is* is love" ("*Er ist aber nicht Allmacht. Er ist Liebe*").

Yet my concern here is to show how Moltmann's good intentions can also lead to difficulties. In particular it is my view that the model of relationship Moltmann is presenting, because it is rooted in a view that we must rewrite the doctrine of the Trinity in a social way, raises difficulties in terms of his understanding of the human being's fundamental relationship with God himself. Barth and Balthasar's models, in their different ways and with different degrees of success, insisted on a clear and fundamental understanding of the human being's dignity not simply as reflecting God to the world through his presence within ourselves. Rather for Barth and Balthasar we also turn to a God outside of ourselves. For Moltmann, however, this kind of emphasis on the individual's relationship with God per se would seem to see God as Lord of history and ourselves as subjects. In short it cuts across his whole project of seeing God's presence *within* creation rather than outside of it as his intention is to move away from the notion of God as a distant monarch in control of his subjects to portray our relationship with God in terms of the equality of persons.

Moltmann's desire to restore to theology a doctrine of "*imago Dei*", in trying to develop a theology of human dignity mirroring God's presence within a community of persons in the earthly Kingdom, leaves insufficient room for the important notion of relating to God not simply as present in all creation but also beyond it. Unlike Balthasar, Moltmann has not appreciated Barth's insistence on theocentrism and Christocentrism, and so will exclude a sufficient notion of the otherness of God. For Moltmann postmodern society no longer needs to restate these preoccupations of the Nazi and post-Nazi era in Europe. What is more important to him is showing God's life-giving Spirit present within creation.

He is surely right that society is searching for a sense of identity as members of the human race who are connected to creation as a whole, and finding a special dignity in their role of forming loving community. But his objection to all forms of hierarchy in understanding the human person leads to an insufficient notion of the human relationship with a God who is saviour. We must now ask of Moltmann who is the God who is present within us as we form the social relationships of our world, with whom, in this everyday social way, we and the world are involved in this intimate mutual relationship. Moltmann's conclusion will turn out to be unsatisfactory. Ultimately for him we find that the social God present in the midst of our world is no more for us than a "friend", and, as we shall see more as we turn

---

[22] Moltmann, *The Trinity and the Kingdom of God*, 197 [Moltmann, *Trinität und Reich Gottes*, 215]. Emphasis his.

to Moltmann's narrative of salvation, this leaves a serious gap in our understanding of our own human condition and dignity in need of a saviour.

For Moltmann friendship is a common concept of the relationship between persons and so of the human being's identity vis-à-vis God. In his work *Spirit of Life* he extols friendship above all other forms of inter-personal communication. Seeing in contemporary culture the exploitation which comes from relationships perceived as unequal, be they between masters and subjects in the workplace, between men and women, or in political society, he finds the only authentic alternative to be "friendship". Friendship is an experience of relationship between persons which is "just there", "simply something we have to discover". Unlike the experience of Lord to subject, friendship "is the opposite of appropriation or the desire to possess ... we do not need to bow down to a friend. We neither look up to him nor down to him".[23] It is the experience of this type of relationship between persons as peers, believes Moltmann, which "is an important stage on the way to the social experience of God".[24] In *The Trinity and the Kingdom of God* Moltmann has in fact already stated that this social experience of God, because it reflects the social understanding of the Trinity to which he has tied himself, represents the authentic way to construe the relationship God's image has with his Creator. All others tend to perpetuate hierarchy and subjugation. But is such an understanding sufficient? What does it mean to say that the God in whose image we are made is no more than a "friend"?

Moltmann's conclusion to *The Trinity and the Kingdom of God*[25] lays out what friendship with God entails. On a positive note such a notion emphasises the importance of developing the mutuality of listening and speaking in conversation with God and trust that God answers prayer. There is much more emphasis on mutual communication and on active participation in the relationship. For Moltmann each human being has a special dignity and is given the unique respect and confidence of a staunch friend, plus responsibility to mirror his presence in the earthly Kingdom. Thus the mutual conversation between us and God has come to the fore in Protestant theology in a way which was not possible for the generation of Barth.

Yet Moltmann's unwillingness to present God in what he would term a monarchical way places humanity on such an equal par with God that, perhaps as is the case between very good friends, the distance between the two is barely recognisable. Thus the roles start to become blurred. Moltmann's stated desire to turn to humanity first to see God's presence within it and to reject the "revealed theology" of Barth had already clouded his notion of the God–human relationship. The descendant pole now becomes less and less discernible in a doctrine of the human person which relies on a doctrine of Trinity expressed above all in terms not of unity but of social communication between persons. The result will reveal

---

[23] Moltmann, *Spirit of Life*, 255.
[24] Ibid., 255.
[25] Moltmann, *The Trinity and the Kingdom of God*, 219–22.

a serious gap in the understanding of the human person's reliance on God. As we proceed to examine Moltmann's narrative theology we will see how there will be insufficient room for a theology of thanksgiving for the saving work God has completed in the death and resurrection of the Son. Because we are friends of God, says Moltmann, "God does not want the humility of servants or the gratitude of children". Rather God wants "the boldness and confidence of friends", who, because they are friends not subjects, "share his rule with him".[26]

Responsibility for being God's presence on earth will be construed in a different way than it was by Barth and Balthasar. "God listens to his friends", says Moltmann, so:

> [b]y virtue of friendship with God in the Spirit, we have the chance to influence God and to participate in his rule. (*Es gibt kraft der Gottesfreundschaft im Geist die Möglichkeit der Einwirkung auf Gott und der Mitwirkung mit seiner Herrschaft*).[27]

Because God is a friend rather than a saviour figure responsibility will actually involve changing God himself. Thus God will cease to be God for us in any traditional sense which respects God's omnipotence.

Moltmann himself would not agree with this evaluation of his model. It must be stated that, in the relationship with God as friend, according to Moltmann, we have the opportunity to discover our true freedom which gives us our special dignity as the "*imago Dei*". Part of my view is that above all the desire to restate the notion of human freedom from the perspective of this doctrine for so long neglected in Protestant theology in particular is certainly to be welcomed. Moltmann is right in seeing such a project as vital in a postmodern society which, for all its apparent liberalism, still exploits the freedom of the human being. It is understandable that, in responding to this challenge, he approaches the doctrine in a different way to the Nazi and post-Nazi generation, which tended in German Protestant circles to emphasise through the pre-eminence of "revealed theology", God's absolute sovereignty, and humanity's reliance on him. Yet it is my view that above all his notion of God as "friend" has fallen into a trap which both Barth and Balthasar had managed to avoid, and that, rather than speak more fully of human freedom, will in fact do the reverse and limit his theology from being able to speak in an integrated way of human dignity before God within the community of persons in the earthly Kingdom.

Moltmann believes that he has made progress in moving from the notion of human persons as "children" of God to being "friends" of God. Yet in doing so it is my view that he has overturned a way of approaching the doctrine which spoke more authentically of true freedom, that is from the perspective above all of the descendant pole, of the revelation of God in itself, in the person of Christ. Both

---

[26] Ibid., 221.

[27] Ibid., 221 [Moltmann, *Trinität und Reich Gottes*, 238].

Barth and Balthasar had defined the freedom we enjoy as God's image on earth first and foremost in terms of our salvation, made possible from outside of ourselves through the Son's victory on the cross. Moltmann, however, in attempting to define the human being's freedom first and foremost through reference to God's presence within us, has left us with a paradox.

He has interpreted Jesus' invitation in John 15:15 to be friends rather than servants as a call not to relate to him so much as the saviour, whom we need to answer our contemporary yearnings for freedom, but as a call to see God in the Spirit dwelling in ourselves. "By virtue of the indwelling of the Holy Spirit, people enter into this new 'direct' relationship with God. The freedom of God's friends does not evolve out of the freedom of God's children."[28] For Moltmann, paradoxically, when we focus again on ourselves to see God our friend within, we discover our freedom. Freedom only becomes possible, he says, "when people know themselves in God and God in them. This is the light of the Holy Spirit".[29] For Moltmann it is in finding God within ourselves that we are meant to find the freedom which God offers. This excludes an important element in the progress towards freedom, namely looking beyond ourselves to experience the process of being freed.

Moltmann's doctrine of "*imago Dei*" has placed too much emphasis on the interior and left insufficient room for an understanding of God himself as also exterior to the human person. This will now become clearer as we proceed to an overall evaluation of Moltmann's model of "*imago Dei*" in itself from the perspective of its chief medium, that is its narrative form. We will now find that, tied as he is to a social doctrine of the Trinity, and averse to the notion of hierarchy in the God–human relationship, the dangers to which we have been referring take still clearer shape. His doctrine of "*imago Dei*" will express God's presence within creation, in the mutuality between God and the world, especially in suffering. Yet God and his image on earth tend to merge in a narrative which fails to distinguish sufficiently creator and creature. Thus ultimately, rather than succeed in his aim of giving a new theological account of human dignity for our contemporary world, Moltmann's narrative will reflect a doctrine of "*imago Dei*" which is insufficiently clear either about the role of humanity, as it searches for salvation yet lacks a sense of sin, or about the role of God, to whom humanity turns in certain hope yet who is divided against himself and whom humanity itself has the power to influence. These problems in turn place in greater relief the lasting contribution of Balthasar who, in reworking Barth's radical Christocentrism into his own narrative, has succeeded where Moltmann has failed, in creating a balanced account of the doctrine in which human dignity is rooted in the mutual relationship played out in the drama of infinite and finite freedom made concrete in God's revelation in Christ.

---

[28] Ibid., 221.
[29] Ibid., 221.

Jürgen Moltmann's Model of "*Imago Dei*" in Itself

The Cross

For Moltmann the significance of the correspondence of the human being to God is expressed above all in his narrative of the cross. Through this Moltmann is able to ground his understanding of the intimacy of the relationship between humanity and the God who in Christ's suffering gives us hope. The full significance of this intimate relationship is thus expressed above all in terms of God's solidarity with human suffering. So Moltmann is able to express how our being placed in this relationship as God's image speaks in a profound way of this ever-present reality of human life, as we search for hope amid the experience of suffering which is so prevalent in today's world.

As we have already noted in our study of Moltmann, there will be problems inherent in his approach. My own view is that he will leave insufficient room in this narrative to express our need to relate to a God beyond our human experience. However, let us put this objection aside briefly, as it is important to uncover the real contribution Moltmann is trying to make to the development of the doctrine. His quest for a more relational model of "*imago Dei*" is in fact attempting to answer a significant contemporary challenge in theology. The development of a narrative expressing the closeness of the relational dynamic between God and humanity will express more forcefully how God's presence in the world gives human life meaning not just in a theoretical way but in the reality of hope amid suffering and death. In other words we can relate to a God who is not just beyond but also within our experience of the struggles involved in life.

Just as Balthasar had attempted to convey this through his narrative of the descent of Christ into the underworld, so Moltmann attempts to do this through his narrative of the cross. In the comparison to Balthasar, however, we find a key distinction. We have seen how Balthasar had found in Barth's Christology the necessary foundations for the development of such a narrative. Moltmann's Christological narrative, however, will differ in its interpretation of Barth in a fundamental way which marks a new avenue of exploration. Moltmann will take a fundamental stance against Barth's understanding of the place of Christ within the Trinity, which he believes will help him to express more appropriately the true significance of God's closeness to the human experience of suffering. From this will flow a narrative of God's indwelling in creation through the dynamic of brokenness in suffering moving towards hope in unity with God.

Moltmann's chief criticism of Barth is that the "*kenosis*" of God in Christ is not expressed in a way in which the misery of humanity is actually caught up in what he wants to call the Trinitarian history of God. The suffering and death of Christ on the cross have insufficient impact on our own experience. Thus, in his major work of narrative theology, *The Crucified God*,[30] he sets out to develop a narrative which aims to express the relationship of God and humanity through the history of the experience of relationship between the persons of the Trinity. The unity of the Trinity is, unlike Barth's *eternally* united Trinitarian narrative, to be discovered in the rupture between the persons as God enters into history in the death of the Son on the cross. This represents a fundamental shift in thinking. Moltmann seems to believe that unity is achieved through the very contradiction of unity, in the dialectical juxtaposition of opposites. A Trinitarian narrative theology of the cross for today needs to move away from the Barthian orthodox self-sufficient Trinitarian God who cannot change or suffer in the economy. Rather we must stress a unifying process within the life of the Trinity which experiences inner disunity as a necessary element. This process has as its central location the seeming abandonment of the Son by the Father on the cross.

The abandonment of the Son by the Father on the cross represents a rupture in the life of God through which the persons of the Trinity will be reunited. Through this Moltmann seems to express, at least at first sight, a more adequate picture of God's solidarity with the human condition which this reunifying process mirrors. God is against God as the human race often suffers at its own hands in its conflicts and divisions. The Trinity experiences mutual suffering in the breaking up of the archetypal Christian family: the Son is abandoned by the Father on the cross and the Son, that is God in God's self, suffers there. But it is out of this very real experience of separation and suffering within God himself that reconciliation comes. Through the new life of the resurrection and the sending of the Holy Spirit comes hope. This hope, however, is not merely theoretical but grounded in reality, as it is, within the very experience of God himself, emerging out of separation, suffering and tragedy.

The relational dynamic of process in the event of the cross has ripped apart the triune God as we in our selves and our communities are sometimes ripped apart, only to find reconciliation through this very dynamic of process later. We have a God who is so intertwined with us in the Trinity on the cross that this God is affected as we are affected. So Moltmann can affirm that this "history of God" is one with our suffering: "to recognise the crucified God", he believes, "therefore means seeing oneself together with suffering creation in the history of God".[31] God's indwelling in creation is in fact seen here and now in the reality of the lived experience of his image on earth, that is in the fundamental experience of human beings moving through brokenness to hope.

Moltmann's narrative of the cross thus suggests an understanding of the doctrine of the "*imago Dei*" in more meaningfully relational terms. In emphasising

---

[30] Moltmann, *The Crucified God: the Cross of Christ as the Foundation of Christian Theology*. Trans. R.A. Wilson and John Bowden (New York and Evanston: Harper & Row, 1974) [*Der gekreuzigte Gott: das Kreuz Christi Grund und Kritik Christlicher Theologie* (Munich: Kaiser Verlag, 1972)].

[31] Moltmann, *The Future of Creation* (London: S.C.M. Press, 1979), 75.

the solidarity of God in human suffering he moves away from understanding humanity's restoration by Christ in terms of individual salvation from sin to stress the Christian hope of reconciliation and healing amid the common experience of suffering. The restoration of human beings to God's image is viewed not simply in terms of Christ's once-and-for-all saving victory on the cross but as a process necessarily involving suffering but moving towards hope. Moltmann has thus found a different way to speak of the presence of God in the world which is mindful of the ebb and flow of human experience.

However, there are important questions to ask about this narrative approach. We must consider the specific question of what he claims about God, as understanding him to suffer and to change opens up various problems in terms of holding to an adequate doctrine of God. Before that, however, we must explore further what he is claiming about humanity's actual position in relation to God. In presenting a doctrine inviting human beings to hope Moltmann depicts humanity in progress towards a discovery of their identity rooted in God. In a new way for Protestant theology, he is emphasising the ascendant pole, the pilgrimage on which humanity finds itself, orienting itself from the perspective of suffering towards salvation.

What does this journey towards hope say about humanity's actual position before God? Because, as we have already seen, God is understood as no more than a friend, the concept of human pilgrimage will be insufficiently rooted in an adequate understanding of the saviour's otherness beyond creation. Because the presence of God is expressed above all within the creation itself, humanity's aim will not be to transcend itself, to discover its divine dignity beyond human weakness. Rather for Moltmann the belief that in the cross God has restored us to his image, while it stresses salvation in speaking more directly about God's solidarity with the human condition in hope amid suffering, does not include an adequate notion of sin. This is a serious omission as in turn it prevents him from speaking adequately of the call to human dignity as good creatures, reflecting the goodness of God, yet invited to an even greater destiny.

Humanity's Position

In order to uncover this nuanced way in which Moltmann understands humanity's actual position before God we must see what lies behind his narrative of the cross. Two other books serve to explain this. In his extended work on the specific theme of eschatology, *The Coming of God*,[32] he develops his understanding of Christian identity in terms of a pilgrimage from suffering towards hope. Here he is developing the ascendant pole, the notion of the human being in a process of movement towards some future divine dignity. As regards the "*imago Dei*" in particular, however, we must consider this theme in conjunction with his specific

---

[32] Moltmann, *The Coming of God: Christian Eschatology* (London: S.C.M. Press, 1996) [*Das Kommen Gottes: christliche Eschatologie* (Gütersloh: Kaiser, 1995)].

study of the doctrine in the seminal *God in Creation*,³³ where he clarifies his account of the eschatological movement towards hope. Here we discover that Moltmann gives insufficient attention to sin and the Fall and that this leads to an inadequate understanding of human identity before God.

Before studying these problems in Moltmann's model, however, we must first of all make a more positive observation. In highlighting the human pilgrimage in hope towards the God who is our salvation Moltmann is part of a movement in twentieth-century theology searching for new ways to depict the profound intimacy of relationship we are offered with God as that which gives our lives consummation, dignity and fullest meaning. Moltmann is attracted to the notion of deification. One section of *The Coming of God* he devotes to the theme of the deification of the world,³⁴ suggesting that the whole of creation, both human and non-human, is in solidarity as a cosmos in the process of transfiguration by Christ into his own body. His narrative does not simply want to say that, through Christ's victory on the cross, humanity is restored to God's image. Rather he intends to show how God's image on earth is called forth into a transforming relationship with God and with each other. God's image is not to be understood in a static way but dynamically, moving towards glory, as it mirrors the Trinity's relationship and movement from suffering through to glory in the narrative of the cross.

Elsewhere in *The Coming of God*³⁵ Moltmann shows his appreciation of this move in twentieth-century theology towards a more dynamic understanding of the human relationship with God. For him Barth had begun to open the doctrine of predestination to a more universal understanding of hope. In emphasising universal salvation he had invited humanity to appreciate the eschatological dimension of their relationship with Christ. We also had noted in our study how Barth's Christocentrism had emphasised the descendant but, in his endeavour to restore the doctrine of "*imago Dei*" and develop it in terms of relationality, he was trying to highlight the element of subjectivity and process in our response to God. However we saw how, in the final analysis, Barth was unable within the constraints of his theological system, to move beyond a static understanding of humanity's restoration to a relationship with God which placed us in relationship with others.

We concluded that Balthasar had given this fuller development to Barth's preliminary work. Through the media of aesthetics and drama he is able to develop a narrative of the mutual relationship between God and humanity against the background of Christ's offer of salvation and the life of infinite freedom which is our destiny. Moltmann seems to recognise the value of Balthasar's work. He now sees himself as part of a similar movement which intends to present a fresh account of the hope promised for all people through the victory of Christ's death and resurrection which at the same time stresses Christ's enduring and free offer of

---

³³ Moltmann, *God in Creation*, 226–42.
³⁴ Ibid., 272–5.
³⁵ Moltmann, *The Coming of God*, 248–55.

friendship with humanity. For him Balthasar's narrative of Christ's descent into the underworld not only stresses the hope of salvation for all but also invites humanity to see Christ as its companion and brother. "By way of a deepened doctrine of Christ's descent into hell", writes Moltmann:

> Hans Urs von Balthasar has tried in the spirit of Origen to mediate between the universal assurance of salvation held by the Eastern Fathers of the church, and the emotional emphasis on freedom of Western theology ... The godless are forsaken by God and in this sense "damned". They experience the hell they themselves have chosen. But Christ's descent into hell says that even in their hell Christ is their companion and brother (*"Höllenfahrt" Christi aber sagt, daß Christus auch in seiner Hölle sein Begleiter und Bruder ist*).[36]

It seems to me that Moltmann's appreciation of Balthasar is right. Balthasar has, through his dramatic account of Christ's descent, highlighted Christ's free offer of brotherhood and friendship with the human race. I would go on to say that this now draws us forward into a dynamic relationship which is characterised by a process of discovery about our true meaning as his presence on earth. Balthasar was emphasising our salvation as restored to God's image on earth, but the theological statement that we are restored, leads us on a pilgrimage through which we discover how we are companions of Christ called to be his disciples on his mission. In this way we discover our divine dignity.

Moltmann's own narrative of the cross is part of this same movement in twentieth-century theology which Balthasar represents. This movement seeks to emphasise how our salvation as the restored image of God invites us on a journey towards discovering our true hope and meaning in Christ. In "the restoration of new creation of the likeness to God", says Moltmann, "since he [Christ] is the messianic *imago Dei*, believers become *imago Christi*, and through this enter upon the path which will make them *gloria Dei* on earth".[37] In a similar way to Balthasar, Moltmann is expressing the incorporation of the human being into Christ's life which leads him towards glory. He is moving away from the static notion of our more passive acceptance of the image restored to embrace a more active understanding of our pilgrimage towards divine destiny.

For Barth this had not come through in his theology as he was still tied to a passive understanding of the effects of Christ on the "*imago*", which has humanity restored through Christ's justification of the sinner but unable to access God. Moltmann, however, wants to break new ground for the Protestant understanding. It is true that "[w]ith his justification", he says, "the sinner receives through grace the righteousness which he lost through sin: he once again becomes God's image on earth".[38] Yet, for him, the full meaning of Luther's "*simul iustus et peccator*"

---

[36] Ibid., 253 [Moltmann, *Das Kommen Gottes*, 282].
[37] Ibid., 226. Emphasis his.
[38] Ibid., 226.

must be expressed through reference to our future calling. Being incorporated into Christ's being means being placed on a journey towards glory which starts with our restoration. "Justification is therefore the beginning of glorification ... is the future completion of justification" (*"Die Rechtfertigung ist also der gegenwärtige Anfang der Verherrlichung ... ist die zukünftige Vollendung der Rechtfertigung"*).[39] So:

> the human being's likeness to God appears as a historical process with an eschatological termination; it is not a static condition. Being human means becoming human in this process (*Die Gottebenbildlichkeit des Menschen erscheint ... als ein geschichtlicher Prozeß mit eschatologischem Ausgang, nicht als ein Zustand. Menschein ist Menschwerden in diesem Prozeß*).[40]

Moltmann is making an important contribution to the history of the doctrine of "*imago Dei*" here. As Barth and Balthasar before him, he has recognised the value of restating the doctrine as an integral part of a narrative theology which attempts to present a message of hope amid suffering to people of today. The doctrine will thus not be relegated to a corner of his theological work as a part of his doctrine of sin and the Fall. In Moltmann's model it is very clear that he does not intend to emphasise the restoration of the "*imago*" against the background of human sin. Rather the doctrine is seen in the context of future hope and divine destiny as we recognise how we are, despite all the suffering which is a part of the human condition, God's good creation, his presence on earth. We might say that here too he is one in aim with Balthasar, who emphasises salvation rather than sin, the future of humanity in relationship with God and each other rather than the relationships destroyed in the past.

However, despite this, it is my contention that Moltmann's contribution has been blighted by his lack of attention to the notion of sin, not simply because it omits an important aspect of the understanding of the Christian person, but because in turn this explains the deeper root of the problem, the lack of space between God and us in a doctrine which at its heart sees God and his image on earth merge into one dynamic of suffering and hope. Through his narrative Moltmann wishes to express our identity as God's image not in terms of salvation from sin but in terms of salvation from suffering. In other words, whereas we do see our divine destiny in the movement from suffering to hope, there is insufficient space for us to relate to God as something other, greater, more perfect than ourselves. Our divine destiny does not involve the possibility of transcending ourselves.

Moltmann's move away from the emphasis on sin seems to me to be directly connected to his search for a fuller understanding of our divine destiny in more relational terms. In *God in Creation*,[41] he states that his reintroduction of the idea

---

[39] Ibid., 226 [Moltmann, *Das Kommen Gottes*, 233].
[40] Ibid., 226–7 [Moltmann, *Das Kommen Gottes*, 233].
[41] Moltmann, *God in Creation*, 234–43.

of "*theosis*" is an affirmation of the value of Orthodox theologies over against those following Augustine. Whereas Augustine, in emphasising the human soul not the whole body, takes as his starting point how human beings are restored from their sins to the image of the Son, Gregory of Nazianzus and those who followed him in the East started from the relationship between the persons in the Trinity.

The Eastern perspective, claims Moltmann, suggests the inter-relational reality of the human condition as opposed to the individualistic one stressed in Augustine's model. "It is not the human individual", he says, "all by him- or herself, that corresponds to the triune God – it is not even the first couple, Adam and Eve; it is the family, as the nuclear cell of every human society".[42] So it is "as a way of overcoming the one-sidedness of Western anthropology" that Moltmann says that he turns to Gregory of Nazianzus, who explained the Trinity as "the original 'nuclear' family".[43] So the Trinity draws us into a relationship through which we are caught up in the dynamic of suffering and of hope in the Trinity, not merely saved from our sin through Christ's victory on the cross.

Whilst this dynamic understanding of human identity is to be welcomed, I believe it is still possible and desirable to include within it a notion of sin. In the contrast he makes between the restoration motif and the more dynamic relational one he models, he seems to have omitted an adequate understanding of human weakness. The notion of the human being's pilgrimage towards a divine destiny would seem to require us to place God also outside of our initial grasp, otherwise we have nothing to attain in any meaningful human terms.

Ultimately for Moltmann our being restored as God's image on earth seems to include the recognition that our sin has been overcome once and for all. The journey on which we embark as "*simul iustus et peccator*" is towards hope in an end to human suffering. This is what the cross means to us. This is our aim in the process of "*theosis*" which culminates in our discovering our divine dignity. However, it would seem to me that such a journey seems to be tied more to the Lutheran doctrine of sanctification which flows from the "*simul iustus et peccator*" than a doctrine of "*theosis*" in the traditional sense. Our recognition that we are in fact God's good creation, his presence on earth, does not seem to include an ongoing call to conquer sin and thus draw closer to God. It is true that God and his restored image are in a much closer dynamic of intimate relationship than Luther or Barth had wanted to admit. However, when we turn to God to discover our divine destiny in a relationship with him, we are really in essence not going further than recognising our position as "*simul iustus et peccator*", only more personally than for Luther and Barth, as now the very presence of God is understood as within ourselves as his image on earth.

Hence as God's image on earth we still see God as fundamentally interior rather than as a God beyond ourselves who shows us the potential for our transcendence. From one of his earliest works, *God in Creation*, Moltmann was concerned to

---

[42] Ibid., 235.
[43] Ibid.

stress the indwelling of God as central to his thought. "The Creator, through his Spirit, *dwells in* his creation as a whole, and in every individual created being ... The inner secret of creation is this *indwelling of God*."[44] It is in our own reflection of a dynamic movement in God that we are drawn into relationship with him. God is close to us as is a friend who shares our suffering and our hope. We are also drawn towards relationship with others with whom we are in solidarity as God's image journeying towards hope. It is above all a social understanding of the God–human relationship which Moltmann wishes to convey. As the human race we are drawn together into this ongoing relationship with a God who invites us on a journey through suffering towards something more fulfilling. Yet, because Moltmann has interpreted the significance of such a journey towards the divine in this way, there is insufficient space to relate to God as an other to whom we move in recognition of our weakness yet potential for transcending it.

Because the negative aspect of human existence has been construed as suffering rather than sin, Moltmann's model of "*imago Dei*" speaks powerfully of hope but does not give due attention to the call to realise our dignity in transcending the world, in virtue and the infinite happiness of oneness with God in heaven. This is the root of Moltmann's problem in portraying a more dynamic understanding of divine destiny. In turn it creates problems for his understanding of the God to whom we relate, as his narrative portrays God as so much a part of human experience that he ceases to be the God of worship in any traditional sense.

God's Position

Moltmann's attempt to speak in a more meaningful way of the intimate mutual relationship between God and his image on earth is based on the assumption that, in order to do so, we must portray God himself in a more dynamic way than has traditionally been the case. A theology which expresses the "*imago Dei*" not as a static doctrine but as one conveying God's solidarity with the world in all its suffering suggests to him a contemporary narrative which highlights to the full the suffering of God himself. If such a narrative is to reflect the dynamism of the transformation from suffering to hope, which is at the heart of the experience of being a human person made in his image, God must be shown to go through this process of transformation too. Hence the God to whom human beings relate is construed as so intertwined with human experience that he suffers and changes. Such an understanding of God presents doctrinal problems. Moreover, this portrayal of the mutable suffering God, prevents Moltmann from developing the adequate picture of God's transcendence which his narrative lacks. Thus, rather than succeed in his intention to convey the fuller significance of being made in God's image, he leaves insufficient room for a fuller picture of human dignity in its capacity for transcendence beyond itself.

---

[44] Moltmann, *God in Creation*, xii.

Revisiting his narrative once more, in turning to his work *The Future of Creation*, we see how these problems emerge. "Is a Christian proclamation of salvation possible at all today", he asks, "without a new proclamation of God?"[45] As Moltmann embellishes and expands his narrative of the cross, he answers this question in the negative as he invites us to see God in a totally new way which he believes is necessary if we are to proclaim more adequately God's salvation for his people.[46] We have already seen how he intended to give a fuller more dynamic account of the Trinity. Now he imagines an inner room off a central room where the Trinitarian God resides. In that inner room we find the Trinity in the Trinity's "*opera*" – all that God does in relation to the economy – and in the Trinity's "*passiones*" – in how the Trinity suffers. These two aspects will be inextricably interconnected through the break between the persons as the Son is totally abandoned by the Father on the cross. The very inner life of the Trinity is torn apart by this rupture on the cross. The Trinity's essential unity is broken through the Trinity's extension in the world.

Only through this revised account of the Trinity as broken within itself does Moltmann believe that he can express adequately how God's image on earth reflects the Trinity. The break-up of the persons within the family of God is a prerequisite for expressing the brokenness of the human condition. This change which occurs within the very being of God is not simply a part of Moltmann's narrative but absolutely fundamental to it. In order to be God at all, it is insufficient simply to state that the Son empties himself in an act of "*kenosis*". Rather we must say that in Christ's "*kenosis*" the Trinitarian God as a whole limits itself in performing what he calls a true act of "*pathos*". God's suffering on the cross, Moltmann concludes, is not merely the God of our traditional narratives of "*leidenschaft*" but also of fully human "*leiden*". A God who does not engage in this process of transformation involving suffering through internal disunity of persons is unable to express who God is. The fullness of God's revelation only comes through the necessary rupture then reunification of the Trinity as God's immersion in creation defines him more fully. It is this mutable, suffering, and above all conditioned picture of God which emerges as the only acceptable picture of the Creator in whose image all human beings are made.

The problems inherent in this view become clear when we place Moltmann in the context of the earlier theologians Barth and Balthasar. We know that Moltmann had intended a very different picture to Barth's. Our own conclusion was that Barth had left us with a somewhat distant picture of the Creator. However, despite the need to develop a fuller picture of the intimacy of the relationship between God and the world, his is still an immutable transcendent God whose salvation is extended to all his creatures to whose image on a fundamental level they correspond as his loved creation. Balthasar's development of a more relational model also

---

[45] Moltmann, *The Future of Creation*, 62.
[46] Here I am summarising the central points in the narrative in *The Future of Creation* inasmuch as they bear out my argument.

insisted on God's transcendence, immutability and universality. In his narrative of the descent into the underworld Balthasar was clear that the Trinity remained one even in its encountering all the negativity in the human response to God's love. For Balthasar the Son is all but abandoned by the Father but never let go as the love of Father and Son, bound by the Holy Spirit is infinite and thus unbreakable.[47] So Balthasar would not want to say that God suffers. O'Hanlon's exhaustive study of the concept of divine immutability[48] puts this well: "it was clear what this modification did not involve. First, God does not change, or become, or suffer in a created, temporal sense. Balthasar time and again rejected any univocal attribution of change to God."[49] Rather it is more appropriate to say that God is immersed in the negativity of the human condition but that he remains one, transcending and overcoming sin and suffering, and thus extending his saving presence to all his creation whom even in its finitude are called to an infinite destiny.

Moltmann has forfeited this more universal and transcendent portrayal of God present in Barth and Balthasar. Rather God's being God is conditioned by the level of his involvement in creation, and in particular by his experience of suffering. It is true that Moltmann is saying that God suffers willingly, out of the choice God makes himself to do so. We might argue that in this case the definition of God is not being limited as God is seen to be choosing freely to express himself in this way. However, in stating the fact that, whether freely or not, God must be defined as one who suffers and changes, Moltmann has moved away from the universal and transcendent God who is infinite to stress God's finitude. The statement that God, whether he does so freely or not, suffers not just in the Son but must suffer and die in all three persons of the Trinity, represents a break with a Christian

---

[47] Cf. Balthasar, *Mysterium Paschale*, 174–81, where, at the heart of the narrative of the descent, Balthasar is clear that the unfolding drama is an act of the Trinity in its unity.

[48] Gerard F. O'Hanlon, *The Immutability of God in the Theology of Hans Urs von Balthasar* (Cambridge: Cambridge University Press, 1990).

[49] Ibid., 131. O'Hanlon takes a more nuanced position on Balthasar's view, based on what he claims is more implicit than explicit in his writing as a whole, which regards him to hold a "modified" understanding of immutability. For him the "liveliness" of the Trinity's action in the world renders God immutable in the sense of his "supra-mutability", that is acknowledging that he cannot change but recognising that this God who enters into the world with such force, and connects with its suffering so powerfully, cannot be limited by static linguistic terms. I would agree that Balthasar's dramatic account of the Trinity's relationship with the world is the basis for a much more dynamic and meaningful understanding of God and of the call extended to his image on earth who approach him as broken and suffering creatures. However, the specific terminology we use when talking of divine immutability is not significant to Balthasar's success in this regard. Rather, it is the very fact that his theology respects fully the doctrine of immutability, as O'Hanlon also shows, that makes the God–human relationship more meaningful to us as people who suffer, as when this is clearly in place, we may speak of God as transcendent, and humanity as called to transcend its own weakness, in all its forms including suffering but also sin, in moving closer to him in his divine perfection.

orthodoxy. For Moltmann's view God is no longer infinite but meets us on our own finite terms as he has been limited in terms of his definition as God himself. Rather than transcending his creation as a whole, he is defined by his experience of involvement in it, and notably through suffering.

It is true that this has enabled Moltmann to express God's presence in his creation in a more meaningful way. God is in total solidarity with the human condition, especially with those who suffer. His image on earth reflects an experience of transformation present in God himself which leads us through suffering to hope, from disunity to unity, from death to life. However, in so doing, he has reduced our understanding of the God in whose image we are all made to a limited and particular projection of God. Rather than God being beyond and universal, the only God who lives up to this name is the suffering, mutable, God.

The limits Moltmann places on God have further ramifications for his portrayal of the relationship between God and his image on earth from the particular perspective of how we understand God's revelation and salvation. Moltmann's intention to develop a more meaningful, accessible and intimate relational model of the "*imago Dei*", had been based on his belief that we must turn to the experience of creation itself in order to define God. In highlighting God's presence in the transformation from suffering through to hope he has defined God's mode of revelation in terms of human experience. As such he has developed the ascendant pole, the experience of humanity's search for God's presence in creation. However, in doing this, he has placed limits not only on our definition of God as transcendent but also on what we consider to be God's revelation.

Moltmann's definition of God in terms of the process from suffering to hope unavoidably includes a similar understanding of revelation. Just as God changes so does revelation as it seems to be transformed from apparent incompleteness through rupture in the death of God on the cross to completeness after the event of the cross. Thus events in the economy of salvation are seen to affect the status of revelation. In Moltmann's understanding we seem to have two stages. We have revelation at point A before the cross, then, after change in God through the effects of total immersion in our world of suffering, the completeness of revelation in point B. Moltmann would want here to claim that point A and point B are each other in the dialectical understanding of mutual relationship he espouses but this still leaves us with a sense of God's incomplete solidarity with us before the cross.

Thus, in turn we are left with the very problem which Moltmann has been trying to solve. A meaningful account of God's dealings with human beings – his love, solidarity and offer of salvation – to all people we say are made in his image – depends not on an all-embracing definition of God himself, but on our own human experience. The more we relate to the cross in our lives, then the more we experience the fullness of revelation, that which has been fulfilled in point B. The more we go through this the more we reflect God's presence as his image on earth. Suffering is a necessary and important part of the human condition, and Moltmann's concentration on the theme is very valuable and timely, in the light of the great experience of suffering in so many parts of the world. However, he has allowed the doctrine of God's revelation to be controlled by this aspect of human experience, rather than to concentrate, as Barth and Balthasar had done, on the very fact that God's love is so great in itself that it is offered to all people in whom his presence resides. In merging God and his creation into one process of suffering moving towards hope he has limited the power of the Christian understanding of salvation as gratuitous. In turn he has placed limits in our own experience on how we define our own special dignity as graced sinners corresponding to God's image. In highlighting the ascendant pole in humanity's search for God within he has omitted to proclaim the all-transforming truth of God's salvific universality.

The critique I have been giving of Moltmann's understanding of God's position within his narrative should not, however, be taken to invalidate the significance of his attempt to develop the doctrine of "*imago Dei*" for our own times. Rather the point I am making is that Moltmann's narrative of the cross in particular engages with a significant contemporary theological challenge. It encourages the theological community not to shy away from trying to express in more meaningful human terms God's solidarity with his image on earth. At the same time, however, through the shortcomings of Moltmann's attempt, we see how his own particular approach does not answer the needs. Moltmann is searching for something very valuable. Like Barth and Balthasar before him he intends to show humanity's potential for goodness in reflecting God's presence on earth. In a word his aim is, like Barth and Balthasar before him, to emphasise humanity's dignity in the light of faith. However, his attempt backfires because, in turning first to the human search for meaning to construct his narrative he has failed to show as fully as he might that humanity's dignity is actually found in the all-embracing truth of God's gift to us in Christ. It is in seeing humanity's relation to God from the perspective of the history of suffering and hope rather than of God's universal offer of salvation through the gift of Christ that he has omitted to include within his narrative an adequate picture of humanity's call to transcendence in the dignity to be found in a divine destiny beyond this world.

Moltmann's contribution has certainly highlighted the key contemporary issue regarding the doctrine of "*imago Dei*". It is at the intersection of this dialogue between God and the world, grace and nature, between the descendant pole emphasising God's love, and the ascendant pole, inviting humanity to freely co-operate with God's grace, that we find tension and debate in the theological community. Theology is always searching for a balance between emphasising God's gracious action, especially in the person of Christ, and humanity's dignity as his image. In all three theologians we have been studying we have found this tension. How much can we revise our understanding of God to speak more concretely of the human condition before God ceases to be a God of transcendence, omnipotence and worship? How far can we speak of the human capacity for God before we elevate humanity itself to the status of divine? The problem for Moltmann is that he fails to keep the balance.

It is true that his doctrine of "*imago Dei*" relates very clearly to the reality of the human condition. The doctrine speaks not of the distance between God and us but is grounded in the reality of human life. This theological picture of the human person thus speaks directly to human beings' real struggles in life and of the search for something more hopeful. This dimension must in general be welcomed as it is striving to ground the doctrine in reality and to show the search for human dignity as part of daily existence. However, for Moltmann the human dimension has not merely grounded the doctrine in reality but actually defined it and in so doing defined how we view God's position. The God who changes becomes the God whose revelation to humanity alters according to our own perception. Thus our true meaning and dignity is no longer found so much in God as in our projection of him. In trying to show how the doctrine of "*imago Dei*" gives contemporary humanity a sense of meaning, Moltmann has twisted the doctrine around. We no longer discover our dignity in the fact that we correspond to the God whom we can be sure gives all people hope in suffering. Rather God corresponds to our own experience of the search for dignity. So Moltmann's valuable contribution has in fact highlighted something very important. In so doing it has highlighted the lasting contribution of both Barth and Balthasar. Through its flaws, it has taught us how, if the doctrine is to succeed in speaking of human dignity at all today, it must be clearly rooted not in our own search for God but in God's descent to us in Christ.

Conclusion

In my conclusion to Chapter 3, having shown how Balthasar's model of the "*imago Dei*" represented a way forward for the contemporary development of the doctrine, I stated that it was now necessary to place his contribution, and that of Barth, more directly in the context of turn-of-the-century theology. In turning to Moltmann in particular we would find a similar desire to that we discovered in Barth and Balthasar to restate the doctrine. Moltmann enshrines the contemporary need to express a firm belief in the dignity of the human person from the perspective of our correspondence to God. However, it is Moltmann's lack of attention to the lessons Balthasar himself had learnt from Barth and his radical Christocentrism, that shed light on some of the challenges a contemporary statement of the doctrine present, and the problems inherent in the particular direction in which Moltmann wishes to take it.

Thus I would conclude that Moltmann's model informs our overall study in two basic ways, the first positive, the second showing us the problems and challenges his approach involves. Firstly, his writing serves to highlight a clear desire to develop a narrative of human dignity vis-à-vis God which prompts theology to emerge from a preoccupation with revealed theology to embrace a more thorough account of human transcendence and divine destiny. Moltmann's contribution here lies in his openness to embrace more anthropocentric themes which had appeared to be in conflict with a theological mindset rooted in the primacy of God's revelation. He recognises that, until now, there was a fear that any theological model which explored human dignity from the perspective of the human capacity for transcendence risked making a god of humanity. Moltmann had the important insight that in today's world this fear has been replaced by a new challenge. Contemporary societies are not trying to make a god of any one race or the human race in general. Rather we live in a world which now devalues the goodness of God's creation, be it human life or the environment as a whole. A contemporary understanding of the "*imago Dei*" can have the courage to forget its fears about giving humanity God-like supreme status and now find ways through theological narrative to be positive about the goodness of God's creation.

Moltmann thus leads Protestant theology into a new era which intends to move away from static notions of God's once-and-for-all salvation of humanity to be open to a more dynamic relational account of our response to God as friend. He is prepared to accentuate this call by focussing on themes previously considered outside the limits of the Protestant theologian. This development must be seen from an ecumenical perspective. In Moltmann we find a contemporary Protestant theologian who shares a similar aim to a contemporary Roman Catholic writer such as Balthasar to give a thoroughly positive and dynamic account of the goodness of creation caught up in an ongoing relationship with a God who shares our suffering and offers us hope as we are caught up in the mystery of his life, death and resurrection in the midst of the world.

In Moltmann's works we see this in a narrative which expresses the presence of the Holy Spirit in the world as the presence of God at the very heart of creation. Moltmann has developed this theme through also reintroducing the idea of "*theosis*" as an affirmation of the value of Orthodox theologies which underline humanity's relationship with and movement towards God. The Eastern perspective gives expression to our direct correspondence with God as his image on earth as we are understood to be conformed to the image of the Son with access to the Father. As such the Trinitarian God is construed as drawing us more closely into a relationship through which we are caught up in the dynamic of suffering and of hope present in God himself.

However, despite these positive aspects of the contribution Moltmann has made, there is a paradox at its heart. This paradox shows us some of the challenges involved in constructing a contemporary doctrine of "*imago Dei*" and places in greater relief the lasting contribution of Balthasar in this regard. The more Moltmann would seem to develop the positive perspective we have been outlining, the more it would become clear that, unlike Balthasar, his move away from Barthian revealed theology has in fact left the foundation of his doctrine insecure. As he fails to ground his doctrine in the radical Christocentrism which informed Balthasar's whole approach, so he presents such an anthropocentric narrative that the distinction in the relationship between God and humanity becomes clouded. His understanding of "*theosis*" does not take sufficient account of humanity's sinfulness and the drama of redemption. Rather it involves an understanding that, as friends of God, we are already saved. We are "*simul iustus et peccator*". Thus we are not called forth so much to transcend ourselves, in fulfilment of a divine destiny, as we are called simply to share friendship with God.

In effect, despite the positive contribution in portraying a God who is clearly close to us and calling us into this ongoing friendship through which he shares his experience of hope and suffering, Moltmann's model of "*imago Dei*" lacks a solid foundation in Christ as our saviour. It is in this way in particular that Moltmann's contribution shows us some of the potential problems theology must first be sure to confront if it is to do justice to a contemporary relational, dynamic, positive account of the fundamental goodness of the human being made in God's image and likeness. Any new narrative of the dignity of the human being must include a clear account of the need for salvation, of human weakness and specifically sin if it is to express more fully humanity's true position vis-à-vis God. Theology needs an account not just of the goodness of the human being as part of God's creation, and not just of our closeness to God and the hope his cross promises, but also of the call to a divine destiny which will transcend our human frailty. To make our reference point more clearly God's call to us in Christ, and not so much our need for friendship and equality with God, will give more scope to the theologian to develop a narrative which reflects more fully the ebb and flow of the human person's pilgrimage on earth as he moves between suffering and tragedy, despair yet hope, and also weakness and sin.

Made in God's image and likeness we are, as Moltmann intends to highlight, made perfectly good and friends with a God who shares our human condition in his Son. However we are also sinners, so not equivalent to God, and so it is as graced sinners that we are now called forth to enter more deeply into the mystery of Christ's cross and resurrection which only has its consummation in our oneness with God in heaven. In short I am saying in my own words that Moltmann's model underlines how important it is that Balthasar's insight be included in a contemporary narrative of "*imago Dei*". The finitude of humanity finds its true meaning and value in the infinite love of Christ who calls us forth. In personal terms human dignity is found not in our quest for God but God's descent to us in Christ.

Chapter 5
Concluding Reflections: Broader Horizons

The overall point of this book has been to show an appropriate way forward for the contemporary presentation of the doctrine of the "*imago Dei*". My research findings, and the recommendations which flow from them, are multi-stranded. However, this study proposes above all a renewed Christocentric understanding of the "*imago Dei*" which, through its emphasis on Christ's descent to earth, holds together two dimensions which in the history of theology have formed a doctrinal, and also specifically ecumenical, divide. These two aspects I have termed the "descendant", that which stresses God's descending to earth in Christ, and the "ascendant", that which focuses on the human person's orientation towards God.

This study of the writings of three influential theologians, each of whom have attempted to revive the doctrine of the "*imago Dei*" for contemporary theological discourse, leads me to the conclusion that Balthasar's interpretation of Barth's radical Christocentrism and its Patristic and Reformation roots shows us how the "descendant" and the "ascendant" may be married in one integrated dynamic. In such a way I conclude that Balthasar's understanding of the "*imago Dei*" represents an important doctrinal and ecumenical achievement which points us towards a fuller understanding of the doctrine.

In doing this, Balthasar in particular enables the Christian community to speak more powerfully of human dignity and vocation. Through greater emphasis on Christ's descent, human identity may now be placed more clearly in the perspective of God's presence within us, thus emphasising the dignity of each human person in whom God, in descending to us in the person of his Son, resides. The dramatic power of Balthasar's narrative portrayal of Christ's descent also enables us to speak of human dignity in terms of the vocation to go beyond ourselves. The fuller picture of human dignity lies in the call to the adventure of transcendence in the ongoing relationship with God in Christ. Our return and ascent to God will be a life of service as we are more fully incorporated into Christ's life and mission.

This study has considered the value of the contribution made by Balthasar against the background of the whole tradition on which he draws. It is especially interested, however, in the resurgence of the doctrine of the "*imago Dei*" in modern theology, and from the standpoint in particular of ecumenical theological dialogue. In the Roman Catholic tradition conciliar and postconciliar teaching is a part of this movement, and against this background my research wishes to make a specifically ecumenical contribution.

My study of Barth was central to the argument as it showed the genesis of Balthasar's Christocentrism. We examined Barth's contribution critically and analytically against the background of the tradition, both Roman Catholic and of the Reformation. We discovered, however, how his model of "*imago Dei*" in itself shows us the problems and the challenges confronting theology when a theological system serves to limit a fuller picture of human dignity. My examination of the relevant sections of Barth's *Church Dogmatics* highlighted an important but neglected dimension to Barth's theological outlook, namely his clear intention to develop a picture of the human being's close relationship with God in Christ. Here I am suggesting a new angle to the relationship between Barth and Balthasar. This suggests how Barth may not have been totally closed to the Catholic understanding that humanity had a natural capacity for God, and that Balthasar's integration of Barth's Christocentrism amounted to a substantial integration of the theology of the Reformation into his own.

In the final analysis, however, we discovered that Barth was confined by his own objections to natural theology. As a result his picture of human identity is placed firmly in the context of Christ but this Christ remains distant. Rather than speak more powerfully of human dignity his view of the human person, through his emphasis on how the image is totally lost at the Fall, remains somewhat sombre. It will be left to Balthasar to develop from Barth's radical Christocentrism an adequate picture of the human person's call to transcendence in the incorporation into Christ's life and mission. This will represent a significant development in the presentation of the doctrine, as it will ground the understanding of the human person in the gratuity of God's love in Christ yet speak equally powerfully of each human person's divine destiny and earthly responsibility. Thus Balthasar finds a way to speak to our contemporary world of the need to proclaim human dignity from twin perspectives. The human being, by virtue of Christ, possesses a divinely-bestowed dignity, which at the same time calls him forward to play his part on Christ's mission and in his own spiritual pilgrimage.

Moltmann also intends to restore the doctrine of "*imago Dei*" to contemporary theological discourse but we discovered that he has approached the question from a totally different angle. In choosing to research Moltmann, I intended to show how this eminent contemporary theologian adds a new dimension to the debate. Although rooted in the theology of the Reformation, he draws on different aspects of the tradition so as to restore a picture of the dignity of humanity as part of a fresh narrative of the goodness of creation as a whole reflecting God's presence on earth. In his writing also we find a tantalising interest in the Eastern doctrine of "*theosis*". This encourages him to speak of humanity as God's image reflecting God's goodness but also on a journey of ascent back to God.

Moltmann, like Balthasar and Barth, wants to show how humanity is in an ongoing relationship with God. Like Balthasar, he learns much from a tradition outside of his own. However, our close study of his theology, with its many implicit as well as explicit references to the doctrine of the "*imago Dei*", serves to underline the importance of Barth's Christocentrism for a contemporary presentation of the doctrine. As Moltmann tries to show the closeness of Christ in his solidarity with human suffering, he pays insufficient attention to the descendant pole. In the final analysis Moltmann thus clouds the relationship between God and his human creation to the extent that human beings do not relate to a God beyond themselves. In such a way his picture of human dignity, called to be Christ to others but not called to the adventure of transcendence, is limited.

Thus, in the final analysis, we see in closer relief the outstanding value of Balthasar's model within the context of the twentieth-century revival and development of the doctrine across an ecumenical divide. In his new Christocentric doctrine of the "*imago Dei*", Balthasar presents a picture of human dignity in which the descendant and ascendant poles are integrated through a dramatic account of the meeting of infinite and finite love in Christ's descent.

My overall appreciation of Balthasar's contribution, however, has been more nuanced. Our study has arrived at its conclusion aware of ambiguities we encountered as we went more deeply into our study of the development of Balthasar's thinking. Nevertheless, in my final analysis, I argue how it is even through his particular and sometimes questionable interpretation of Barth and of the whole tradition, that Balthasar makes a contribution to theology which shows us a way forward for the doctrine of "*imago Dei*". It is true that Balthasar's own interpretation of Barth does not always seem to match Barth's own views. We raised important questions here. At times it seemed that Balthasar was placing a Catholic construct on Barth's Protestant system. The impetus for Balthasar's turn to Christocentrism in theology is clearly that of Barth's but he is also strongly influenced by sources in the Patristic tradition whom he interpreted in a different way to him.

In particular we concluded that he understood Augustine very differently, focussing on the Latin Father's more relational and teleological strands of thought rather than those which stressed humanity's inability to be saved. In the tradition we saw that Barth tended to agree with a Lutheran interpretation of Augustine emphasising justification by faith. Balthasar emphasised Augustine's idea of the human way back to God and our eventual "*deificatio*". In addition to Augustine, Irenaeus was a very significant influence on Balthasar, leading him to a picture of human capacity for God which seemed to be totally contrary to Barth's. Whilst rooted in Christ's "*recapitulatio*" of humanity, Balthasar's interpretation of the tradition leads him to give much more scope to the teleological, participative and relational, that is to the ascendant pole, to humanity's capacity for God.

Such themes might seem totally unacceptable to Barth. Above all the fact that Barth's Christocentric picture of the human person's relationship with God is rooted in the "*analogia Fidei*", and so in the unequivocal rejection of "*analogia entis*", would seem to make constructive dialogue between the two theologians and their respective traditions fruitless. Thus, we might conclude that Balthasar's integration of the Reformation tradition which formed the basis of Barth's turn to Christocentrism in its emphasis on the descent of Christ, was less substantial.

Yet, as we proceeded to trace the development of Balthasar's doctrine through his particular reading of Barth, we found that he had appreciated nuances in his thought suggesting possibilities which pushed him in the particular direction he chose to go. His appreciation of Barth's efforts to express a more relational understanding of "*imago Dei*" rooted in radical Christocentrism leads him to develop his own model in a way which he realises Barth, given the limits of his own theological system, would not. Balthasar's deep appreciation of Barth, however, regards him as pioneering a new movement in Protestant theology from which we can glean much.

This is a movement which refocuses Lutheran Christocentrism on two important aspects. The first is Christ's presence in human life, that which speaks of the human person's special dignity as bearing Christ to the world. The second lies in the quest for a new Christocentric theological aesthetic expressing human identity in terms of a mutual relationship between Christ and the believer. Barth's tendency to begin to rethink the "*imago Dei*" in this way is not singular to him. We saw through our study of Moltmann how both these themes are equally important to a contemporary writer. Moltmann too intends to expand the understanding of mutual relationship between God and us, and to focus on Christ's presence within us. It is Balthasar, however, through his particular understanding of the nuances in Barth's thought who, in a powerful way through the medium of drama, finds the way to place Christ's appearance, the "*Gestalt*", and his image in creation, the "*Bild*", in one dramatic encounter expressed in the dynamic of love.

Balthasar's understanding of the doctrine thus speaks, in a new powerful way through the dramatic interplay of finite and infinite love, of the very core of human identity. The meeting of the beloved and the lover in the Christian believer's relationship with Jesus Christ underpins our special dignity, vocation and mission, on the earth, and enables us to speak of the hope of transcendence. In turn this shows the enduring importance of the doctrine of the "*imago Dei*" which is currently being echoed on the wider theological horizon. We have seen how this has been stressed in Roman Catholic teaching in the postconciliar period, which intends to restate the doctrine in a way which centres clearly on Christ yet speaks of the human vocation in an exalted way. We have seen how this is enshrined in particular in the Dogmatic Constitution on the Church of the Second Vatican Council, *Lumen Gentium*, and in the recent document of the International Theological Commission, *Communion and Stewardship: Human Persons Created in the Image of God*.

Deus Caritas Est and the Interface of *Agape* and *Eros*

Against the background of this study, however, a particular section is also due here, regarding the first encyclical of Pope Benedict XVI, *Deus Caritas Est*.[1] This groundbreaking Encyclical shows all the more clearly how the focus of the "*imago Dei*" doctrine which I have been advocating, is part of a movement of renewal which promises to have much impact ecumenically and pastorally. In *Deus*

---

[1] Pope Benedict XVI, *Deus Caritas Est* (Vatican City: Libreria Editrice Vaticana, 2006).

Caritas Est Pope Benedict invites us to ground the identity of the human being in Jesus Christ in a way which highlights, in a very similar way to Balthasar, the mutual dynamic of love between Christ and us. For the Pope the descent of Christ and our ascent to him are expressed in terms of *"agape"*, Christ's perfect love for us, and *"eros"*, the desire which calls us forward in love. Both are necessary, says Pope Benedict: *"eros* and *agape* -ascending love and descending love- can never be completely separated. The more the two, in their different aspects, find a proper unity in the one reality of love, the more the nature of love in general is realized."[2]

For the Pope this theme is clearly chosen as one which can speak profoundly to the contemporary world of what is at the very heart of a proper understanding and living out of the dignity of the human vocation rooted in Christ. He intends to bring us back to Christ's love for us so we may look at ourselves, loved infinitely by him, and called forward to transcend ourselves in our relationship with him and with others. The reintroduction of the theme of the dynamic encounter of *"agape"* and *"eros"* in Christ, which forms the theological background to this call, shows more clearly the enduring significance of Balthasar's work.

Balthasar also uses these terms *"agape"* and *"eros"* love to characterise the eternal drama of God's love for humanity played out in the appearance and descent of Christ. This too grounds human identity and draws us, out of our longing for meaning, into a relationship of love which will now define us as Christian disciples. For Balthasar it is in this encounter that the *"eros"* of our longing for the meaning of our earthly existence as God's image is echoed in the *"agape"* of the perfect image in the Christ who meets us. In such a way, Balthasar has prefigured what Pope Benedict attempts to do in *Deus Caritas Est*, to present an understanding of human identity as the *"imago Dei"* which gives to each human person an active role in God's plan. This, however, is rooted not in the quest for human meaning in itself, as we look towards our future glory, but in the descent of Christ to us. This is a timely theme in a world where so many are searching for a sense of value, dignity and identity, but in which the figure of Jesus Christ has become less significant.

Both the Pope and Balthasar have been addressing the question of contemporary Christian identity from the perspective of *"agape"* and *"eros"* love in a way which intends to confront human desire with the truth of the infinite love of Jesus Christ. For Pope Benedict the passionate nature of the love of God in Jesus Christ for us gives us a sense of our special dignity as beloved and enkindles the desire to show this love to others. This is a key message for our generation. Moreover, the mutuality of *"agape"* and *"eros"* are so significant for him, in a sense, says the Pope, we may also call God's love for us *"eros"*, because the *Logos* "is … a lover with all the passion of a true love", yet this love, finding

---

[2] Ibid., no. 7.

its fulfilment in God's becoming one like us in Jesus Christ, "is so purified as to become one with *agape*".[3]

This contribution to contemporary theology, however, is not confined to postconciliar Roman Catholic theology. The reintroduction of these motifs "*agape*" and "*eros*" show more clearly how here the ecumenical bridge Balthasar has been making between Roman Catholic and Reformation thought is beginning to show a way forward for a theological perspective which speaks to the very heart of contemporary humanity. The motifs "*agape*" and "*eros*" had been perceived as forming a divide between Roman Catholics and Lutherans as they express totally different ways of attempting to present an understanding of the human person's Christian identity and vocation.

In the 1940s this was highlighted in the work of the Lutheran theologian Anders Nygren, *Agape and Eros*.[4] This seminal study asserted that the New Testament understanding of Christ's unconditional love "*agape*", as the perfect model of love for humanity, was diametrically opposed to an understanding of love as "*eros*". For Nygren "*eros*" represents the human desire to ascend to God, and is characterised in particular in Roman Catholic theology in the understanding of grace working through human nature. For Nygren "*agape*" excludes this notion of "*eros*" as Christ's death on the cross fully and adequately expresses Luther's doctrine that we are justified by our faith alone in this truth. "*Eros*" is inextricably connected with the egoism of human desire for another. Whilst he does not say that "*eros*" amounts to Pelagianism or hedonism, Nygren does make a connection between the human desire for salvation and a Roman Catholic understanding of our ascent to God through participation in the life of grace.

At this point, however, it is useful to turn to Barth, but, given our study of him, we need not be surprised to find how his view is split between two camps. On the one hand he follows clearly the teaching of Luther, in principle agreeing with Nygren, defending his argument that Christ's "*agape*" and human "*eros*" were fundamentally antithetical. "Even a superficial glance at the two phenomena and concepts, or rather at the realities of the two types of love", he says, "necessarily discloses that we have to do here with two movements in opposite directions, so that there can be no harmony but only conflict between them".[5] Yet, as we have seen in this study, Barth is also trying to develop a more reciprocal understanding of God's relationship with the human person, and so it is that, in his discussion of "*agape*" and "*eros*", he raises the question of whether "*eros*" can be totally discarded. His answer is that it cannot as it represents the reality of human desire

---

[3] Ibid., no. 26. Balthasar also describes God's love for us in terms of the passion of an "*eros*" which is a "divine *ekstasis*", discussing in *Glory of the Lord I*, 120–121, the notion of "*eros*" in God in the same author as referred to by Pope Benedict, in *Deus Caritas Est*, no. 9, that is Pseudo-Dionysius, the Areopagite.

[4] Anders Nygren, *Agape and Eros* (London: S.P.C.K., 1953).

[5] Barth, *CD IV/2*, 736. For Barth's fuller discussion of Nygren see Barth, *CD IV/2*, 727–51.

for God, yet it must be understood from the perspective of God's "*agape*" which in Christ frees "*eros*", and draws it out of itself to love more fully:

> The concrete content of this declaration ... of the antithesis between *agape* and *eros*, is to the effect that God simply espouses the cause of man, and therefore even the man who loves erotically. This is how it is when he calls him out of the kingdom of *eros*, and into the kingdom of His love ... For it is a matter of his liberation when God loves him.[6]

This continuity will also be Balthasar's point, just as it also is a key message of *Deus Caritas Est*. The full force of God's infinite "*agape*" love in Christ does not exclude our finite way of loving but draws us in more closely. As Balthasar puts it, Christ's victorious love on the cross calls us to "glory" "out of the profanity of a worldly life to a new 'pneumatic' existence".[7] Balthasar has recognised the force of this "*agape*", expressed so strongly in the theology of the Reformation, as the foundation of an understanding of Christian life. "*Agape*" and "*eros*" come together but in a new way which proclaims how Christ's infinite love transforms all our finite human desires. The drama of this encounter transcends the dualistic understanding of "*eros*" as expressing the egoism of human desire for God, as it speaks more powerfully of how "*eros*" is transformed through "*agape*", of how the beloved may be transformed through encounter with the one who loves. Thus, in expressing the human person's creation in God's image in these terms Balthasar has begun to break through the perceived dualism surrounding the motifs "*agape*" and "*eros*" in the Lutheran and Roman Catholic traditions.[8]

It is fascinating that Pope Benedict, a former colleague of Balthasar with a similar appreciation of the tradition, should choose to reintroduce these two motifs in his first Encyclical. The Pope does not mention the ecumenical debate specifically. However, what is more important is the message which ensues. Both he and Balthasar before him can speak to the whole of contemporary humanity

---

[6] Ibid., 749.

[7] Balthasar, *GL I*, 124.

[8] A note is necessary here on the debate over "*agape*" and "*eros*" in the 1940s, as the first Roman Catholic response to Nygren's book was given by Martin D'Arcy in his work *The Mind and Heart of Love: Lion and Unicorn: a Study in Eros and Agape*, 2nd edn (London: Fontana, 1954, 1962). D'Arcy's reply to Nygren traced the "*eros*" motif in the history of thought, and concluded that if "*eros*" was not incorporated into theological anthropology, a proper understanding of humanity would not be possible. So for D'Arcy "*agape*" and "*eros*" were equally significant. Balthasar, however, is making a different point. He is not merely returning to a teleological God–human picture which ensures that it expresses the desires of humanity in response to God's grace. Rather Balthasar brings to the God–human drama the full force of "*agape*" as understood in the tradition of Barth and the Reformation. Thus he approaches the question not from D'Arcy's perspective of humanity's desire but from God's "*agape*".

from the perspective of a renewed Christocentrism which wants to proclaim Christ's infinite love as the answer to humanity's deepest desires. Restating from this perspective how the human person is created in God's image connects all Christians with the basic human need to love and be loved, which for believers of all Churches and traditions has its fullest meaning in the person of Christ who loved us fully.[9]

Closing Recommendations

As we come to the end of this study I would like to make some concluding remarks and recommendations. These recommendations advocate, above all, the enduring importance of the "*imago Dei*" doctrine from the perspective of the theological task faced by the churches' united mission to speak to contemporary humanity about the identity and vocation of the Christian. I will divide these remarks into three sections. The first recommends a doctrine of "*imago Dei*" which centres clearly on Christ and in such a way underlines the fundamental dignity of the human person. The second and the third turn to how we must see this in terms of the twin poles, the descendant, expressing God's relationship with humanity, and the ascendant, expressing our response to God.

My first recommendation is that as Christian churches and communities together we appreciate more and more how a truly Christ-centred doctrine of

---

[9] Pope Benedict's Encyclical appears to be encouraging a resurgence of interest in the theological understanding of Christian love, as various articles and talks have, in the last few years, attempted to explain the Pope's work. The Pope himself has emphasised the theme once more in his Message for Lent 2007: Pope Benedict XVI, *Message of His Holiness Pope Benedict XVI for Lent* (www.vatican.va/holy_father/benedict_xvi/messages/pont-messages/2007/docu). Here he is calling the faithful to appreciate God's love in Christ's sacrifice on the cross as both "*agape*" and "*eros*". Once again God's passionate love for humanity calling us to respond in love is the central message as the Pope reflects on the call of the Christian to conversion and discipleship. This book is not the place for a wider discussion of this theme of Christian love. However, I have intended to show here how an appropriately balanced understanding of the human person created in God's image, reflecting the descendant and ascendant poles, makes a contribution to the broader and especially contemporary ecumenical debate which touches directly on the theological themes reintroduced by Pope Benedict. For a most comprehensive commentary on the Encyclical itself and its theological and philosophical background, see the article by Avery Cardinal Dulles, "Love, the Pope, and C.S. Lewis" (*First Things* 169, January 2007). In this article the author also recognises the ecumenical possibilities against the background of the 1940s debate involving Nygren and D'Arcy. Recognition of this theological background is clearly invaluable to the ecumenical reception of the Pope's work, as this can be a platform for a study of more contemporary writers, such as Balthasar, who bring a different perspective to the ecumenical debate, which in turn can foster a greater mutual understanding of the insights contained in the respective writings of Roman Catholics and theologians of the Reformation.

"*imago Dei*" can speak to contemporary humanity of its special dignity. This is the fundamental lesson Balthasar learned from Barth and from Reformation theology. The "*imago Dei*" doctrine must focus its attention on the power of Jesus Christ in each individual human person's life. Jesus Christ must be at the beginning, the core, and the end of our teaching of the doctrine as Christians together, because the "*imago Dei*" should reflect above all Christ's presence in the world shining through us.

This firm belief in a renewed Christocentric understanding of the human person's special dignity is at the centre of postconciliar Roman Catholic teaching. In particular, Pope John Paul II constantly underlined that at the centre of the Christian message was the dignity of the human person as one in whom Christ resides. This was highlighted throughout his pontificate, starting with his 1979 Encyclical *Redemptor Hominis*,[10] in which he first of all declared Jesus Christ as "the Redeemer of man" to be the "fundamental and essential response" to the question of how we should approach the "new advent of the Church" at the end of the second millennium.[11] In this, his first Encyclical, John Paul II goes on to underline how it is Jesus Christ who "fully reveals man to himself":

> If we may use the expression, this is the human dimension of the mystery of the Redemption. In this dimension man finds again the greatness, dignity and value that belong to his humanity. In the mystery of the Redemption man becomes newly "expressed" and, in such a way, is newly created. He is newly created![12]

John Paul II developed this theme throughout his pontificate in a way which gave substance to his promotion of the dignity of the human person. We have seen how the teaching of Pope Benedict, in particular in his first Encyclical *Deus Caritas Est*, is stressing in explicitly theological terms the rooting of human dignity in Christ. His predecessor brought this theme to the fore of pontifical teaching as a key message the Church must present afresh to the world. John Paul II's more philosophical approach to the understanding of the human person had consequences for his teaching on our moral responsibilities as citizens because it focussed not on the human person per se but on Christ in whose image and

---

[10] Pope John Paul II, *Redemptor Hominis* (Vatican City: Libreria Editrice Vaticana, 1979).

[11] Ibid., no. 7.

[12] Ibid., no. 10. Pope John Paul is here echoing the teaching of *Gaudium et Spes*, no. 22, when it declares that Christ is the "'image of the invisible God' (Col. 1:15), is himself the perfect man who has restored in the children of Adam that likeness to God which had been disfigured ever since the first sin. Human nature, by the very fact that it was assumed, not absorbed, in him, has been raised in us also to a dignity beyond compare" (*GS*, no. 22). As we commented in our study of the doctrine in Vatican II teaching, in Chapter 1, this means that Christ not only puts us right with God but in doing so this constitutes our vocation and special dignity as new creatures made in God's image.

likeness he is made. Understanding the human person in this way, he was able to present this key message to the world on matters of Christian morality in the Encyclical *Veritatis Splendor*:

> People today need to turn to Christ once again in order to receive from him the answer to their questions about what is good and evil. Christ is the Teacher, the Risen One who has life in himself and who is always present in his Church and in the world. It is he who opens up to the faithful the book of the Scriptures and, by fully revealing the Father's will, teaches the truth about moral action. At the source and summit of the economy of salvation, as the Alpha and the Omega of human history (cf. Rev 1:8; 21:6; 22:13), Christ sheds light on man's condition and his integral vocation. Consequently, "the man who wishes to understand himself thoroughly – and not just in accordance with immediate, partial, often superficial, and even illusory standards and measures of his being – must with his unrest, uncertainty and even his weakness and sinfulness, with his life and death, draw near to Christ. He must, so to speak, enter him with all his own self; he must 'appropriate' and assimilate the whole of the Reality of the Incarnation and Redemption in order to find himself. If this profound process takes place within him, he then bears fruit not only of adoration of God but also of deep wonder at himself".[13] [14]

In other words John Paul II's moral teaching, stressed so strongly in *Veritatis Splendor*, had as its foundation the profound belief that Jesus Christ defines the Church's understanding of the human person's responsibilities as a moral agent. This fundamental belief, offered in *Redemptor Hominis* as a basis for Christian renewal at the end of the second millennium, is enshrined in a doctrine of the "*imago Dei*" which centres on Christ and the recognition of human dignity which flows from this. Thus the Pope declares at the start of *Veritatis Splendor* that "[t]he splendour of truth shines forth in all the works of the Creator, and, in a special way, in man, created in the image and likeness of God".[15]

Following on from John Paul II, Pope Benedict sets out to convey a similar message. Pope Benedict's general tone is more dialectical and less humanist but we find in his pronouncements the same basic truth emphasised by his predecessor. Thus in his introduction to his first Encyclical he declares:

> Being Christian is not the result of an ethical choice or a lofty idea, but the encounter with an event, a person, which gives life a new horizon and a decisive direction. Saint John's Gospel describes that event in these words: "God so loved the world that he gave his only Son, that whoever believes in him should

---

[13] *Redemptor Hominis*, no. 10.

[14] Pope John Paul II, *Veritatis Splendor* (Vatican City: Libreria Editrice Vaticana, 1993), no. 8.

[15] Ibid., Blessing.

... have eternal life" (3:16) ... Since God has first loved us (cf. 1 *Jn* 4:10), love is now no longer a mere "command"; it is the response to the gift of love with which God draws near to us.[16]

In other words the present Pope, like John Paul II, is conveying a very important message to redirect our attention to Jesus Christ, as it is from our encounter with him that we may understand more fully our own Christian identity and responsibility. Pope Benedict, however, develops this still further, in recognising the importance of stressing in theological terms what I have in this study termed the descendant pole, the primacy of God's love for us, "*agape*" love. This is the infinite love Balthasar speaks of in his theological narrative. It is the love of God for us in giving us his Son, Jesus Christ. This appeal to locate an understanding of the core of our identity in Christ's infinite love for us is for Pope Benedict "both timely and significant". "In a world where the name of God is sometimes associated with vengeance or even a duty of violence, this message is both timely and significant", he declares. "For this reason", he explains, "I wish in my first Encyclical to speak of the love which God lavishes upon us and which we in turn must share with others".[17]

I would thus conclude that theology should not only be concerned to express the doctrine of the "*imago Dei*" afresh from the perspective of Jesus Christ, but should do so in a way which stresses this descendant pole. In such a way the doctrine invites us to appreciate Christ's love for us. We must place the "*imago Dei*" against the background not primarily of our ascent to God but first and foremost from the perspective of the descent to earth of the God in Jesus Christ who in his infinite love for us intends to draw us into a personal encounter with him which affects all our relationships with our fellow humans. To do this we need a theological narrative which places God's descent before our ascent, God's love in Christ as fundamental and primary. The pre-eminence of God's descent to us then leads into a mutuality of the two movements as God's giving his Son for us not merely identifies us as made in his image but beckons us to draw closer to him and to become more like him.

This way of approaching the doctrine echoes a movement in theology discernible in particular in the much broader field of ecumenical dialogue. Central to my own thesis has been my view that Balthasar has gleaned and assimilated into his own theology the core insight of the primacy of the descendant pole which he has found in Barth and the theology of the Reformation. Balthasar's whole approach here suggests a fresh and more fruitful ecumenical methodology than has been the case in the past. Since the Second Vatican Council in particular, Roman Catholic theologians have been keen to move away from the view that traditions are diametrically opposed to each other. This is a very positive development. However, it is a development which may have a less helpful consequence, as, if

---

[16] *Deus Caritas Est*, Introduction.
[17] Ibid., Introduction.

not checked, it can lead theologians to play down the strength of different views and positions, in order to marry aspects of one tradition with another in order to arrive at an agreed statement.

In Balthasar's approach we see a historical development here in the way we approach ecumenical dialogue. Rather than look for a theological compromise, Balthasar shows us, in his reception of Barth and the Reformation, how to accept the core insight of a theological narrative as it stands within its own tradition. Similarly, he shows us that this should not lead us to divest our own tradition and the teaching of the Church of any of its riches and fullness. We may conclude that the fuller picture of human dignity is missing in the Reformation understanding of the "*imago Dei*" and still recognise the core insight of that theological tradition. Thus we learn from Balthasar that to move forward in ecumenical dialogue requires us, in a sense, to take a step back. He teaches us to listen and to learn from the tradition of the other, to be receptive to it, and so to move on from the stage of ecumenical dialogue which looked more for compromise. It is a movement which captures the insight of what the other has to say and how it enriches us yet still expresses our own position as boldly as possible. In order to clarify what I mean it is necessary to give some examples from the history of the Lutheran–Roman Catholic dialogue in particular.

Lutheran theologians of the pre-war period, such as Gustav Aulén and Philip Watson,[18] had presented a view that preaching the power of Christ's descent to us necessarily included a belief that we were justified by faith alone. The view that the two theological systems were opposites was perpetuated in the "*agape*" and "*eros*" debate between Anders Nygren and Martin D'Arcy to which we alluded in the last section of this chapter.[19] Then in the 1970s and 1980s a major shift took place. It was in this period following Vatican II that Roman Catholic theologians in particular such as Cornelius Ernst[20] and Roger Haight,[21] attempted to show how Lutheran and Roman Catholic understandings of the human person's relationship with God were at root not so different but presented different emphases.

The view of these theologians may be taken to stress how Lutheranism emphasises the descendant pole, while Roman Catholicism the ascendant. Both,

---

[18] Gustav Aulén, in his seminal work *Christus Victor* (London: S.P.C.K., 1931) argues that Luther's model of the atonement is the most authentic, as it proposes a picture of Christ as victor over sin, whereas other models, especially in the Roman Catholic tradition, emphasise the storing up of merit and sinful humanity's ascent to God. Philip Watson, in his work *Let God be God! An Interpretation of the Theology of Martin Luther* (London: Epworth Press, 1947) presents the classical understanding of Luther's teaching on justification by faith alone as properly theocentric and diametrically opposed to the Council of Trent's egocentric definition of grace as faith informed by love.

[19] Cf. footnote 8, this chapter.

[20] Cornelius Ernst, *The Theology of Grace* (Notre Dame, IN: Fides Publisher, 1974).

[21] Roger Haight, *The Experience and Language of Grace* (New York, Ramsey, NJ and Toronto: Paulist Press, 1979).

however, proclaim the truth about Jesus Christ. On a positive note the work of this period was very fruitful as it opened up theology to the possibility of ecumenical dialogue across the traditions. We could agree that both ways of approaching the issue were on one level valid and so talk to one another. This was able to happen on an official level through various agreed statements, which were extremely fruitful for the ecumenical process. It culminated in an important breakthrough in the *Joint Declaration on the Doctrine of Justification*[22] of 1999, which recognised the value in both traditions, as it declared:

> In faith together we hold the conviction that justification is the work of the triune God. The Father sent his Son into the world to save sinners. The foundation and presupposition of justification is the incarnation, death and resurrection of Christ. Justification thus means that Christ himself is our righteousness.[23]

The process of arriving at agreement, however, necessarily involved a considerable measure of theological compromise. For example, ARCIC II, the Second Anglican-Roman Catholic International Commission, produced an agreed statement, *Salvation and the Church*,[24] which, while coming to a measure of agreement on previously divisive points of issue, did so at the expense of a compromise on the question of justification and sanctification, seeing them as part of the same movement. The Commission concluded that "[t]he balance and coherence of the constitutive elements of the Christian doctrine of salvation had become partially obscured in the course of history and controversy", but now "[w]e have also realised the central meaning and profound significance which the message of justification and sanctification, within the doctrine of salvation, continues to have for us today".[25] "As justification and sanctification are aspects

---

[22] The Lutheran World Federation and the Roman Catholic Church, *Joint Declaration on the Doctrine of Justification* (Vatican City: Libreria Editrice Vaticana, 1999).

[23] Ibid., no. 15.

[24] The Anglican Consultative Council and the Secretariat for Promoting Christian Unity, *Salvation and the Church: an Agreed Statement by the Second Anglican-Roman Catholic International Commission (ARCIC II)* (London: Church House Publishing; London: Catholic Truth Society, 1987). It should be pointed out here that I am using ARCIC II as an example of the methodology in an ecumenical dialogue during the 1980s for the purpose of my recommendations for a fresh contemporary outlook. There is not scope here for a fuller treatment of the methodology of ecumenical dialogue, which would then necessarily take account of the Lutheran–Roman Catholic dialogue elsewhere. For a fuller commentary on the process, see the published proceedings of the 1995 Rome Conference on this in: *Catholic-Lutheran Relations Three Decades after Vatican II: Conference at the International Bridgettine Centre, Farfa Sabina, 12–15 March 1995*, Peder Nørgaard, ed. (Vatican City: Libreria Editrice Vaticana, 1997).

[25] Ibid., no. 32.

of the same divine act, so also living faith and love are inseparable in the believer", declared the Commission.[26]

This was intended as a statement which recognises the value in the Lutheran idea of justification by faith alone and in the Roman Catholic doctrine of grace as faith informed by love. In other words it recognised the importance of the descendant and the ascendant poles. However, such a general acceptance of the significance of both views tends to avoid the essential dichotomies between the two positions. It leads to a certain large agreement, crystallised in such a general statement as "[I]nasmuch as we are recreated in his 'own image and likeness', God involves us in what he freely does to realise our salvation".[27] Thus one might conclude that, in the interests of agreement, the Commission has been unable to appreciate the insights of both traditions more fully.[28]

Balthasar's prophetic approach can prompt us to make a new shift as we move into a new period of ecumenical dialogue now 50 years after Vatican II. The key is that, rather than look so much for agreement, he is first and foremost searching the tradition for insight, for flashes of beauty and of truth. It is because of this shift that he is much more appreciative of the full force of the descendant pole, of the Reformation's insistence on human incapacity in the face of the gratuity of justification. As a result, although it might seem at first sight paradoxical, it is in recognising this and in working with the real insights and also the shortcomings and falsities of the Reformation position, that he could move ecumenical dialogue to a new level of understanding.

His particular contribution is that his reading of Barth helps him, through discernment of what is the major insight but also of what in his theology is still lacking, to develop a doctrine of the "*imago Dei*" which proclaims to contemporary humanity all the more powerfully the core truth contained in the teaching. This core teaching is God's love for us in the descent of his Son, Jesus Christ. The value of seeing the descendant as primary to the ascendant represents new possibilities for ecumenical dialogue because, rather than simply seeing the different emphases in what were in the past perceived as opposite theological systems, it has heard and recognised the core insights for what they are.

Thus we are learning a new way forward for ecumenical dialogue in the twenty-first century. This is closely linked to a general movement which has been called "receptive ecumenism", a process of theological dialogue now gaining

---

[26] Ibid., no. 19.

[27] Ibid., no. 19.

[28] The official response of the Sacred Congregation for the Doctrine of the Faith recognised this, in concluding that there had not in fact been "substantial agreement", as the Commission had not considered in sufficient depth key differences between the traditions on the definition of "faith", on the distinctions between justification and sanctification, and freedom and merit, as well as the central role of the Church in salvation. See Sacred Congregation for the Doctrine of the Faith, *Observations on ARCIC II's "Salvation and the Church"* (Vatican City: Libreria Editrice Vaticana, 1988).

currency, which, recognising the fruits and the shortcomings of the post-Vatican II quest for agreed statements, reflects again on the nature of truth and solidarity between Christians. Among others "receptive ecumenism" has two important aims which I would highlight from my study as a way forward. Firstly, it intends to listen more carefully to the other, and, secondly, to express our own position more boldly. In general it looks less for compromise as for insight and meaning.[29] Such a perspective on ecumenical dialogue can move us forward into the next stage of growing closer together, as we enter more deeply into a mutual understanding of the substantial agreement which has now been achieved in the *Joint Declaration on Justification*. It also echoes the intention of Pope John Paul II in his Encyclical, *Ut Unum Sint*, when he declares that "[t]he unity willed by God can be attained only by adherence of all to the content of revealed faith in its entirety. In matters of faith, compromise is in contradiction with God who is truth".[30]

However, the future of a doctrine of "*imago Dei*" which is ecumenically inspired must also recognise aspects of another's tradition which are undeveloped. Barth's doctrine on its own lacks a necessary understanding of our ascent to God in the adventure of transcendence. We learn from him the powerful insight that we must proclaim Christ's love for us first, but for a fuller picture of human dignity which speaks adequately not just of the gift but of the promise of life in Christ we need to stress the ascendant pole too. Because Jesus Christ is a real person the promise of transcendence gained through a lifelong relationship with him is attainable. Moreover, my study has led me to the conclusion that such a "receptive ecumenism" will be especially fruitful if it addresses these central matters of our Christian faith regarding the essential dignity, responsibility and vocation of the human person. In doing this in particular, theology can take up the call of Pope John Paul II in *Ut Unum Sint*, when he recognises how "[t]he capacity for 'dialogue' is rooted in the nature of the person and his dignity ... Dialogue is an indispensable step along the path *towards human self-realization*, the self-realization both of *each individual* and *of every human community*".[31]

How, then, can theology address this best today? The fact that we are given such a special gift through Christ's love for us poured out for the salvation of the world is not to be expressed simply as a dogmatic truth but must be expressed as an invitation to participate in a process of conversion through which we connect

---

[29] The term "receptive ecumenism" was applied to the methodology of two large international symposia on the future of ecumenical dialogue, held in Durham, UK, in January 2006 and January 2009. As a theme in ecumenical methodology it has been gaining currency in the last decade, such as, for example, in its substantial treatment in the proceedings of the 1995 Rome Lutheran–Catholic Conference. For more background see: Paul D. Murray, "On Valuing Truth in Practice: Rome's Postmodern Challenge" (*International Journal of Systematic Theology* 8/2, April 2006), 163–83.

[30] Pope John Paul II, *Ut Unum Sint* (Vatican City: Libreria Editrice Vaticana, 1995), no. 18.

[31] Ibid., no. 28. Emphasis his.

with this love and pass it on to others. Any philosophy or anthropology which tries to find a way to God without first recognising the power of God's grace is to be rejected. Yet, at the same time, we need to develop an adequate notion of our human dignity and vocation which places us on mission with Christ as disciples in relation with each other. This allows for recognition of the innate human quest for relationship with the infinite as the basis for all human relationships and of our identity as the "*imago Dei*".

The general approach we find in theologians such as Moltmann and Balthasar can help us to find a way of presenting doctrine which allows truth to be proclaimed through a narrative which brings the insights of doctrine alive for the reader. The narrative of the mysteries of the cross, of Holy Saturday, and of the resurrection, show us in themselves how the lover and the beloved are called to be in a mutual relationship in which the beloved is called to be actively engaged and so gradually discover his true destiny. From an ecumenical perspective in particular, it is fascinating to see how in the last 30 years or so, in both Catholic and in Protestant theology, there has been a renewed interest in narrative theology.

We may see Moltmann's narrative of the cross and Balthasar's of the descent into the underworld as part of a movement which intends to proclaim doctrine not so much through systematic theology but in narrative form. It was theologians in the 1980s such as Hans Frei and George Lindbeck[32] who made this deliberate turn away from the exclusive development of systematic theology to use narrative as the chief medium. This is not just a development within theology but more broadly part of the movement in the history of ideas away from more systematic categories towards modes of expression which embrace the fluidity of the narrative.

An important figure here is the French philosopher Paul Ricoeur, who saw the value of narrative for our understanding of human identity.[33] For Ricoeur telling our personal and our communal narratives enables us to see our horizons more clearly, so to understand ourselves better, and to prompt us to expectation of personal fulfilment. Theology can speak of the dignity of the human person all the more meaningfully and creatively through narrative. It enables theology to situate the quest for a personal identity in the central mysteries of God's becoming man, and so to invite the human being to see his eternal horizon realised in Christ. Narrative also has ecumenical significance as it helps theology to develop its invitation to recognise the insights of doctrine across traditions and present them in a way which may enable the reader to encounter these truths as a lived response to the Gospel. Proclaiming God's love through retelling the great mysteries of our salvation helps to highlight above all the element of movement, dynamic and

---

[32] Cf. Hans W. Frei, *The Eclipse of Biblical Narrative: a Study in Eighteenth and Nineteenth Century Hermeneutics* (New Haven and London: Yale University Press, 1974), and George A. Lindbeck, *The Nature of Doctrine: Religion and Theology in a Postliberal Age* (Philadelphia: Westminster Press, 1984).

[33] Cf. Paul Ricoeur, *Time and Narrative* (Chicago: Chicago University Press, 1984, 1988).

drama in the God–human relationship, through creation, sin, suffering and death, to the expectation of new life. Through this the human being may discover what it means to be created in the "*imago Dei*". The Christian narrative reveals to him how his creation as God's image gives us a share in the drama of the divine life.

Such a theological narrative must affirm our human identity as the beloved whom we intend to draw into this divine encounter. It must include the ascendant pole, the promise of fulfilment in our divine destiny. Human dignity reaches its goal in oneness with God in heaven. This is the fullest experience of love and relationship for which our lives on earth are a preparation. As such Balthasar's understanding of the doctrine represents such a significant contribution as it speaks through narrative drama of the mutuality and movement of the descendant and ascendant pole, infinite and finite love, "*agape*" and "*eros*", of human identity rooted in Christ's love of us drawing us more deeply into vocation, mission, and ultimately preparing us for our final destiny. The mutuality of the descendant with the ascendant unlocks the key to the enduring importance of the doctrine, now echoed in the postconciliar interest in a narrative theology which focuses clearly on Christ yet speaks of human destiny in the divine in as exalted a way as possible.

Closing Summary

To summarise, I would want to recommend that the doctrine of the "*imago Dei*" is best maintained and restated in a theological narrative which holds together the descendant and the ascendant pole in a mutual drama of love. To be created in the "*imago Dei*" means above all that we are loved infinitely by Christ who draws us into a life of love ultimately fulfilled in our divine destiny. The best way forward for the doctrine is to capture in theological narrative the mutuality of the descendant and the ascendant, drawn together in the drama of infinite and finite love. This expresses what is at the heart of the identity of the Christian. Moreover, I would suggest that this way of approaching the doctrine also represents a significant ecumenical way forward.

Most importantly the doctrine must be rooted in Jesus Christ. It is the presence of Jesus Christ in each human person which gives him his special dignity as created in the "*imago Dei*". The doctrine must speak to a contemporary world which yearns to connect with what ultimately defines us, that is the person of Jesus Christ. Pope Benedict, in his message to participants in the Conference "Only Love is Credible", marking the centenary of the birth of Balthasar, expressed this most basic yet most profound point succinctly. In commenting that Balthasar perceived in the drama of the Triduum narrative the "'logic' of revelation", he concludes: "God becomes man so that man can live the communion of life with

God. In Christ, the ultimate and definitive truth is offered in answer to the question that everyone asks himself or herself."[34]

Pope Benedict here is echoing Balthasar's call to humanity to accept the logic of the Christian mystery, and thus to surrender to God's love poured out for us in the Son. It is in so doing that the human being discovers that he is an image of God. It is in surrendering to Christ's love in our vulnerability, we discover our infinite horizon and our special dignity, and we are called forth to join him as his disciples. It is the infinite love of God for us in the person of Christ which is the foundation and the fulfilment of the Christian life. It is that powerful and consoling message which we must aim to present in the doctrine of the "*imago Dei*", just as Balthasar did so powerfully in this section of *Theo-Drama III*:

> it is not simply that the *imago* is a foundation on which heaven builds the *similitudo* in an entirely different style: rather, it is created man, as the conscious subject he is, who is given *his* true purpose in the divine, triune life. In that trusting self-surrender to God that we call the faith that hopes and loves, and which Christ performed on earth in an exemplary way, as our prototype (Heb 12:2), man both transcends himself and lives in Christ, or allows Christ to live in him: "It is no longer I who live, but Christ who lives in me; and the life I now live in the flesh I live by faith in the Son of God, who loved me and gave himself for me" (Gal 2:20).[35]

---

[34] Pope Benedict XVI, *Message for the Centenary of the Birth of Fr Hans Urs von Balthasar*, www.vatican.va/holy_father/benedict_xvi/messages/ pont-messages/2005/docu.

[35] Balthasar, *TD III: The Dramatis Personae: the Person in Christ* (San Francisco: Ignatius Press, 1992), 528. Emphasis his.

Bibliography

I. Primary Sources

1. Selected Writings of Barth

Barth, Karl. *Church Dogmatics I/1, The Doctrine of the Word of God*. Trans. G.W. Bromiley. 2nd edn. Edinburgh: T&T Clark, 1936, 1975 [*Kirchliche Dogmatik I/1: Die Lehre vom Wort Gottes*. Zurich: Evangelischer Verlag A.G. Zollikon, 1932, 1964].

Barth, Karl. *Church Dogmatics II, The Doctrine of God, Part 1*. Trans. T.H.L. Parker, W.B. Johnston, Harold Knight and J.L.M. Haire. Edinburgh: T&T Clark, 1957 [*Kirchliche Dogmatik II: Die Lehre von Gott: Erster Halbband*. Zurich: Evangelischer Verlag A.G. Zollikon, 1936].

Barth, Karl. *Church Dogmatics II, The Doctrine of God, Part 2*. Trans. G.W. Bromiley, J.C. Campbell, Iain Wilson, J. Strathearn McNab, Harold Knight and R.A. Stewart. Edinburgh: T&T Clark, 1957 [*Kirchliche Dogmatik II: Die Lehre von Gott: Zweiter Halbband*. Zurich: Evangelischer Verlag A.G. Zollikon, 1942].

Barth, Karl. *Church Dogmatics III, The Doctrine of Creation, Part 1*. Trans. J.W. Edwards, O. Bussey and H. Knight. Edinburgh: T&T Clark, 1958 [*Kirchliche Dogmatik III: Die Lehre von der Schöpfung: Erster Teil*. Zurich: Evangelischer Verlag A.G. Zollikon, 1945].

Barth, Karl. *Church Dogmatics III, The Doctrine of Creation, Part 2*. Trans. G.W. Bromiley. Edinburgh: T&T Clark, 1960 [*Kirchliche Dogmatik III: Die Lehre von der Schöpfung: Zweiter Teil*. Zurich: Evangelischer Verlag A.G. Zollikon, 1948].

Barth, Karl. *Church Dogmatics III, The Doctrine of Creation, Part 3*. Trans. G.W. Bromiley and R.J. Ehrlich. Edinburgh: T&T Clark, 1960 [*Kirchliche Dogmatik III: Die Lehre von der Schöpfung: Dritter Teil*. Zurich: Evangelischer Verlag A.G. Zollikon, 1950].

Barth, Karl. *Church Dogmatics IV, The Doctrine of Reconciliation, Part 1*. Trans. G.W. Bromiley. Edinburgh: T&T Clark, 1956 [*Kirchliche Dogmatik IV: Die Lehre von der Versöhnung: Erster Teil*. Zurich: Evangelischer Verlag A.G. Zollikon, 1953].

Barth, Karl. *Church Dogmatics IV, The Doctrine of Reconciliation, Part 2*. Trans. G.W. Bromiley. Edinburgh: T&T Clark, 1958 [*Kirchliche Dogmatik IV: Die Lehre von der Versöhnung: Zweiter Teil*. Zurich: Evangelischer Verlag A.G. Zollikon, 1955].

2. Selected Writings of von Balthasar

von Balthasar, Hans Urs. *Dare we Hope that "All Men be Saved?" with a Short Discourse on Hell*. Trans. David Kipp and Lothar Krauth. San Francisco: Ignatius Press, 1988 [*Was dürfen wir hoffen?* Einsiedeln: Johannes Verlag, 1986; *Kleiner Diskurs über die Hölle*, Ostfildern: Schwabenverlag A.G., 1987].

von Balthasar, Hans Urs. "Der Begriff der Natur in der Theologie". *Zeitschrift für Katholischen Theologie* 75 (1953): 453–61.

von Balthasar, Hans Urs. *Engagement with God*. Trans. J. Halliburton. London: S.P.C.K., 1975 [*In Gottes Einsatz leben*. Einsiedeln: Johannes Verlag, 1972].

von Balthasar, Hans Urs. *Explorations in Theology III: Creator Spirit*. Trans. Brian McNeil. San Francisco: Ignatius Press, 1993 [*Skizzen zur Theologie III: Spiritus Creator*. Einsiedeln: Johannes Verlag, 1967].

von Balthasar, Hans Urs. *The Glory of the Lord: a Theological Aesthetics I, Seeing the Form*. Trans. Elizabeth Leiva-Merikakis. Edinburgh: T&T Clark, 1982 [*Herrlichkeit: Eine Theologische Ästhetik I: Schau der Gestalt*. Einsiedeln: Johannes Verlag, 1961].

von Balthasar, Hans Urs. *The Glory of the Lord: a Theological Aesthetics V, The Realm of Metaphysics in the Modern Age*. Trans. Oliver Davies, Andrew Louth, Brian McNeil, John Saward and Rowan Williams. San Francisco: Ignatius Press, 1991 [*Herrlichkeit: Eine Theologische Ästhetik III/1: Im Raum der Metaphysik: Teil 1: Altertum*. Einsiedeln: Johannes Verlag, 1965; *Herrlichkeit: Eine Theologische Ästhetik III/1: Im Raum der Metaphysik: Teil 2: Neuzeit*. Einsiedeln: Johannes Verlag, 1965].

von Balthasar, Hans Urs. *The Glory of the Lord: a Theological Aesthetics VI, Theology: The Old Covenant*. Trans. Brian McNeil and Erasmo Leiva-Merikakis. San Francisco: Ignatius Press, 1991 [*Herrlichkeit: Eine Theologische Ästhetik III/2: Theologie: Teil 1: Alter Bund*. Einsiedeln: Johannes Verlag, 1967].

von Balthasar, Hans Urs. *Mysterium Paschale: the Mystery of Easter*. Trans. Aidan Nichols. Edinburgh: T&T Clark, 1990 [*Mysterium Salutis: Grundriss Heilsgeschichticher Dogmatik*. Einsiedeln: Johannes Verlag, 1985].

von Balthasar, Hans Urs. "A Résumé of My Thought". *Communio: International Catholic Review* 15 (Winter 1988), reproduced in ed. Schindler, David L., *Hans Urs Von Balthasar: His Life and Work*. San Francisco: Ignatius Press, 1991: 1–5.

von Balthasar, Hans Urs. *Theo-Drama: Theological Dramatic Theory II, The Dramatis Personae: Man in God*. Trans. Graham Harrison. San Francisco: Ignatius Press, 1990 [*Theodramatik II/1: Die Personen des Spiels: Der Mensch in Gott*. Einsiedeln: Johannes Verlag, 1976].

von Balthasar, Hans Urs. *Theo-Drama: Theological Dramatic Theory III, The Dramatis Personae: the Person in Christ*. Trans. Graham Harrison. San Francisco: Ignatius Press, 1992 [*Theodramatik II/2: Die Personen des Spiels: Die Person in Christus*. Einsiedeln: Johannes Verlag, 1978].

von Balthasar, Hans Urs. *Theo-Drama: Theological Dramatic Theory IV, The Action*. Trans. Graham Harrison. San Francisco: Ignatius Press, 1994. [*Theodramatik III: Die Handlung*. Einsiedeln: Johannes Verlag, 1980].

von Balthasar, Hans Urs. *The Theology of Karl Barth*. Trans. Edward T. Oakes. San Francisco: Ignatius Press, 1992 [*Karl Barth: Darstellung und Deutung Seiner Theologie*. Cologne: Verlag Jakob Hegner, 1951, 1962].

3. Selected Works of Moltmann

Moltmann, Jürgen. *The Coming of God: Christian Eschatology*. Trans. Margaret Kohl. London: S.C.M. Press, 1996 [*Das Kommen Gottes: christliche Eschatologie*. Gütersloh: Kaiser, 1995].

Moltmann, Jürgen. *The Crucified God: the Cross of Christ as the Foundation of Christian Theology*. Trans. R.A. Wilson and John Bowden. New York and Evanston: Harper & Row, 1974 [*Der gekreuzigte Gott: das Kreuz Christi Grund und Kritik Christlicher Theologie*. Munich: Kaiser Verlag, 1972].

Moltmann, Jürgen. *The Future of Creation*. Trans. Margaret Kohl. London: S.C.M. Press, 1979 [*Umkehr zur Zukunft*. Munich and Hamburg: Siebenstern Taschenbuch Verlag, 1970].

Moltmann, Jürgen. *God in Creation: an Ecological Doctrine of Creation*. Trans. Margaret Kohl. London: S.C.M. Press, 1985 [*Gott in der Schöpfung: ökologische Schöpfungslehre*. Munich: Kaiser Verlag, 1985].

Moltmann, Jürgen. *The Spirit of Life: a Universal Affirmation*. Trans. Margaret Kohl. Minneapolis: Fortress Press, 1993 [*Der Geist des Lebens: Eine ganzheitliche Pneumotalogie*. Munich: Kaiser Verlag, 1991].

Moltmann, Jürgen. *Theology of Hope: on the Ground and the Implications of a Christian Eschatology*. Trans. James W. Leitch. New York and Evanston: Harper & Row, 1967 [*Theologie der Hoffnung: Untersuchungen zur Begründung und den Konsequenzen einer Christlichen Eschatologie*. Munich: Kaiser Verlag, 1966].

Moltmann, Jürgen. *The Trinity and the Kingdom of God: the Doctrine of God*. Trans. Margaret Kohl. London: S.C.M. Press, 1981 [*Trinität und Reich Gottes: zur Gotteslehre*. Munich: Kaiser Verlag, 1980).

II. Magisterial Sources

Benedict XVI, Pope. Encyclical Letter. *Deus Caritas Est*. Vatican City: Libreria Editrice Vaticana, 2006.

Benedict XVI, Pope. *Message for the Centenary of the Birth of Fr Hans Urs von Balthasar*. www.vatican.va: 2005.

Benedict XVI, Pope. *Message of His Holiness Pope Benedict XVI for Lent 2007*. www.vatican.va: 2007.

The Council of Trent, *Decree on Original Sin, Decretum super peccato originali*. Ed. Tanner, N., *Decrees of the Ecumenical Councils* II, Trent – Vatican II. London: Sheed and Ward; Washington, DC: Georgetown University Press, 1990: 657–800.

First Vatican Ecumenical Council, Dogmatic Constitution on the Catholic Faith, *Dei Filius*. Ed. Tanner, N., *Decrees of the Ecumenical Councils* II, Trent – Vatican II. London: Sheed and Ward; Washington, DC: Georgetown University Press, 1990: 804–811.

International Theological Commission of the Sacred Congregation for the Doctrine of the Faith. *Communion and Stewardship: Human Persons Created in the Image of God*. Vatican City: Libreria Editrice Vatican, 2002: www.vatican.va.

John Paul II, Pope. Encyclical Letter. *Evangelium Vitae*. Vatican City: Libreria Editrice Vaticana, 1995.

John Paul II, Pope. Encyclical Letter. *Fides et Ratio*. Vatican City: Libreria Editrice Vaticana, 1998.

John Paul II, Pope. Encyclical Letter. *Redemptor Hominis*. Vatican City: Libreria Editrice Vaticana, 1979.

John Paul II, Pope. Encyclical Letter. *Ut Unum Sint*. Vatican City: Libreria Editrice Vaticana, 1995.

John Paul II, Pope . Encyclical Letter. *Veritatis Splendor*. Vatican City: Libreria Editrice Vaticana, 1993.

Sacred Congregation for the Doctrine of the Faith. *Observations on ARCIC II's "Salvation and the Church"*. Vatican City: Libreria Editrice Vaticana, 1988.

Second Vatican Ecumenical Council, Dogmatic Constitution on the Church, *Lumen Gentium*. Ed. Flannery, A., Vatican Collection 1, *Vatican Council II: The Conciliar and Post Conciliar Documents*. Dublin: Dominican Publications, 1992: 350–426.

Second Vatican Ecumenical Council, Dogmatic Constitution on Divine Revelation, *Dei Verbum*. Ed. Flannery, A., Vatican Collection 1, *Vatican Council II: The Conciliar and Post Conciliar Documents*. Dublin: Dominican Publications, 1992: 750–765.

Second Vatican Ecumenical Council, Pastoral Constitution on the Church in the Modern World, *Gaudium et Spes*. Ed. Flannery, A., Vatican Collection 1, *Vatican Council II: The Conciliar and Post Conciliar Documents*. Dublin: Dominican Publications, 1992: 903–1001.

III. Complementary Sources

The Anglican Consultative Council and the Secretariat for Promoting Christian Unity. *Salvation and the Church: an Agreed Statement by the Second Anglican-Roman Catholic International Commission (ARCIC II)*. London: Church House Publishing; London: Catholic Truth Society, 1987.

Augustine, St. *Confessions*. Trans. Henry Chadwick. Oxford: Oxford University Press, 1992.
Augustine, St. *De Diversis Quaestionibus*. Ed. Migne, J.-P., *Patres Latini, Tomus* 40. Paris: Garnier Fratres et J.-P. Migne Successores, 1887.
Augustine, St. *Enchiridion on Faith, Hope and Love*. Trans. Albert C. Outler. Philadelphia: Westminster Press, 1955.
Aquinas, St Thomas. *De Veritate*. Ed. Bourke, Vernon J., *Opera Omnia, Tomus IX*. New York: Musurgia Publishers, 1949.
Aquinas, St Thomas. *Summa Theologiae*. New Blackfriars edn. Volume 2, *Existence and Nature of God*. Trans. Timothy McDermott. London and New York: McGraw-Hill Book Company, 1964.
Aquinas, St Thomas. *Summa Theologiae*. New Blackfriars edn. Volume 11, *Man*. Trans. Timothy Sutter. London and New York: McGraw-Hill Book Company, 1970.
Aquinas, St Thomas. *Summa Theologiae*. New Blackfriars edn. Volume 13, *Man Made to God's Image*. Trans. Edmund Hill. London and New York: McGraw-Hill Book Company, 1964.
Aquinas, St Thomas. *Summa Theologiae*. New Blackfriars edn. Volume 16, *Purpose and Happiness*. Trans. Thomas Gilby. London and New York: McGraw-Hill Book Company, 1969.
Aquinas, St Thomas. *Summa Theologiae*. New Blackfriars edn. Volume 26, *Original Sin*. Trans. T.C. O'Brien. London and New York: McGraw-Hill Book Company, 1965.
Aquinas, St Thomas. *Summa Theologiae*. New Blackfriars edn. Volume 30, *The Gospel of Grace*. Trans. Cornelius Ernst. London and New York: McGraw-Hill Book Company, 1972.
Aulén, Gustav. *Christus Victor*. Trans. A.G. Hebert. London: S.P.C.K., 1931.
Aulén, Gustav. *Das Drama und Die Symbole. Die Problematik des Heutigen Gottesbildes*. Götingen: Vandenhoek and Ruprecht, 1964.
Bauckham, Richard. *The Theology of Jürgen Moltmann*. Edinburgh: T&T Clark, 1995.
Beer, T. *Der Fröhliche Wechsel und Streit. Grundzüge der Theologie Martin Luthers*. Leipzig: Benno, 1974.
Bonner, G. "Augustine's Conception of Deification". *Church and Faith in the Patristic Tradition*. Aldershot: Variorum, 1996: 369–86.
Bromiley, George. *Introduction to the Theology of Karl Barth*. Grand Rapids: William B. Eerdmans Publishing Company, 1979.
Brunner, Emil. *Dogmatik II: Die Christliche Lehre von Schöpfung und Erlösung*. Zurich: Zwingli-Verlag, 1950.
Butler, Christopher. *The Theology of Vatican II*. London: Darton, Longman and Todd, 1981.
Calvin, John. *Institutes of the Christian Religion*. Trans. Ford Lewis Battles. Philadelphia: Westminster Press, 1960.

Cihak, John. "Balthasar and Anxiety: Methodological and Phenomenological Considerations". Convegno Internazionale per il centenario della nascita di Hans Urs von Balthasar, Rome, 6–7 October 2005. www.ignatiusinsight.com/features2005/jcihak_hubanxiety_dec05.asp.

Clark, Mary T., ed. *An Aquinas Reader*. London: Hodder & Stoughton, 1974.

Clifford, Richard J. and Murphy, Roland, E. "Genesis". Ed. Brown, Raymond E., Fitzmyer, Joseph A. and Murphy, Roland E., *The New Jerome Biblical Commentary*. London: Geoffrey Chapman, 1989: 8–43.

dal Covolo, Enrico and Tosso, Mario. *Attrati dall'Amore: Riflessioni sull'Enciclica Deus Caritas est di Benedetto XVI*. Rome: Libreria Ateneo Salesiano, 2006.

D'Arcy, Martin. *The Mind and Heart of Love: Lion and Unicorn: a Study in Eros and Agape*. 2nd. edn. London: Fontana, 1954, 1962.

Dorrien, Gary. *The Barthian Revolt in Modern Theology*. Louisville: Westminster John Knox Press, 1999.

Dulles, Avery. *Models of Revelation*. New York: Orbis Books, 1979, 1992.

Dulles, Avery Cardinal. "Love, the Pope, and C.S. Lewis". *First Things* 169 (January 2007).

Egúzkiza Mutiloa, Ion. *El hombre creado a imagen de Dios en la teología del siglo XX: Las aportaciones de la teología positiva y su recepción en el Concilio Vaticano II*. Rome: Pontifical University of the Holy Cross, 2005. Doctoral dissertation.

Erhueh, Anthony O. *Image of God in Man. An Enquiry into the Theological Foundations and Significance of Human Dignity in the Pastoral Constitution on the Church in the Modern World, "Gaudium et Spes"*. Rome: Urbanian University Press, 1987. Doctoral dissertation.

Ernst, Cornelius. *The Theology of Grace*. Notre Dame, IN: Fides Publisher, 1974.

Farrugia, Mario. "Gn1: 26–27 in Augustine and Luther: 'Before you are my strength and my weakness'". *Gregorianum* 87, 3 (2006): 487–521.

Frei, Hans W. *The Eclipse of Biblical Narrative: a Study in Eighteenth and Nineteenth Century Hermeneutics*. New Haven and London: Yale University Press, 1974.

Gilkey, Langdon. *Message and Existence: an Introduction to Christian Theology*. New York: Seabury, 1979.

Gounelle, André. "L'homme, image de Dieu". *Foi et Vie* 87 (1988): 27–40.

Greshake, Gisbert. *Gnade als konkreten Freiheit. Eine Untersuchung zur Gnadenlehre des Pelagius*. Mainz: Matthias-Grünewald, 1972.

Greshake, Gisbert. *Gottes Heil – Glück des Menschen. Theologische Perspektiven*. Freiburg im Breisgau: Herder, 1983.

Gunton, Colin. "Karl Barth's Doctrine of Election as Part of his Doctrine of God". *Journal of Theological Studies (New Series)* 25 (1974): 384.

Haight, Roger. *The Experience and Language of Grace*. New York, Ramsey, NJ and Toronto: Paulist Press, 1979.

Harrison, Carol. *Beauty and Revelation in the Thought of Saint Augustine*. Oxford: Clarendon Press, 1992.
Hemming, Lawrence P. *Benedict XVI: Fellow Worker for Truth – an Introduction to His Life and Thought*. London: Burns and Oates, 2005.
Henrici, Peter. "Hans Urs von Balthasar: A Sketch of His Life". *Communio: International Catholic Review* 16 (1989): 306–50.
Horst, F. *Face to Face: the Biblical Doctrine of the Image of God*. Munich: Kaiser Verlag, 1950.
Hranić, D. *L'uomo imagine di Dio nell'insegnamento di Giovanni Paolo II (1978–1988)*. Rome: Gregorian University, 1993. Excerpt from the Doctoral Dissertation.
Hunsinger, George. *Disruptive Grace: Studies in the Theology of Karl Barth*. Grand Rapids: William B. Eerdmans Publishing Company, 2000.
Jennah, Daniel. *L'homme créé à l'imago Dei: Essai d'une théologie de la rassemblance*. Strasbourg, 2000. Doctoral Dissertation.
Jüngel, Eberhard. *Caritas fide formata: Die erste Enzyklika Benedikt XVI.- gelesen mit den augen eines evangelischen Christenmenschen*. Unpublished paper given to the Pontifical Theological Academy, Rome, 2006.
Jüngel, Eberhard. *Karl Barth: A Theological Legacy*. Philadelphia: Westminster Press, 1986.
Kelly, J.N.D. *Early Christian Doctrines*. 4th edn. London: Adam & Charles Black, 1958, 1968.
Ladaria, Luis. *Antropologia teologica*. Trans. G. Occhipinti and C. Dotolo. Piemme: Casale Monferrato (AL) and Rome: Gregorian University Press, 1998.
Ladaria, Luis. "Humanity in the Light of Christ in the Second Vatican Council". Ed. Latourelle, René, *Vatican II: Assessment and Perspectives*. New York and Mahwah: Paulist Press, 1989.
Ladaria, Luis. *Introduzione alla antropologia teologica*. Trans. G. Occhipinti. Piemme: Casale Monferrato (AL), 1992.
Lidums, Gatis. *The Doctrine of Imago Dei and Its Relation to Self-Transcendence in the Context of Practical Theology*. Helsinki, 2004. Doctoral Dissertation.
Lindbeck, George A. *The Nature of Doctrine: Religion and Theology in a Postliberal Age*. Philadelphia: Westminster Press, 1984.
Lochbrunner, Manfred. "L'amore trinitario al centro di tutte le cose". *Rivista Internazionale di Teologia e Cultura: Communio* 203–4 (2005): 105–16.
Löser, Werner. *Eros und Agape*, Unpublished Lenten Sermon in Mainz Cathedral, 12 March 2006.
Löser, Werner. "Wort und Wort Gottes in der Theologie Hans Urs von Balthasars". *Theologie und Philosophie* 80/2 (2005): 225–48.
Lossky, Vladimir. *In the Image and Likeness of God*. London: Mowbray, 1974.
Luther, Martin. *D. Martin Luthers Werke: Kritische Gesamtausgabe*, Volume 54. Weimar: Böhlau, 1938.

The Lutheran World Federation and the Roman Catholic Church. *Joint Declaration on the Doctrine of Justification.* Vatican City: Libreria Editrice Vaticana, 1999.

McCormack, Bruce L. *Karl Barth's Critically Realistic Dialectical Theology: its Genesis and Development 1909–1936.* Oxford: Oxford University Press, 1995.

McCormack, Bruce L. "The Role of God's Gracious Election in Karl Barth's Theological Ontology". Ed. Webster, John, *The Cambridge Companion to Karl Barth.* Cambridge: Cambridge University Press, 2000: 92–110.

McDade, John. "The Trinity and the Paschal Mystery". *The Heythrop Journal* 29 (1988): 175–91.

McGrath, Alistair, ed. *The Christian Theology Reader.* Oxford: Blackwell, 1995.

Macquarrie, John. *Principles of Christian Theology.* London: S.C.M. Press, 1977.

Maloney, George. *Man the Divine Icon.* Pecos: Dove Publications, 1973.

Mersch, Emile. *La Théologie du Corps mystique.* Paris: Desclée de Brouwer and Brussells: Edition Universelle, 1946.

Migne, J.-P., ed. *Patrologiae Graecae, Tomus VII.* Paris: Garnier Fratres et J.-P. Migne Successores, 1882.

Murphy, Roland E. "Introduction to the Pentateuch". Ed. Brown, Raymond E., Fitzmyer, Joseph A. and Murphy, Roland E., *The New Jerome Biblical Commentary.* London: Geoffrey Chapman, 1989: 3–7.

Murray, Paul D. "On Valuing Truth in Practice: Rome's Postmodern Challenge". *International Journal of Systematic Theology* 8/2 (April 2006): 163–83.

Nichols, Aidan. "An Introduction to Balthasar". *New Blackfriars* 79/923 (1998): 2–10.

Nichols, Aidan. *No Bloodless Myth.* Edinburgh: T&T Clark, 2000.

Nichols, Aidan. *The Theology of Joseph Ratzinger: an Introductory Study.* Edinburgh: T&T Clark, 1988.

Nichols, Aidan. *The Word has been Abroad: a Guide through Balthasar's Aesthetics.* Edinburgh: T&T Clark, 1998.

Nørgaard, Peder, ed. *Catholic-Lutheran Relations Three Decades after Vatican II: Conference at the International Bridgetine Centre, Farfa Sabina, 12–15 March 1995.* Vatican City: Libreria Editrice Vaticana, 1997.

Nygren, Anders. *Agape and Eros.* London: S.P.C.K., 1953.

Oakes, Edward. *Pattern of Redemption: the Theology of Hans Urs von Balthasar.* New York: Continuum, 1994.

O'Collins, Gerald. *Christology: a Biblical, Historical, and Systematic Study of Jesus.* Oxford: Oxford University Press, 1995.

O'Donnell, John. "Hans Urs Von Balthasar: the Form of His Theology". Ed. Schindler, David L., *Hans Urs Von Balthasar: His Life and Work.* San Francisco: Ignatius Press, 1991: 207–20.

O'Donnell, John. *Hans Urs von Balthasar.* London: Geoffrey Chapman, 1992.

O'Donnell, John. *The Mystery of the Triune God.* London: Sheed and Ward, 1988.

O'Hanlon, Gerard F. *The Immutability of God in the Theology of Hans Urs von Balthasar.* Cambridge: Cambridge University Press, 1990.

Otto, Stefan. "Der Mensch als Bild Gottes bei Tertullian". *Münchener Theologische Zeitschrift* 10 (1959): 276–82.
Ouellet, Marc. "The Message of Balthasar's Theology to Modern Theology". *Communio: International Catholic Review* 16 (1989): 270–99.
Pinto de Olivera, Carlos-J. "Image de Dieu et dignité humaine". *Freiburger Zeitschrift für Philosophie und Theologie* 27 (1980): 401–36.
Ratzinger, Joseph (Pope Benedict XVI). *Introduction to Christianity*. San Francisco: Ignatius Press, 1990.
Ratzinger, Joseph (Pope Benedict XVI). V*olk und Haus Gottes in Augustins Lehre von der Kirche*. Münchener Theologische Studien, II.7. Munich: Karl Zink Verlag, 1954.
Ricoeur, Paul, *Time and Narrative*. Chicago: Chicago University Press, 1984, 1988.
Sachs, John R. "Current Eschatology: Universal Salvation and the Problem of Hell". *Theological Studies* 52 (1991): 227–54.
Sachs, John R. "*Deus semper major – Ad majorem Dei gloriam*: the Pneumatology of Hans Urs von Balthasar". *Gregorianum* 74 (1993): 631–57.
Saward, John. "The Christocentricity of John Paul II". *Communio: International Catholic Review* 18 (1991): 332–55.
Saward, John. *The Mysteries of March: Hans Urs von Balthasar on the Incarnation and Easter*. Washington, DC: The Catholic University of America Press, 1990.
Schepers, M.B. "Lutheranism". Editorial Staff at the Catholic University of America, Washington, District of Columbia. New York: McGraw-Hill Book Company, 1967: 1091–8.
Schönborn, Christoph. *Die Christus-Ikone. Eine theologische Hinführung*. Fribourg: Editions Universitaires, 1984.
Scola, Angelo. *Hans Urs Von Balthasar: a Theological Style*. Edinburgh: T&T Clark, 1995.
Schindler, David L. "The Dramatic Nature of Life: Liberal Societies and the Foundations of Human Dignity". *Communio: International Catholic Review* 33 (Summer 2006): 183–202.
Schwager, Raymund. "Der Sohn Gottes und die Weltsünde. Zur Erlösungslehre von H. Urs von Balthasar". *Zeitschrift für Katoloische Theologie* 108 (1986): 5–44.
Schwager, Raymund. *Jesus in the Drama of Salvation*. Trans. J.G. Williams and Paul Haddon. New York: The Crossroad Publishing Company, 1999.
Striet, Magnus and Tück, Jan-Heiner, eds. *Die Kunst Gottes verstehen*. Freiburg, Basel and Vienna: Herder, 2005.
TeSelle, Eugene, *Augustine the Theologian*. New York: Herder and Herder, 1970.
Tilliette, Xavier. "Le Samedi-Saint speculative et la descente aux enfers". *Revue Catholique Internationale: Communio* XXX/2 (2005): 83–9.
Vriezen, T.C. *Theologie des Alten Testaments in Grundzügen*. Wageningen: Veenman und Zonen, 1956.

Ward, Graham. "Kenosis: Death, Discourse and Resurrection". Gardner, Lucy, Moss, David, Quash, Ben and Ward, Graham, *Balthasar at the End of Modernity*. Edinburgh: T&T Clark, 1999: 15–68.

Ward, Graham. "Barth, Modernity, and Postmodernity". Ed. Webster, John, *The Cambridge Companion to Karl Barth*. Cambridge: Cambridge University Press, 2000: 274–95.

Watson, Philip. "Book Review of Martin D'Arcy, *The Mind and Heart of Love: Lion and Unicorn: A Study in Eros and Agape*. 2nd edn. London: Fontana, 1954, 1962". *London Quarterly Review* (January 1947).

Watson, Philip. *Let God be God! An Interpretation of the Theology of Martin Luther*. London: Epworth Press, 1947.

Watson, Philip. "Some Theological Implications of Agape and Eros". *The Expository Times* 49 (1938): 537–40.

Wenham, Gordon J. "Genesis". Ed. Dunn, James D.G. and Rogerson, John W., *Eerdmans Commentary on the Bible*. Grand Rapids and Cambridge, UK: William B. Eerdmans Publishing Company, 2003: 32–71.

Glossary

Christocentric	Centred on Christ
The Council of Trent	A council of the Roman Catholic Church held in the period following the Protestant Reformation (1545–1563)
Encyclical	A letter from the Pope addressed to all people of good will
Exegesis	Critical interpretation of scripture
Jesuit	A member of the Society of Jesus
Patristic	Relating to the Fathers of the Early Church
Postconciliar	After Vatican II
Prevenience	Belief in the priority of God's action in the world
Salvific	Regarding salvation
Septuagint	The Greek version of the Old Testament
Society of Jesus	A Roman Catholic religious order of priests and brothers
Thomist	The school of thought of St Thomas Aquinas
Vatican I	A nineteenth-century council of the Catholic Church
Vatican II	The most recent council of the Catholic Church (1962–1965)

Index

Adam 12–13
  second, Christ as 13
analogia entis 32
  Aquinas 53–4, 60, 80
  Barth's rejection of 54–5, 79, 80, 161
analogia fidei, Barth 55, 63, 79, 161
Anselm, St 48, 49
  Proslogion 47
Aquinas, Thomas, St
  analogia entis 53–4, 60, 80
  on "*imago Dei*" 14–16, 60–67
  works
    De Veritate 15, 61
    Summa Theologiae 15, 54
ascendant/descendant dimensions, "*imago Dei*" 129, 130, 159, 161, 166, 170–71, 172, 175
Augustine, St 41–2, 56
  Barth on 32, 50
  Barth's interpretation of 57–60
  on evil 10
  on the Fall 10
  on "*imago Dei*" 8–11, 94, 150
    influence on Balthasar 94–8, 113, 161
  on salvation 11
  theology of humanity 10
  works
    De Diversis Quaestionibus 8
    De Trinitate 9
    Enchiridion on Faith, Hope and Love 10, 57
Aulén, Gustav 170

Balthasar, Hans Urs von 4, 40–41
  Benedict XVI on 175–6
  on Christ as God's *Gestalt* 34–5, 84–5, 106, 162
  and the *Bild* 110–16, 118, 162
  on *eros* and *agape* 163, 165, 175
  on "*imago Dei*" 36–8, 43, 83–6, 98, 100–110, 113, 115, 120–28, 159, 176
  ascendant/descendant dimensions 161
  Augustine's influence 94–8, 113, 161
  Barth's influence 98–119, 172
  critical analysis of 89–119
  drama, use of 116–19
  ecumenical contribution 124–6
  human response 122–4
  Irenaeus' influence 89–94, 161
  narrative 86–9
  reorientation in God 120–22
  Speyr's influence 35
  theological formation 33–4
  works
    "A Résumé of my Thought" 83, 121
    Creator Spirit 69–70
    Glory of the Lord series 85, 86, 105, 108, 110, 113, 117
    Theo-Drama series 36, 86, 92, 93, 94, 95, 106, 110, 113, 115, 118, 176
    The Theology of Karl Barth 99
baptism, and "*imago Dei*" 22
Barmen Theological Declaration (1934) 132
Barth, Karl
  analogia entis, rejection of 54–5, 79, 80, 161
  analogia fidei 55, 63, 79, 161
  on Augustine 32, 50
  Christocentrism 99, 101–2, 103, 106, 107, 110, 112, 114, 115, 116, 147, 160, 162
  Church Dogmatics 29, 31, 32, 45, 50, 64, 75, 76, 110, 114, 160
  on double predestination 31

on election 30, 43
on *eros* and *agape* 164–5
on faith 52, 76–7, 77–8
on "*imago Dei*" 31–3, 43, 45–81, 100, 104, 105, 159–60, 173
   critical analysis of 67–78, 80–81
   influence on Balthasar 98–119, 172
   rejection of Roman Catholic position 60–67
   relational doctrine 46, 48–9
   tensions 45–6
theological formation 29
Word of God doctrine 45, 46
Benedict XVI, Pope (Joseph Ratzinger) 1
on Balthasar 175–6
Deus Caritas Est 2–3, 162–3, 165, 167, 168–9
on *eros* and *agape* 163, 163–4
Brunner, Emil 92

Calvin, John
double predestination 105, 106
on faith 20
on "*imago Dei*" 20–22
Institutes of the Christian Religion 20
Cathecism of the Catholic Church 7–8
Christocentrism 166
   Barth's 10, 99, 101–2, 103, 106, 107, 110, 112, 114, 115, 116, 147, 160, 162
   definition 187
   and "*imago Dei*" 123, 159, 166, 166–7, 169, 175
   Moltmann's 129, 131
Clifford, Richard J. 6, 7
Council of Trent 19, 187
   Decree on Justification 25
   and "*imago Dei*" 22–4
   and salvation 24
creation epics 7
cross, the
   and Moltmann's "*imago Dei*" 144–6, 148, 155
   and rupture of Trinity 145, 152

D'Arcy, Martin, on *eros* and *agape* 165fn8
double predestination 20–21
   Barth on 31

ecumenism, receptive 172–3, 173fn29
election doctrine, Barth on 30, 43
Ernst, Cornelius 170
eros and *agape*
   Balthasar on 163, 165, 175
   Barth on 164–5
   Benedict XVI on 163, 163–4
   D'Arcy on 165fn8
   Nygren on 164
evil, Augustine on 10

faith
   Barth on 52, 76–7, 77–8
   Calvin on 20
   as gift 51–2
   and prayer 49
   see also analogia fidei
Fall, the 6, 7, 20
   Augustine on 10
Farrugia, Mario 9
Frei, Hans 174
friendship
   Moltmann on 141
   presence of God as 135, 141, 142

Genesis
   authorship 6–7
   editorial traditions 6
glossary 187
God
   Balthasar's reorientation of "*imago Dei*" in 120
   human, relationship 25–6, 75–6, 77, 79, 112–13
   immutability 153
   knowledge of 20
   position in "*imago Dei*" theology 151–6
   presence as friendship 135, 141, 142
   as revealed in Christ 133–4
   and suffering, Moltmann on 38, 39, 40
grace, primal 96
Gregory of Nazianzus 134
   "*imago Dei*", Augustine, comparison 150
   on the Trinity 150
Gregory of Nyssa 94, 95, 113
Greshake, Gisbert 97
Gutwenger, Engelbert 99

Index

Haight, Roger 170
hell, Christ's descent into 148, 153
Holy Spirit, in *"imago Dei"* model 134
human, God, relationship 25–6, 75–6, 77, 79, 112–13
human identity
    and *"imago Dei"* 19, 174
    and Jesus Christ 26, 87, 113
    and the Trinity 150
Hunsinger, George 71, 72, 80–81

identity *see* human identity
"imago Dei"
    Aquinas on 14–16, 60–67
    ascendant/descendant dimensions 129, 130, 159, 161, 166, 170–71, 172, 175
    Augustine on 8–11, 94
        Gregory of Nazianzus, comparison 150
        Irenaeus, comparison 13–14
    and baptism 22
    Calvin on 20–22
    and Christocentrism 123, 159, 166–7, 169, 175
    and Council of Trent 22–4
    Genesis 5
    God's position 151–6
    and human
        dignity 1
        identity 19, 174
    and the Incarnation 90
    Irenaeus on 12–14, 90–91, 113
    Luther on 17–19
    meaning 175
    and narrative 86–9, 175
    and salvation 149
    and Vatican II 24–7
    see also under Balthasar; Barth; Moltmann
Incarnation, the
    and *"imago Dei"* 90
    purpose 13
International Theological Commission, *Communion and Stewardship* 73, 120, 121, 123, 128, 162
Irenaeus 134
    Adversus Haereses 13, 90
    on *"imago Dei"* 12–14, 90–91, 113
    influence on Balthasar 89–94, 161

Jesus Christ
    and the Father, abandonment by 145
    God as revealed in 133–4
    as God's *Gestalt*, Balthasar on 34–5, 84–5, 86, 106, 118, 162
    hell, descent into 148, 153
    and human identity 26, 87, 113
    paschal mystery 74
    as second Adam 13
John Paul II, Pope
    Evangelium Vitae 2
    Fides et Ratio 66–7, 68, 80
    Redemptor Hominis 1, 167, 168
    Ut Unum Sint 173
    Veritatis Splendor 168
justification doctrine
    Luther 18–19, 20, 38, 50, 102, 103, 106–7, 148–9, 172
    Lutheranism, Roman Catholicism, comparison 170–71
    declaration on 171, 173

Kelly, J.N.D. 12
kenosis 144, 152

Lindbeck, George 174
Luther, Martin
    on *"imago Dei"* 17–19
    justification doctrine 18–19, 20, 38, 50, 102, 103, 106–7, 148–9, 172
    Lecture on the Letter to the Romans 105
    sanctification doctrine 150
Lutheran Formula of Concord 17
Lutheranism 17

Moltmann, Jürgen
    Christocentrism 129, 131
    on friendship 141
    on God and suffering 38, 39, 40
    on God's presence as friendship 135, 141, 142
    on *"imago Dei"* 38–41, 43, 129–36, 144–58
        ascendant/descendant dimensions 129, 130

the cross narrative 144–6, 148, 155
God's position 151–6
humanity's position 146–51, 160
Orthodox theology, incorporation of 134–5
paradox 157–8
relational model 129, 133, 134, 136–43, 154
and salvation 149
significance 156–7
theosis 150, 157, 160
and the Trinity 137–8, 152
theological formation 38
works
The Coming of God 146, 147
The Crucified God 38, 145
The Future of Creation 152
God in Creation 131, 133, 136, 147, 149, 150
The Spirit of Life 135, 138
The Trinity and the Kingdom of God 136, 141
Murphy, Roland E. 6

narrative
ecumenical significance 174
and "*imago Dei*" 86–9, 175
theology 174
value of 174
natural theology 56
and Nazis 131
revealed theology, dichotomy 131
Nazis, and natural theology 131
New Jerome Biblical Commentary 6
Nygren, Anders, on *agape* and *eros* 164

Oakes, Edward 105
O'Donnell, John 85, 88
O'Hanlon, Gerard F. 153
Origen 19
Otto, Stephan 93

Pelagianism 41, 61
Pelagius 95, 96, 97
prayer, and faith 49

Ratzinger, Joseph 93
Introduction to Christianity 68–9

Volk und Haus Gottes 93
see also Benedict XVI, Pope
revealed theology 132, 142
Ricoeur, Paul 174
Ritschl, Albrecht 51

salvation
Augustine on 11
Calvinist 21
and Council of Trent 24
and "*imago Dei*" 149
and suffering 39
Salvation and the Church 171
sanctification doctrine, Luther 150
Schleiermacher, Friedrich 29
Scola, Angelo 88
self-realization 173
Speyr, Adrienne von, influence on Balthasar 35
suffering
and God, Moltmann on 38, 39, 40
and salvation 39

Tertullian 91, 95
theosis, in Moltmann's "*imago Dei*" 150, 157, 160
Trinity, the
Gregory of Nazianzus on 150
and human identity 150
and "*imago Dei*" 137–8, 152
rupture of, on the cross 145, 152

Vatican I 63, 187
De Revelatione 54
Dei Filius 80
Vatican II 19, 187
documents
Dei Verbum 65, 80
Gaudium et Spes 24, 25, 26, 27, 42, 68, 121
Lumen Gentium 24, 26, 27, 42, 68, 74, 162
and "*imago Dei*" 24–7

Watson, Philip 170
Wenham, Gordon J. 7–8
Wobbermin, Georg 50
Word of God doctrine, Barth 45, 46

Printed in Great Britain
by Amazon